Issues in Development, Environment and Bio-diversity Conservation

Dr. Mohinder Slariya

Series

"Advances in Environmental Sociology"

Volume: V

Preface

The 2030 Agenda for Sustainable Development, scheduled to be adopted by UN General Assembly, sets forth an ambitious sets of universal goals and target to tackle the issues and challenges facing the world today because of development. The Agenda-2030 is going to integrate the economic, social and environmental dimensions and will be crucial for new development agenda. Development which in laymen sense can be defined as a "process of desired change" has a detrimental impact on environment which further is one of the most important and inseparable component of bio-diversity. While targeting development issues related to environment and biodiversity conservation always remain unaddressed and unlistened by the policy makers as well as by the policy executors at local/national as well as at international level.

To highlight issues related to development an international conference on *Development, Environment and Bio-diversity Conservation: Issues and Challenges,* popularly known as "Chamba Climate Meet-2014" has been organized with national and international collaborations and many scholars coming from different parts of globe had discussed and raised the issues of immediate concerns and being published in form of a series "Advances in Environmental Sociology" and this volume is fifth in series. This volume is comprises of 14 chapters contributed by eminent professors, researchers and budding researchers coming from different parts of the world.

The first chapter is contributed by an eminent environmental sociologist who is presently serving as a director of Asia Climate Change Education Centre, Jeju, South Korea and his contribution on a desirable approach to establishment of climate change policy is a new step for policy formation. The second chapter has been contributed by a scholar Abhay Kanwar Singh from Indian Institute of Technology, Bombay on issue of development and water governance and its crises which is in form of case studies from India continent. Issues of development in relation to earthquakes in context of growing cities which is responsible to increase the possibilities of disasters, is an attempt of budding scholar Ms.

Amrita Singh in form of a case study of 18th September, 2011 earthquake. The fourth chapter has been contributed by senior faculty Dr. Ashwani Luthra and he has highlighted issues and options for development in hilly areas focusing on spatial and transportation concerns in wake of climate change. Rivers have been badly targeted for development on the one hand and on the other climate change is also affecting them a lot, the next chapter contributed by Paresha Baria and Sanjay Yadav is a case study of lower tapi basin, which is an attempt of the contributors to highlight issues at local level by generalizing it national and international levels.

Difference between modern and traditional urban planning and impact of climate change is the content of chapter sixth contributed by Bishowdev Bhattarai is a case study of city planning in Kathmandu valley and highlighted logically earlier we were more developed as compared to today. The seventh chapter is contributed by Prof. Jitender Prasad focusing on some reflections on food security, poverty, inequality & marginalization, which is responsible for all sorts of disparities and problems. Agriculture has been corner stone of rural Indian economy but in wake of climate change it is facing changes now, Dr. Tilak Raj from Panjab University Chandigarh is highlighting this issue in chapter entitled, impact of climate change on traditional farming systems in Himachal Pradesh, he is of the view that because of climate change traditional farming is changing which is putting threat to food security. Solid urban waste management is a major threat in number of metropolitan cities not in India but in whole world, the next chapter contributed by Kokila Yadav is a case study of existing municipal solid waste management scenario in Faridabad city. A contribution from Rajshahi University, Bangladesh by Md. Aminul Islam, is a critical analysis of role of grameen bank in the socio-economic and ecological development of rural women.

Rainfall plays very crucial role in rural as well as in urban economy and it's predictability can change the whole scenario and could be very helpful to arrive at some conclusions. The next chapter is an attempt of Prof. Sanjay Yadav who analytically compared rainfall wetness in Gujarat by using seasonality index of different time periods. Savita Ahatwal a scholar from Panjab University has contributed her chapter focusing on population growth, environment and food security in India. The next chapter is contributed by Sohina Singh et.al on renewable energy and green buildings is an assessment of hindrances and catalysis associated with implementation of renewable energy in green buildings and this chapter is a detailed description of hindrances which are threatening govt. plans to convert building to green buildings. The last chapter is a description of traditional use of medicinal plants from ethno-medico botanical perspective contributed by Prof. Summit and Vishal. Contributors are of the view that need of the hour is to go-back to Mother Nature for treatment and they emphasized that such traditional medicinal plants should be conserved.

I am thankful to all contributors and all collaborators of Chamba Climate Meet-2014 who gave me this chance to work for them and enable to make this small academic contribution. I am thankful all direct/indirect hands who remains with me in whole project, hands are numerous and it is very difficult to put them all on record in this limited space as it seems very difficult for me to quantify their contributions. Last, but not least I am thankful to whole family for their emotional support starting from my mother, wife, son and daughter.

I will be very happy to respond to any quarry/question at mkslariya@gmail.com. I wish this little contribution proves beneficial to all readers.

Chamba, Himachal Pradesh, India: 28th of December, 2015

(Dr. Mohinder Kumar Slariya)

Table of Contents

Chapter-I

A Desirable Approach to Establishment of Climate Change Policy

Dai-Yeun Jeong*

Abstract

Climate change is responded by policy by government, green management by enterprise, environmental movement by civil organization, and environmentally friendly behavior by citizen in everyday life. United Nations Framework Convention on Climate Change is also a response to climate change at global level in collaborative network among nations. This paper focuses on firstly the development of framework to identify the real impact of climate change, and followed by what components should be included in the formation of climate change policy, the framework on the introduction of governance system in the decision-making process of climate change policy, and finally the methodology for analyzing the efficiency and effectiveness of climate change policy.

Keywords: Climate Change Policy, Effectiveness Analysis, Efficiency Analysis, Framework

* Director of Asia Climate Change Education Center, South Korea
Emeritus Prof. of Environmental Sociology, Jeju National University, South Korea

Introduction

Environmental problems are categorized into local and global one (Jeong, 2004: 163-164). The former is defined as the environmental problems impacting on the area around the source of pollution such as soil pollution, while the latter is defined as the environmental problems impacting on world-wide areas regardless of the source of pollution such as climate change, acid rain, ozone depletion, and desertification. Climate Change is known as the most important environmental problems in terms of its seriousness and impact on nature and humans.

Global warming is the cause of climate change. There are two groups of scholars arguing the cause of global warming. One is those arguing the natural factors (eg. Sylvestre, 2000: 273-275; Flannery, 2005: 78; Ruddiman, 2007: Chapters 3-4; Choi, 2008: 325-329). The other is those arguing the emission of greenhouse gases induced by human activity in the process to improve material affluence and convenience in everyday life (eg. Kraus et al, 1992: 4, 28; Miller, 2002: 452-453; IPCC, 2007). However, United Nations Framework Convention on Climate Change (UNFCCC) takes a stand that 80% of the current global warming is caused by human-induced greenhouse gas emission and 20% by natural factors (Jeong, 2009). Domestically, there are five major agents responding to climate change. They are government, enterprise, environmental organization, and citizens. Government approaches climate change by policy, enterprise by green management, civil organization by environmental movement, and citizen by environmentally friendly behavior in everyday life.

This paper will focus on climate change policy being developed and implemented. The target of climate change policy is changing and/or changed climate. There are a wide range of possible policies responding to climate change policy. Each policy will be different in terms of its effectiveness and efficiency. Therefore, it is necessary to adopt effective and efficient policy within the limited resource mobilization with which each national and local government is faced.

In such a context, this paper will examine and explain a desirable approach to establishment of climate change policy. Climate change policy should be developed on the basis of the vulnerability to climate change. In this sense, the framework for identifying the vulnerability to climate change will be developed firstly. As the second step, the components as the formation of climate change policy will be examined. As the third step, a framework of governance system that should be employed in the process of climate change policy will be developed. Finally, the methodology for analyzing the efficiency and effective analysis of climate change policy will be developed.

A desirable Approach to establishment of climate change policy

1. The 1st Step: Identifying Vulnerability to Climate Change
Controversy surrounds climate change policy because of uncertainties in climatic effects, impacts, mitigation costs and their distributions. Nonetheless, climate change policy has been developed and implemented at local, national, and global level. In particular, international climate change policy at global level over 30 years is divided into five periods (Gupta, 2010): the pre-1990 period, the period leading up to the adaptation of the Climate Change Convention, the period of the Kyoto Protocol until US withdrawal, the period focusing on the entry into force of the Kyoto Protocol, and the post-2008 period that coincides with the financial crisis. They are important in that they have functioned as a guideline for local and national governments to develop their climate change policy.

The first step for establishing climate change policy should be to identify the vulnerability to climate change either at local or national level. The ordinary use of the term 'vulnerability' refers to the capacity to be wounded, i.e. the degree to which a system is likely to experience harm due to exposure to a harm. However, the scientific use of 'vulnerability' has its roots in geography and natural hazards research but this term is now a central concept in a variety of research contexts such as natural hazards and disaster management, ecology, public health, poverty and development, secure livelihoods and famine, sustainability science, land change, and climate impacts and adaptation. The term 'vulnerability' is used in many different ways by various scholars (for detail, see Fussel, 2007). However, according to IPCC (2007) from a climate change perspective, vulnerability is defined as 'the degree to which a system is susceptible to, or unable to cope with, adverse effects of climate change, including climate variability and extremes". This implies that IPCC definition includes three components of vulnerability - exposure to climate change, sensitivity to climate change, and adaptive capacity.

Exposure is defined as a degree of climate stress upon a particular unit analysis; it may be represented as either long-term change in climate conditions, or by changes in climate variability, including the magnitude and frequency of extreme events. In short, exposure is the change in climate itself such as sea level rise, precipitation and temperature changes, and so on. Sensitivity is the degree to which a system will be affected by, or responsive to climate stimuli. Sensitivity is basically the biophysical effect of climate change; but sensitivity can be altered by socio-economic changes. Adaptive capacity refers to the potential or capability of a system to adjust to climate change, including climate variability and extremes, so as to moderate potential damages, to take advantage of opportunities, or to cope with consequences. As the name suggests, adaptive capacity is the capability of a system to adapt to impacts of climate change.

The three components do not exist independently, but exist in a causal relationship. The relationship is that the real impact of climate change at a region or nation occurs by exposure to climate change through sensitivity and adaptation capacity to climate change. This means that exposure is independent variable, sensitivity and adaptation capacity are intermediate variables, and real impact is dependent variable. Adaptation capacity should be treated as a component of sensitivity rather than as an independent variable from sensitivity. This is because as IPCC (2007) states, the state of sensitivity can be altered by socio-economic changes, and that the determinants of socio-economic adaptation capacity include wealth, technology, education, institutions, information, infrastructure, and social capital, etc. (Brooks, et al., 2005). Brooks and his colleagues cover a wide range of factors including even non-socio-economic ones as the determinants of adaptation capacity. Thus, societal adaptation capacity would be more fit than the term 'socio-economic adaptation capacity'. In addition, natural adaptation capacity also exists. For example, even though two regions are exposed to the same quantity of precipitation, real impact of precipitation is different according to whether the region is geographically steep or flat.

Synthesizing the above discussions, human activity for improving material affluence and convenience in everyday life is one of the causes arising climate change through greenhouse gas emission, and each region and nation are exposed to climate change. However, the real impact of climate change occurs by the exposure through sensitivity being composed of natural and socio-economic adaptation capacity. The vulnerability to climate change should be assessed on the basis of the real impact of climate change in a region and nation. In order for the climate change policy to be effective and efficient in each region and nation, adaptation and mitigation policy should be developed on the basis of the assessment of vulnerability. Such a mechanism among the components of vulnerability to climate change is diagramed as in Figure 1.

The assessment of vulnerability can be classified into two categories. One is composite assessment, and the other is assessment by sector. The former is the assessment of vulnerability at national and local level as a whole (eg. Moss et. al, 2001), the latter is the assessment of vulnerability on ecosystem, health, and agriculture, etc. (Hwang and Byun, 2011).

Fussel (2005, 21-22) distinguishes two different interpretations of vulnerability to climate change. One is 'end-point', and the other is 'starting-point'. 'End-point' interpretation represents the net impact of climate change for a given level of global climate change, taking into account feasible adaptation. This interpretation is consistent with the integrated framework of vulnerability research. It is most relevant for the development of mitigation policy and for the prioritization of international assistance. 'Starting-point' interpretation assumes that addressing (internal socioeconomic)

Figure 1: Showing Framework for Developing Climate Change Policy

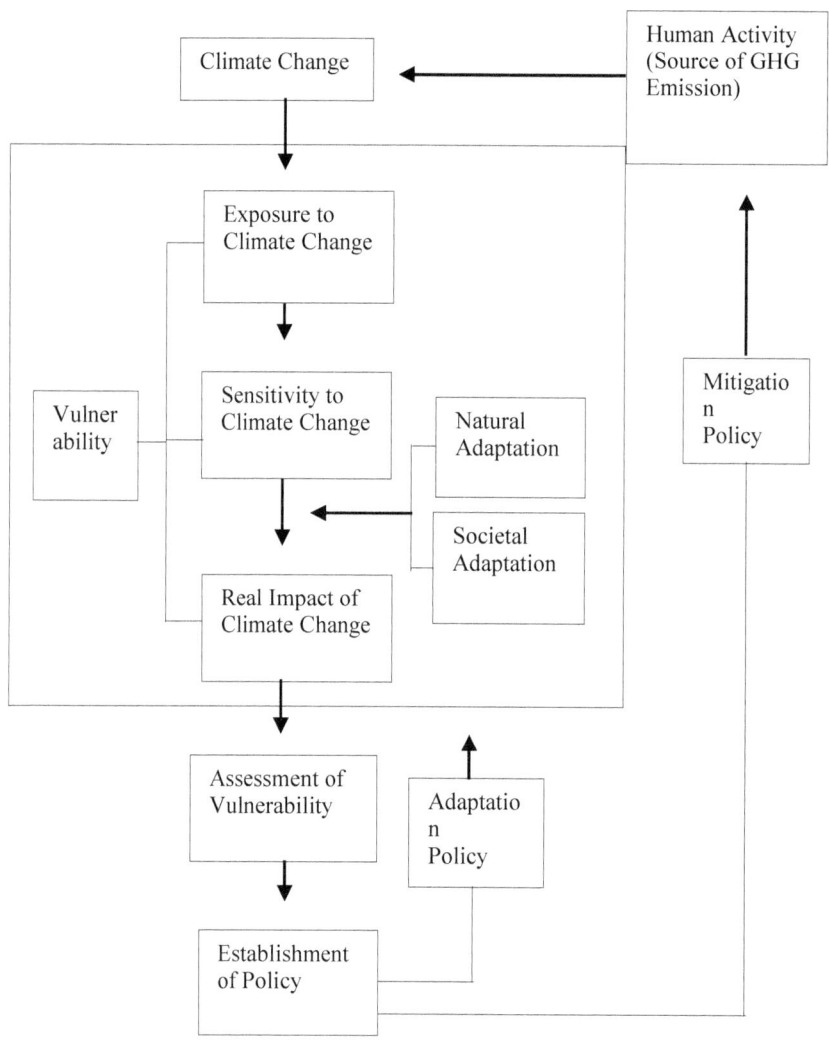

vulnerability to current climate variability will also reduce vulnerability to future climate change. This interpretation is largely consistent with the social constructivist framework and addresses primarily the needs of adaptation policy.

The 2nd Step: Forming the Components of Climate Change Policy

It is not easy to define the concept of policy because it has a wide range of theoretical and empirical implications. In a word, however, policy is defined as a course or principle of action adopted or proposed by a government, party, business or individual. In this definition, 'government, party, business or individual' are the agents developing and implementing policy, while 'course or principle of action' is the connotation of policy. Reviewing the definitions of the connotation being included in policy since the 1970s, the meanings of policy can be classified into the following three categories (Jeong, 2004: 316-317).

First: Policy is an action plan projecting value and its practice. This implies that policy has a goal, and action is a means to achieve the goal. Second: Policy is a guide of future-oriented action. The goal of this guide is to achieve public interest, mobilizing the best fit means. Third: Policy is an explanation disclosing the coercive goal, means, agent, and target. This implies that coercion is a core meaning of policy. The above conceptual meanings of policy imply that policy is composed of at least four components. They are target, goal, means, and implementation.

There are similar terms to policy such as strategy and measure, etc. It is not easy to distinguish the difference among them, because they are in exchangeable use. However, examining strictly, their meanings are different in that they are in conceptual hierarchy (Jeong, 1997). For example, strategy is a genetic concept including other sub-concepts, while policy is a specific concept being included in strategy. Strategy generally involves setting goals, determining actions to achieve the goals, and mobilizing resources to execute the actions. A strategy describes how the ends (goals) will be achieved by the means (policies). In this sense, policy is a means to achieve strategy. This is like the relationship between objective and goal in that goal is set up within the boundary of objective. Meanwhile, measure is a sub-concept of policy. For example, mitigation policy for reducing greenhouse gas emission is composed of a wide range of measures such as saving energy at home, reducing car driving, and launch carbon labeling institution, etc.

This session is to seek for the desirable formation of the components of climate change policy. As explained above, at least four components of climate change could be drawn from the conceptual meanings of climate change policy - target, goal, means, and implementation. When these four components are applied to the development of climate change policy, the desirable policy formation would be as below.

Target

Target is a reference object to attain an intended goal through the process of selecting it and matching the appropriate response to it on the basis of operational requirements, capacities and limitations. All of the vulnerable sectors being identified from the assessment can be not selected as targets of climate change policy, because of financial, technological, and operational capacity and limitations inherent in local and national government. Therefore, it is inevitable to select limited number of vulnerable sectors as the target of climate change policy. The priority of selection should be based on in order of more vulnerable sector, availability of applicable technology, and availability of finance, etc. Each local and national government would be different in the selection of vulnerable sectors as the target of climate change policy according to the differences in the priority of selection.

Goal

Goal is defined as the result or achievement towards which effort is directed. If this definition is applied to climate change policy, the goal of climate change policy would be defined as an observable and measurable end result having one or more targets of climate change policy to be achieved within a given fixed timeframe. Different goal of climate change policy is set up by policy. Broadly, the goal of mitigation policy is different from that of adaptation policy.

Broadly, the goal of mitigation policy is to reduce or eliminate the long-term risk damaged from climate change. In such a context, for example, the goal of mitigation is set up as a reduction target of greenhouse gas emission by sector such as industry, transportation, home, and commerce, etc. In detail, for example in transportation, the reduction target is set up by the kind of car such as bus, passenger car, and truck, etc.

Meanwhile, the goal of adaptation policy focuses on how to adapt to the consequences of climate change as a real impact. Adaptation policy can be classified as many as the vulnerable sectors selected. Overall, the goal of adaptation policy is to protect human well-being in the face of climate change, to reduce many of its adverse impacts, and to enhance beneficial impacts. Like mitigation policy, different goal of adaptation policy is set up by the sector selected in terms of what and how to do for adaptation (for detail, see Burton et. al, 2004).

However, there is an emerging discourse of limits to such adaptation (Adger et. al, 2009). The limits are a set of immutable thresholds in biological, economic or technological parameters. There are at least four propositions concerning the limits to adaptation. First, any limits to adaptation depend on the ultimate goals of adaptation underpinned by diverse values. Second, adaptation need not be limited by uncertainty around future foresight of risk. Third, social and individual factors limit adaptation action. Fourth, systematic undervaluation of loss of places and culture disguises real, experienced but subjective limits to adaptation. These four are mutable rather than independent.

Means

Generally, means is defined as how a result is obtained or an end is achieved. If this definition is applied to climate change, the means of climate change is the measures of climate change being mobilized for achieving the goal of mitigation and adaptation polices. In other words, individual project being launched for implementing mitigation and adaptation policy corresponds to the means of climate change policy. For example, if the goal of mitigation policy is set up to reduce the emission of greenhouse gas by 10% within a given fixed timeframe, an alternative means to adopt for achieving the goal is to reduce energy use, to increase energy efficiency, and/or to supply new and renewable energy.

Effective and efficient means should be adopted in relation to the achievement of goal (Jeong, 2009). The adopted means is the determinant of how successfully the goal is achieved. In this sense, effectiveness is the degree to which the goal is achieved through the process of match between the goal and its achievement. In other words, effectiveness implies 'doing the right thing for achieving goal'. Meanwhile, efficiency is the extent to which the adopted means achieves its goal without wasted resources, effort, time, or money. In other words, efficiency connotes using the smallest quantity of resources in the process of achieving goal. In this sense, efficiency is the degree of the match between the goal and thee adopted means in terms of rationality and/or relevance, and implies 'doing thing the right way for achieving goal'.

The 3rd Step: Introduction of Governance System in the Decision-making Process

Government is the agent developing and implementing climate change policy which has a legal force. A lot of empirical observations reveal that conflicts are expressed by the variety of social groups and stakeholders in the process of the policy being implemented. The conflicts prevent or delay implementation of climate change policy itself or reduce policy effectiveness. However, no formal system for resolving the conflict is institutionalized after the policy having been launched. The main cause of the conflict is that the policy is developed as a top-down processing with less consideration of different perspectives on the issues related to the policy, stakeholders' interest, and citizens' opinion, etc.

Conflict resolution is a skill based in good communication practices and an understanding of inter-personal and inter-organizational dynamics - therefore, successful implementation of conflict resolution policies and procedures needs to be institutionalized in the process of climate change policy being developed. As is known, such an institutional strategy is governance system as a desirable decision-making process of policy. The governance system is based on policy coordination, integration of policy means, sharing participation and responsibility, and cooperative efforts to resolve problems through the network among variety of agents having interest and concern (Leroy and Arts, 2006; Koh, 2009). The major advantage of governance system is to internalize potential conflicts in advance through drawing a social consensus before a policy being decided and implemented.

There are a wide range of governance systems according to the issues in relation to establishment of policy, resolution of specific problem, and social conflict, etc. The desirable governance system would be different by issue of which social consensus needs to be drawn. In relation to the establishment of climate change policy, a desirable governance system would be diagramed as (Figure 2, Jeong, 2004: 342).

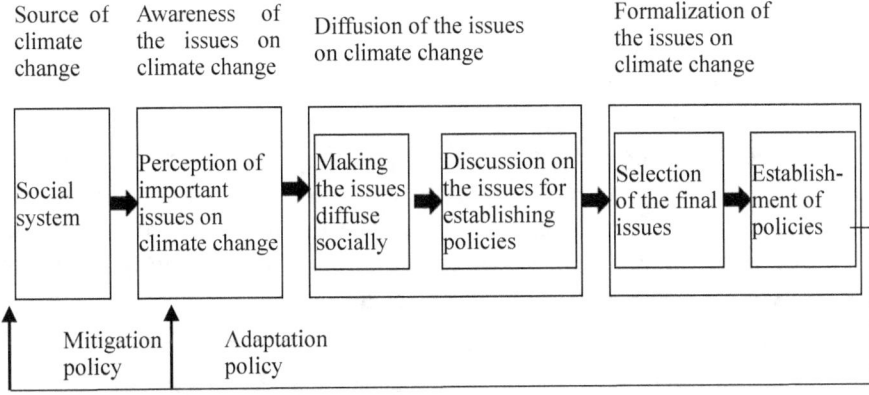

Figure 2: Showing A Desirable Governance System for Establishing Climate Change Policy

Figure 2, consists of four major components. 'Social System' is the source of human-induced climate change. After exposure to climate change, societal components such as government, citizens, social groups, and experts, etc. becomes aware of the wide range of issues on climate change. Among them, some issues are perceived as important ones. This is the stage of 'Awareness of the Issues on Climate Change'. The perceived issues to be important are diffused socially and are discussed explicitly and implicitly by societal component. This is the stage of 'Diffusion of the Issues on Climate Change'. In this stage, what issues should be included in the establishment of policy are diffused socially. After this stage, the final issues to be included in the establishment of policy are selected, and they are established as mitigation or adaptation policy. This is the stage of 'Formalization of the Issues on Climate Change'. Mitigation policy is applied to social system as the source of human-induced climate change, while adaptation policy is applied to the perceived important issues on climate change.

There are two important points government should consider in the introduction of governance system diagramed in Figure 2. One is the decision on the participants in the governance system. There are a variety of potential participants to invite. The example includes experts, civil organization, stakeholders, and residents, etc. The other is the decision on the stage of participation. For example, it should be decided whether to participate them from the stage of 'discussion on the issues to be established as policy' or at the stage of 'establishment of policy'.

The 4th Step: Analyzing Policy Effectiveness

The effectiveness of climate change policies established through the stages in Figure 2 should be examined before they are fixed as the final ones to be implemented and after they are implemented. The former is efficiency analysis of financial investment, and the latter is effectiveness analysis of all policies as a whole.

Efficiency Analysis of Financial Investment: The projects being implemented for achieving the goal of climate change policy require a lot of finance, and each project has different effectiveness in terms of, for example, reduction quantity of greenhouse gas. It is possible to compare between the invested fiancé and the potential reduction quantity of greenhouse gas. This is the efficiency analysis of financial investment. It may be argued that the policy reducing more emission of greenhouse gas with less financial investment is more efficient policy. Thus, efficiency analysis of financial investment has a function as guide for the decision of policy priority. This analysis results in more beneficial effect on the policy that can be measured quantitatively, can be done by individual policy, and needs because most local and national governments have a limited availability of finance.

Table 1 is an example of efficiency analysis of financial investment which has been done for Jeju Province, South Korea (Jeong, 2014). The potential reduction quantity is estimated, using IPCC default emission factor by source of greenhouse gas.

Table 1 Showing Example of Efficiency Analysis of Financial Investment - Jeju Province, South Korea

Policy Implemented	Budget (USD million)	Potential Reduction Quantity (ton)	Budget for Reducing 1 ton (USD)
Afforestation (6,500ha)	93	38,350	2,430
Supply of Clean Energy	104	227,372	460
Substitute of Traffic Signal with Light Emission Diode (LED)	3	9,735	310
Substitute of 50,000 Cars with Electric Ones	1,500	191,100	7,849

As is identified from Table 1planting tree in an area of 6,500ha requires USD93million, and the potential carbon sink is estimated as 38,350 ton a year. The budget for reducing 1 ton from afforestation is estimated as USD2, 430. With such a methodology using IPCC default emission factor, 'Substitute of Traffic Signal with LED' is the most efficient in financial investment, and followed by 'Supply of Clean Energy' and 'Afforestation (6,500ha). 'Substitute of 50,00 Cars with Electric Ones' is the most expensive policy.

Effectiveness Analysis of All Policies as a Whole: Climate change policies are implemented on the basis of individual policy. However, their effectiveness is achieved as a whole set of policies. Nonetheless, it is quite rare to conduct the effectiveness of all policies as a whole after the policies are implemented. It is no doubt that implementation of policy itself is not the purpose of launching policy. Thus, it is necessary to analyze how successfully the policies achieve the goal being set up.

The effectiveness of all policies as a whole may be analyzed in various frameworks. However, a simple and desirable framework of the effectiveness analysis can be drawn on the basis of the paths of effectiveness being achieved from the implementation of policies, using the existing theoretical and/or empirical concepts related to climate change. Jeong (2011) developed the framework as <Figure 3> which can be applied to the effectiveness of mitigation policies.

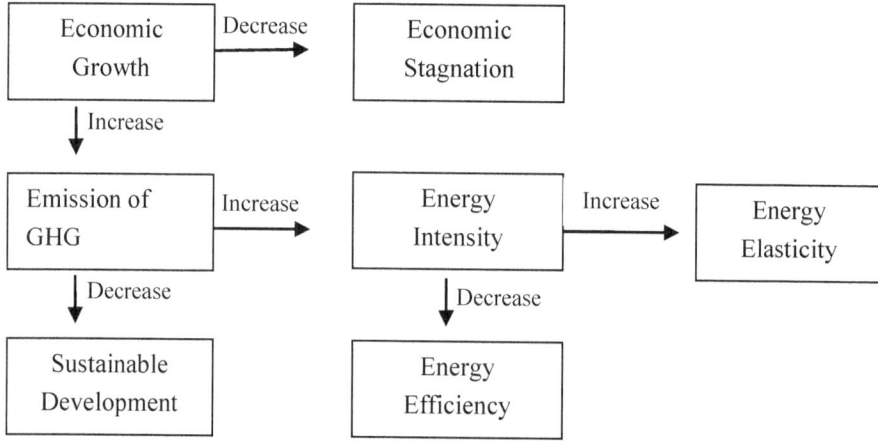

Figure Showing Framework for Analyzing the Effectiveness of All Climate Change Policies as a Whole

Figure 3 is based on the following logical paths. Decrease in 'Economic Growth' goes to 'Economic Stagnation' that results in no increase in 'Emission of Greenhouse Gas (GHG)'. Meanwhile, increase in 'Economic Growth' accompanies increase in 'Emission of GHG)'. Liu (2005) proved empirically that the correlation between increase in economic growth and CO^2 emission is 0.70 at global level.

However, if 'Emission of GHG' decreases or does not increase during 'Economic Growth', this means that climate change policies having been implemented contribute to 'Sustainable Development' as their goal set up intends. Meanwhile, in spite of climate change policies having been implemented, if 'Emission of GHG' increases during 'Economic Growth', this leads us to examine 'Energy Intensity' which is a crossroads towards 'Energy Efficiency' or 'Energy Elasticity'. If 'Energy Intensity' decreases, this means that climate change policies contribute to 'Energy Efficiency'. However, 'Energy Intensity' increases, this means increase in 'Energy Elasticity' implying that climate change policies having been implemented are ineffective.

Conclusion- Capacity building

This chapter aimed at developing a desirable approach to establishment of climate change policy. In relation to this objective, this paper suggested the identification of vulnerability to climate change as the first step, the components in the formation of climate change policies as the second step, the introduction of governance system in the process of climate change policies being developed as the third step, and efficiency and effectiveness analysis of climate change policies as the fourth step before and after they are implemented.

Even though the policies responding to climate change are developed through the four stages, each local government or national government is faced with some constraints in implementing the final policies. The constraints impede the successful implementation of the policies to be launched. Therefore, the policies should be implemented together with the strategies to overcome the constraints. This may be termed capacity building. The capacity building can be categorized into internal and external one.

The Internal Capacity Building: This includes increase in financial capacity and development of advanced technology. This is because a lot of budget is necessary for launching climate change policies, and the clean energy requires advanced technologies. A cooperative network with business enterprises, civil organization, mass media, and citizens should be established. This is because all climate change policies are related with their ordinary activities. This means that climate change policies can't be achieved successfully without social consensus with them as the major societal components. The final one is change of the current socio-economic system to a new one. This may be termed a social system approach in that the existing social system as the source of greenhouse gas emission should be attempted to be restructured. The major targets of the restructuration include change in economic market system in terms of production and distribution, change in citizens' lifestyle in terms of purchase and consumption behavior, and change in cultural ethos from consumerism to environmentalism.

The External Capacity Building: Climate change is a global environmental problem in that climate change occurs from both internal and external source of greenhouse gas emission. In this sense, it would be necessary to establish a cooperative network with other regions and countries. The network would function, at the least, as sharing mutual understanding, information exchange, and collaborative activities. Sharing mutual understanding includes the seriousness of climate change, the necessity of collaborative response to climate change, and the effectiveness of collaborative response to climate change, etc. Information exchange includes the state of climate change, the data related to climate change, and the training program necessary for climate change education, etc. The fields of collaborative activities are mutual personnel exchange of administrative and professional staffs, collaborative research, and holding professional academic conferences on a joint base, etc.

References

1. W. N. Adger, S. Dassai, M. Goulden, M. Hulme, I. Lorenzoni, D. R. Nelson, R. O. Naess, J. Wolf, and Wreford, Are There Social Limits to Adaptation to Climate Change? Climate Change, 93(3-4), 2009, 335-354

2. N. Brooks, W. N. Adger, P. M. Kelly, The Determinants of Vulnerability and Adaptive Capacity at the National Level and the Implications of Adaptation, Global Environmental Change, 15(2), 2005, 151-163.

3. I. Burton, E. Malone, and S. Hug, Adaptation Policy Framework for Climate Change: Developing Strategies, Policies and Measures (Cambridge: Cambridge University Press, 2004).

4. D. G. Choi, Understanding of Earth. (Seoul: Seoul National University Press, 2008).

5. T. Flanny, Tim, The Weather Makers: How Man Is Changing the Climate and What It Means for Life on Earth (New York: Grove Press, 2005).

6. Hans-Martin Fussel, Vulnerability in Climate Change Research: A Comprehensive Conceptual Framework (Breslauer Symposium, No. 6, University of California International and Area Studies, University of California, 2005).

7. -----. Vulnerability: A Generally Applicable Conceptual Framework for Climate Change Research, Global Environmental Change, 17(2), 2007, 155-167.

8. P. Gupa, A History of International Climate Change Policy, Wiley Interdisciplinary Reviews: Climate Change,1(5), 2010, 636-653.

9. H. S. Hwang and B. S. Byun, Building Vulnerability Index on Climate Change: Focused on Seoul Metropolitan City, Journal of Environmental Policy and Administration (Korea Environmental Policy and Administration Society), 19(4), 2011, 93-119.

10. IPCC (Intergovernmental Panel Climate Change). Climate Change 2007: Synthesis Report (London: Cambridge University Press, 2007).

11. D. Y. Jeong, Dictionary of Social Science Methodology (Seoul: Baek-Ui Publishing Co., 1997).

12. -----. Environmental Sociology (Seoul: Acanet, 2004).
13. -----. A Critical Evaluation of Climate Change Measure Being Implemented in Jeju, South Korea, Journal of Social Research (Institute of Social Research, Korea University, South Korea), 10(1), 2009, 151-181.
14. -----. An Effectiveness Analysis of Climate Change Policy in South Korea, Journal of Environmental Impact Assessment (Korean Society of Environmental Impact Assessment), 20(5), 2011, 585-600.
15. -----. Methodology for Analyzing the Effectiveness of Climate Change Policy, The 3rd Asia Climate Change Education Center International workshop on The Effectiveness of Climate Change Strategy, Jeju, South Korea, 2014, 31-44.
16. K. Koh, A Study on Priorities to Enhance Local Environmental Governance Capacity, Journal of Environmental Policy and Administration (Korea Environmental Policy and Administration Society), 17 (2), 2009, 72-114.
17. F. Kraus, B. Wilfrid Bach, and K. Jonathan, Energy Policy in the Greenhouse (New York: John Wiley and Sons, 1992).
18. P. Leroy and B. Arts, Institutional Dynamics in Environmental Governance, in B. Arts and P. Leroy (Ed.), Institutional Dynamics in Environmental Governance (Dordrecht, The Netherlands: Springer, 2006) 1-19.
19. X. Liu, Explaining the Relationship between CO^2 Emission and National Income - The Role of Energy Consumption, Economic Letters, 87(3), 2005, 325-328.
20. T. G. Jr. Miller, Living in the Environment: Principles, Connections, and Solutions (Belmont, CA: Wadsworth, 2002).
21. R. H. Moss, E. L. Brenkert, and A. L. Malone, Vulnerability to Climate Change: A Quantitative Approach, Prepared for the US Department of Energy, 2001.
22. W. F. Ruddiman, Earth's Climate: Past and Future. New York: W. H. Freeman and Company, 2007).
23. H. Sylvestre, Quel Climate Pour Demain? (Paris: Les Editions Calmanny-Levy, 2002).

Chapter-II

Water Governance and its Crises: Case Studies from India

Abhay Vir Singh Kanwar*

Abstract

India is the second fastest growing economies of the world but in summers its claims of high growth becomes self-evident. Mismanagement of water as commons is not only manifested at local level but also at national level, which not only entails into legal strife between the center and the state but also between two states. Scenario of such sort succeeds into environmental injustice for large chunk of population of this country.

Reciprocating to the above scenario, the undertaken academic probe will delve into "water as commons". The issue of water miss-governance at national level in India will be gauged through Garrett Hardin lenses of "tragedy of commons". To structure it further, the paper will put forth few case studies in India: the Kaveri river dispute between Karnataka and Tamilnaidu, pollution of river Yamuna in Delhi and unprincipled privatization of Sheonath and other rivers in Chattisgarh.

The paper will detail about the history of each issue with special reference to its genesis and will move on to its legal complications and its unfortunate impact on the effected communities. With reference to the governance, discussions in the paper will also elucidate about the solutions of top bottom and bottom to top approach that can be practically realized that can cater to the problems. On the closing note, role of judiciary, how it can negotiate with the diverse stakeholders and mediate between market, state and citizens will also be delved into.

Keywords: Active Citizenship, Commons, Environmental Justice, Environmental Security

* *Research Scholar, Department of Humanities and Social Sciences, Indian Institute of Technology, Bombay India*

Introduction

"Destruction is a man's will; Nevertheless Prevention is also a man's will, its man's choice to choose between Destruction and Prevention)" Babu Rajan.

A life in a low carbon community with ample commons as implicit guarantor of jobs, justice and human flourishing with in the finite capacity of our planet seems to be a utopian and unachievable vision thus it stands as a paradox with reference to contemporary planetary environmental fiasco. Blending the axed history of environment as well as the elephantine policy regimes of the modern governance which seems to cater to utopian vision of regulating commons by prioritizing public welfare offers us several lenses to introspect the multiple realms, be it be the realm of various social movements by the indigenous to protect their rights on commons or the domain of prestigious academia which constitutes the well red intellectuals that have tried to address the issues of commons or the strife between government and natives over the ownership of commons.

History has been a witness that every century has its own debates. If 15th century was a era of confrontation between church and science then 16th century stood a witness to fall of divine theory and 17th to 19th century marked the strife between state and masses followed by industrial revolution. 20th century was a disaster in its own sense as its roots were embedded in plan market and revolution and it marked the death of three utopias science socialism and development. Lewis Mumford defines them as Kakatopias, Utopias that smell of death and genocide [Vishavanathan Shiv 2000]. As we move towards 21st century it is also caged in the unfulfilled promises of development and the impure ambitions of science and contrived form of socialism which not only took toll on human subsistence but also has maimed the environment at planetary scale which has ensued into the depletion of the environmental resources [commons] at an unprecedented scale as compared to the long human environmental history. In the last two centuries there have been several academicians and committed social activist who have exhausted the theme of environment sustainability and has given an alternative to address the questions of sustainable development. To name a few Francisco Alves Mendes Filho, better known as Chico Mendes was a

Brazilian rubber tapper and an environmentalist. He thought to preserve Amazon forest and also fought for human rights of the Brazilian peasants'. Kenule Ken Beeson Saro Wiwa was a Nigerian author environmental activist, and winner of the Right Livelihood Award and the Goldman Environmental Prize. He was a member of Ogoni people whose homeland was targeted for crude oil extraction and the extractions done for oil resulted into huge environmental debacle. Dian Fosseywas an American zoologist who took an extensive study of gorilla groups over the 18 years and was the ardent supporter of conservation of natural habitat for animals (vidhyaasree, 2011). Above mentioned were just the tip of the iceberg who has strengthened the foundations of environment conservation. To name a few more there is Vandana Shiva Amit Jethwa Ramachandra Guha, Anil Agarwal and Sunita Narain, etc. of all the environmentalists and their propounded frameworks when Garrett Hardin in 1968 marked a crucial departure in his theory of "tragedy of commons" to address the issues of public resources which she addressed as commons, since then they have garnered a lot of debate in both in academic as well as policy circles.

"Commons", according to the Digital Library of the Commons (DLC), refers to shared resources in which each stakeholder has an equal interest. These commons have two main characteristics: they are rivalrous which means one person's use depletes the resource therefore depriving others of the enjoyment of the resource. The other characteristic is that they are non-excludable which means that they cannot be divided into parts and therefore are open to all. This therefore calls for collective use and management of such resources in order to minimize the risk of emerging conflict among users. In the framework of tragedy of commons the author elaborates over one of the most critical problems of the society. The problem of the resource accounting in a public domain. In an economic version it is a depletion of a shared resource by individuals, acting independently and rationally according to each one's self-interest, having an understanding that depleting the common resource is compromise with the group's long-term best interests (Hess 2008). This concept is in accordance to the concept of sustainable development. Concept of commons may include land, atmosphere, oceans, rivers, fish stocks, and national parks etc. in this way Garrett Hardin's contributions introduce new lenses to scan the contemporary environmental crises across the globe.

It started off in England and Europe but the instinct to hoard and accumulate subsume the globe like an overrun machine by plowing colonialism as a tool. History of environmental degradation in India can be traced back to the history of British colonialism [Guha Ramchandra 2000] and even in 21st century its remnants have been powerful enough that India faces heat from all the corners on an environmental front. Developmental projects both on land and air with a myopic appraisals have ensued into abatement in the rich and valuable resources of the country which have not only flustered the sociopolitical fabric but projects of such sort have proved to be unyielding both on economic as well as environmental front. By plowing the lenses of tragedy of commons we can very well discern how the rich resources of the country in terms of land and air in general and water in particular has subsided due to unrestricted and illicit access when it is home to only 2.2% land mass, 4% freshwater resources and 16% population of the world.

In the last two decades, in India commons irrespective of land, water and air have all of sudden emerged as a sight of conflict, be it be two states, state or its masses or two groups of communities. Thus they have received a considerable attention from judiciary in particular and bureaucracy, academicians, national planners, social activists and the multitude of justice seekers in general. As land and water are commons, they are one of the most crucial resources of the country. To comprehend their contention, technically they are divided into common pooled resources and common property. Common pooled resources are the once in which everybody can have unrestricted access irrespective of community. These properties are immune from individual ownership. On the other hand common properties are those which have communal or individual ownership (Liz Alden Wily, 2011). Since common pooled resources are more prone to ownership disputes due to unrestricted access patterns, consequently it becomes comparatively arduous to unearth their sustainable and enduring alternatives. In a developing country like India, with its emerging legal apparatus, when it comes to national resources, water reserves falls in the category of common pooled resources and thus manifest highly mismanaged profile not only at local level but also at national level.

The Kaveri water war stands a witness, how water as a resource is a point of contestation between the two states of Karnataka and Tamilnaidu. The conflict between the two states dates back to the British rule when they ruled the two states of Mysore and Madras for a short period in the middle of the 19th century. Several plans were drawn to use the water of the river but the drought followed by famine in mid-1870 brought every plan to halt. The plan was revised in 1881 by Mysore. Mysore's revision of its irrigation projects faced resistance from madras which was followed by a conference in 1890 which helped Mysore in dealing in its agricultural projects as well as it would also layed practical security against injury to interests" and eventually the Agreement of 1892 was signed [Meenakshi Sundaram SS, Raghavan P, and Singh A. 2010]. In 1910 Mysore came up with a plan to construct a dam which was resisted by madras presidency.

In 1914 Mysore was granted permission to go ahead with the project. Several negotiations took place in 1924, 1929, 1933. In 1956 when states were reorganized on linguistic demographics, it simply changed the equations and made the dispute more demanding as Kerala and Pondicherry also jumped into the fray but primarily the dispute remained between Karnataka and Tamilnaidu. There were many rounds of interstate discussions but nothing could come out of a stalemate. The formation of constitution of tribunal which was followed by interim award and riots, the crises of 1995 1996 were not in a position to handle the situation. Even after the high drama of 2002 when the judgment came in 2007 the issue is still unresolved. The crucial issue of access to water is still rolling like a bone of contention amongst tribunal, Supreme Court, Kaveri river authority and Indian government with no closing and sustainable alternative.

Apart from political and legal front *The Aam Adami,* common man has faced the heat in the recognition of ownership rights over commons as In the decade of nineties both Karnataka and Tamilnadu were struck by vilent attacks and demonstrations against each other's people due to which Tamils had to flee away from Bangalore . Again in 2002 the flare took up the ugly tern which resulted in accusations and counteraccusations in both the states. The anger of the people spilt on the streets in Karnataka. When Tamilnadu filed a contempt petition various cross sections of society from both states were on the streets. Tamil TV channels and screening of Tamil films were blocked in Karnataka. Also all buses and vehicles from Tamil Nadu were barred from entering Karnataka creating public nuisance.

Apart from the Kaveri water war at the national level, most of the rivers in India are either has an history of legal battle or prone to pollution. When it comes to pollution Yamuna River is one of the most polluted rivers in the world. River Yamuna has a length of 1370 km and is one of the longest tributary of river Ganges. It arises from Yamunotri in the Uttarakhand Himalaya regions. It flows through Uttrakhand, Haryana, Delhi and Uttar Pradesh before it merges with Ganges in Allahabad. Over the decades Yamuna has become much polluted especially due to Delhi who dumps 57% of its waste in the river. Everyone including big industries, Factories, Peoples living in colonies, slums and rural areas pollute this holy river. In addition, the water in this river remains stagnant for almost nine months in a year, aggravating the situation.

Agricultural residues, insecticides and pesticides also contribute to the pollution of the river. Also People wash their clothes, utensils and defecate in the river and pollute it. Delhi being a national capital bears 22km of the river which is just 2% of its length; with in that 2% it contributes to 70% of the pollution load of the river. It discharges about 3,684 MLD (million liters per day) of sewage through its 18 drains into the river [Deepshikha Sharma and Arun Kansal]. The pollutions levels has gone to an extent that at downstream Okla., the DO (dissolved oxygen) level declined to 1.3 mg/l with the BOD (biochemical oxygen demand) at 16 mg/l, indicating considerable deterioration in water quality. It is declared as a dead river as it can't support any form of life. Due to unplanned and unrestricted dumps it now releases ammonia and hydro sulphide gas into air which is responsible for breathing problems further resulting into bronchitis, asthma and headache. It is being taken care of by several organizations like Central Pollution Control Board (CPCB), Delhi Pollution Control Committee (DPCC), State Pollution Control Board (SPCB), Delhi Jal Board (DJB) and Japan International Cooperation Agency (JICA). What has been seen regarding the maintenance of Yamuna is that governments has taken temporary interest in the cleaning of the river but a concrete and concerned approach is missing. There have been lumps of investments in the Yamuna express way as well as Delhi Chandigarh express way but from last 15 years the river is crying for help as there is lack of political will or inefficient policies and people's ignorance, the river is dying slow death.

As the two case studies mentioned above unfurl the saga of mismanagement both in terms of legal alternatives as well as action oriented approach, the case study of Sheonath River evidently manifests the spillover effects of miss governance in terms of an illicit nexus between state machinery and private players. The unlawful contract of such sort eroded the legitimate rights of the indigenous to harness the water of the river as a resource and it further ensued into injustice not only at socioeconomic level but also at an environmental note. Sheonath river flows through Borai in Durg district, Chhattisgar government in 2001 commissioned the project and handed it over a stretch of Sheonath River to private players to manage water distribution without setting up independent regulatory authorities that could establish guidelines under which private player can manage a common resource. Actually this project was initiated in 1998 under the Madhya Pradesh industrial Development Corporation It was responsible to cater the industrial needs of the various upcoming water intensive business endeavors in the region.

The government body with an intention to supply water to the region lying between two district headquarters, Durg and Rajnandgaon instead of erecting regulations fraudulently gave a river on a long lease of 22 years to Radius Water, a division of Kailash Engineering. The private company to cater to the business needs of the region erected a 4m high dam through a technique called the Flood Regulating Barrier System along a 3.5 km stretch of the river (Das Binayak, Pangare Ganesh: 2006). The cost of the project was 9 crore for providing 30 million leters of water per day, with an investment of 4 crore it had an capacity of providing 6 million letter per day of which Chhattisgarh state industrial development corporation bought only 4 million liters per day at Rs 6.60 for 1000 liters of water and for common effluent treatment plant CETP, price was fixed at Rs 3.6 per 1000 liters of water. When this business deal was signed, a clause in it mentioned that the villages downstream would get water supply free of cost. The strife between locals and water Management Company did not start immediately. It got triggered after few months when the local fishermen were apprised off the prohibition imposed on fishing within 200 meter zone from the barrage. Arrangement of such sort ensued into banning of fishing and clear guidelines to the farmers that they can't lift water from the river with the help of motor pumps. These restrictions were actively endorsed by district administration accompanied by Chattisgarh state industrial development corporation's verdict which also outlawed the installation of tube wells in the region. It opened up as a Pandora's Box with two prominent types of complaints. The first one was with reference to abatement in the ground water levels and another one was with reference to noncompliance of the contract of providing free water to the villagers by the Radius Water.

Within the state of Chhattisgarh, Sheonath River is not the only version of siphoning of public resources, especially water. Many other rivers which were the lifeline of the agricultural state were caged in the private hands at the cost of irrigation and daily needs of communities. Apart from the case of Sheonath River, rivers like Kelo, Kurkut, Shabri, Kharun, and Maand also share the same fate. In 1991 Jindal Steel and Power Ltd set up a sponge iron factory around Kelo with a capacity of producing 5 lakh tonnes of iron every year. As it expanded, it set up a power plant too. In 1996 it made a bid to lift water from the river which was refused by government on the pretext that it would cause water shortage. With the persistence of Jindal, government not only bent to the proposal but also endorsed Jindal's proposal to erect a check dam which enabled Jindal to lift 35,400 cubic meters of water every day (Putul Alok Prakash: 2008).

As such a unprecedented stashing of public resources preceded into water crunch, amongst the impacted communities were the farmers of Bonda Tikra and Gudgahan as their lands were taken in the name of another irrigation project and the only way they could irrigate the fields were from the waters of Kelo. Such a scenario resulted into socioeconomic backfiring of the various projects erected by Jindal.

As there were large demonstrations, protests and rallies by the tribal farmers which were also against various other projects like acquisition of extra land for its 1000MW power plant set in 143 acres which effected more than 6,000 families in 15 villages. Taking cognizance of the anger of the people, the chief minister in 2004 ordered the work on the dam to be stopped, contrary to that, ignoring to the legal orders, Jindal resumed the work after one weak. It was not Jindal alone who overstepped the legal sanctions issued by the state's chief minister but an entire bureaucracy including police and local judicial authorities which lined up to give illicit wavers to corporate giant rather than standing by the side of people. The local bureaucrats often called the village people and threatened them to be jailed, if they opposed the construction of the dam. It was accompanied by police whom intimidated people of disputes followed by local judicial authority which maintained that land in the end belonged to the government.

The saga of looting of public resources is further reiterated when various other rivers in Chhattisgarh were confided in the private hands. A large part of the Shabri River that flows through Naxalite-affected Dantewada in Bastar district is under the occupancy of Essar Steel Chhattisgarh Ltd. which has a pipeline from Dantewada to the port of Vishakhapatnam in Andhra Pradesh to send iron ore with the help of the water pressure of the river. Industrial houses such as Monnet Ispat and Neco Jaiswal have private dams on the Kharoon River in Raipur. Neco Jaiswal lifts 3 mgd and Monnet Ispat 2 mgd water from the Kharoon. Lafarge India possesses rights to 0.75 mgd of water of the Sheonath River. Bajrang Ispat & Power Ltd, SKS Ispat, and M/s South Asian Agro Ltd are in the queue to acquire proprietary rights over the river.

The meaning of commons or common property has got a considerable attention after Garrett Hardin's significant contribution in the essay "tragedy of commons" published in 1968. In the essay harden flags of the certain problems of unrestricted access to the resources resulting into their depletion which further does not have a technical solution but their solution lies in the judicious change in the techniques of natural sciences. He very clearly indicated that these changes do not demand the change in the human values and ideas of morality. His primary focus was the natural resources of the earth and the well fare state. He elaborated over the problem of individuals of acting irrationally, according to their own self-interest resulting in temporary or permanent depletion of the resources which further imbalances the equations between the altruistic once and the free riders.

As unrestricted access to commons by some group of individuals result in accruing the returns of the commons to a particular section of individuals and when it comes to bearing the maintenance cost of the commons the entire community has to suffer due to accumulated gains. Drawing from Garrett Hardin's essay, it can be clearly discerned how India's rivers are evading from public eye and depleting at unrestrained pace which has resulted and is resulting into tragedy of commons.

As commons has been classified into common pooled resources and common properties on the bases of ownership, Kaveri water war is the fitting case to demonstrate, how water as a common resource is disputed. Water can be classified as a common pooled resource within the context of Kaveri water war and the case of Yamuna pollution. Being a common pooled resource, it can have unrestricted access without any claims to ownership. The Kaveri flows from Karnataka to Tamilnadu.

Tracing the history of the dispute, water has always been a bone of contention between the two states, each accusing one another of depriving the benefits to each other. In India water comes under state subject and over 130 years have passed both states has not been in a position to reach to a consensus. Situation of this kind has simply eroded the rights of communities of each state of using the water as per their needs. In pre modern times communities use to be the owner of the resources but in the current scenario both states have not been in a position to reach up to a sustainable alternative. Now the question arises that, should the ownership rights of the river left entirely to the community? It would certainly not be possible to give away the matter in the hands of communities as the natives won't be in a position to utilize the river in its full capacity due to techno centric development. As River Yamuna is also a common pooled resource, its ownership rests with state government of Delhi.

In last 15 years it has been seen how government along with various agencies has miserably failed to restore Yamuna to its original form. It has turned into a tragedy of commons as when it comes to using Yamuna everybody from industrialists to jal board to the slum dwellers benefit from the river in what so ever capacity they can but on the question of maintenance only state government along with some crucial and dedicated agencies are working for the cause of Yamuna. To address the problem of Kaveri as well as Yamuna, they both need altogether a different approach. On one hand, Kaveri issue needs to be addressed from top to bottom approach on the other hand Yamuna needs a change from bottom to top. On the binding note, as propounded by harden no technical solution can address this issue of commons if they have to be restored to judicious use. An apt consensus has to be reached between the Karnataka government and government of Tamilnadu of river Kaveri is to be used in a cautious manner. On the other hand, Delhi government has to ensure such mechanisms through which they can reach to public to spread the awareness about the sound use of river Yamuna as a common resource.

Since rivers falls under the common pooled resources as per the legal apparatus of India as well as pre-colonial community laws, in the case of Chhattisgarh, rivers could have been fallen under the ownership of the local people. Drawing from this standpoint when Madhya Pradesh government today's Chhattisgarh government was outsourcing the rivers in private hands; the people could very well have been taken into confidence. But according to the reports, the things at ground zero went exactly diametric. Both MPAKVN, a government's appointed body and the top management of Radius Water, a water management companies were illicitly hand and glove with each other in eclipsing one of the most vital public resource. In the legal unearthing of the facts, the water management company neither confirmed to the conditions required for minimum capital required for erecting a project nor it had an adequate experience with reference to water management mentioned in the tender.

On the other hand MPAKVN, a government's appointed body kept things in dark and did not took permission, did not even informed the concerned departments like revenue and irrigation before entering into a contract with Radius Water. It ensued into concealing of the deal from public eye in which river was handed over to private entity. The issue came to light when the illegal deals done started exuding the spillover effects In terms of water scarcity and several imposing legal restrictions from people's point of view. With reference to water scarcity, the geography of Chhattisgarh depicts an average of 126 ponds in every village and receives 1400 mm rains every year. Since it has five river basins: Mahanadi, Godavari, Ganges, Narmada and Brahmani Kachar, and several rivers like;Mahanadi, Sheonath, Indravati, Jonk, Kelo, Arpa, Sabri, Hasdev, Eib, Kharun, Peri, and Maand -- water scarcity should not be a problem in the state. But water scarcity is one of the primary problems in the state. As after the privatization of the rivers, people are not only strictly prohibited to use the rivers for fishing purposes but also forbidden to use water even for the drinking purpose.

Scenario of such sort has ensued into several debates of who is the generic owner of the river? Which is further accompanied by polemics between environment, development of indigenous aspirations and industrial growth.

India from its colonial period had been witness to the crises of water governance and even after six and half decades of independence, it has not in a position to ascertain a sustainable alternative as the water in india primarily falls under state subject, many states either due to paucity of resources or political strife have not been in a position to optimize rivers in a judicious demeanor. Given the global stature of India with reference to its economic credibility, water disputes at national level have flagged off a debate of inclusion of water under concurrent list. Before comprehending the debates of water, it is crucial to be apprised of the actual constitutional provision. In a general parlance, water in India is state subject. But the position is not as simple.

The primary entry in the Constitution relating to water is indeed Entry 17 in the State List, but it is explicitly made subject to the provisions of Entry 56 in the Union List which enables the Union to deal with inter-State rivers if Parliament legislates for the purpose. Which means that if parliament considers the development and regulation of river in the public interest, it can enact a law which can give executive and legislative powers over that river. Since independence no such law have been passed by the parliament due to sociopolitical strains between the center and the state. It has ensued into a dead letter. from the vide spectrum of academicians, bureaucracy, national planners, social activists and multitude of justice seekers, scholars from the vintage point of decentralized government ascertain that water should not be a part of concurrent list. As it is not only averse to the federal structure but also detrimental to the political machinery which may proceed into backfiring. Apart from that inclusion of water in the concurrent list would facilitate central government to make laws on the water as a resource.

Given the facilitation of making laws on water when it will be in the concurrent list seems a futile legal alternative as central government can already regulate it when it "water" under union list in the entry 56. The workable alternative can be to rework on, how can make river boards as effective regulatory bodies which can work in an apolitical demeanor. On the other hand there is a strong push to include water in concurrent lists and centralize it. as to many policy makers water essentially cannot be reduced to merely to rivers, it is also in several forms as a resource like: ponds and lakes, springs, groundwater aquifers, glaciers, soil and atmospheric moisture, wetlands etc. to them decision of putting water in the hands of states have proved into a temporal decision, given the water crunch in today's scenario. The unanticipated climatic variations have further aggravated the problem of water management which calls for active participation of all stakeholders which should be steered primarily by the central government, given its resources and constitutional stature.

State after state and river after river in India, the story of unwarranted corporate loot and stashing of the public resources in the name of management have become an order of the day in most of its parts, especially in the developing ones. Example construction of Narmada dam on the river Narmada, various hydro projects in Himachal Pradesh, and usurping of river Ganges. With the advent of the scenario of liberalization and globalization in the economic spheres, commons have all of sudden emerged as a sight of conflict. People find it extremely arduous to confront the techno centric and neoliberal forces offered both by state and market, if they want to maintain possession over commons. On the other hand the new grammarians of globalization drew the inspiration to accumulate to avoid the tragedy of commons. The illicit amassing of public resources further ensues into market fundamentalism to which citizens are coerced to subjugate.

In such a scenario neither the state nor the market caters to the needs of the citizens. Now the question arises, in the prepossessed system of injustice in which cries for integrity are lost in the chambers of power and corruption, where do we go from here? Laws and courts of any country are two pillars on which the society in entirety rests. As laws on one hand derived from the customs details the society about the default contracts and put forth various legal regulations, courts on the other hand with the help of fare and just mechanisms fill in the spaces of injustice and abide by the given laws. They "courts" not only reduce the transaction costs from injustice to justice but also ensure "the rule of law".

When India in the world has one of the longest constitution, on the same hand it is accompanied by lack of implementation. The lack of implementation of laws questions both the government apparatus as well as the functioning of judiciary. In the recent years there has been increasing ambivalence towards Indian judicial system. As there has been increase in judicial activism on the same hand there has been a decline in the public faith due to the working of the courts with reference to the delaying of the cases (Galanter (1984: 500).

When commons have emerged as a sight of conflict at an unprecedented level, it is high time for the judiciary to act as a lender of last resort in terms of granting justice to the citizens. It will not only secure once legitimate right to justice but it will also help to preserve the commons. As addressing the questions of commons, there is dire need to retain the commons as they are the rich resources of the country. Rather they must be preserved judiciously so that they become sustainable and long-lasting. One of the most imperative tasks that India needs to achieve is to formulate strict and clear-cut laws to regulate commons in the favor of actual public good, by empowering the judiciary and by ensuring its implementation if it wants to achieve undisputed development.

References:

1. Arrunada Benito, Andonova Veneta, Judges' Cognition and Market Order, Review of Law and Economics, 2008, 4(2), 665-92
2. Bhagwati, P, N., Dias, C, J., the Judiciary in India: A Hunger and Thirst for Justice.
3. Gajaweera, N., Bangalore, a Global City? Virtual Realities and Consumer Identities, Equations July 2006.
4. Guha, R., Environmentalism, a Global History, Oxford University Press.
5. Hardin, G. (1968). The Tragedy of the Commons. Science, 162(3859), 1243-1248. http://www.sciencemag.org/content/ 162 /3859/1243.full
6. Iyer R. Ramaswamy, Should water be moved to Concurrent List? June 18, 2011 Updated: June 23, 2011 01:31 IST
7. Meenakshisundaram, SS., Raghvan, P, M., Singh, A., Backgrounders on Conflict, The Cauvery Conflict., National Institute of Advanced Studies Conflict Resolution Programme, 2010.
8. Paley, N., The Cauvery Water War, Division of Environmental Studies University of California Davis, CA 95616 USA, URL: nwpelkey@ucdavis.edu
9. Pangare Ganesh, Das Binayak. Privatization in Chhattisgarh, a River Becomes Private Property, Economic and Political Weekly February 18, 2006
10. Pustule Alok Prakash, 2008, News and analysis on social justice and development issues in India, Privatization unlimited: Rivers for sale in Chhattisgarh, www. infochangeindia.org
11. Sharma, D., Kansal, Arun. Current condition of the Yamuna River - an overview of flow, pollution load and human use.
12. Visvanathan, S., A Letter to the 21st Century Author(s), Economic and Political Weekly, Vol. 35, No. 1/2 (Jan. 8-14, 2000), pp. 12-15.URL: http://www.jstor.org/stable/4408791

Chapter-III

Growing cities and Increasing Disaster: A Case Study of 18th Sept. 2011 Earthquake

Amrita Singh*

Abstract

Because of the development and change in society, disasters are augmented. Sikkim is a place which is prone to earthquakes and still the growth of buildings which is taking place is at high pace. This paper aims to explore a number of lessons learned from the disaster experienced in Sikkim in response to the earthquake of 2011. The basic objective of the paper is to examine the pattern of change due to the development and the result of the same after 2011 earthquake. It also examines the determinants and dimensions of public awareness of, and response to earthquake vulnerability in order to design more effective public communication strategies and mitigation policies. This study uses mixed methodology approach to explore a variety of potentially salient influences on awareness and adaptations to the vulnerability of earthquake. The required data were collected from direct questionnaire based primary field study as well as through interviews. The survey comprised of 200 households representing both residential and non-residential (schools, institutions, etc.). It discusses the shortcomings of disaster preparedness measures of the people in the context of development relationship. Through the investigation and survey of the earthquake, the paper also outlines the possible measures which can be done to educate people with the help of government and NGO's.

Keywords: Coping Capacity, Disaster, Hazard, Mitigation, Vulnerability Assessment.

* *Department of Geography and Natural Resource Management, Sikkim University, India.*

Introduction

The basic problem in the area is the vulnerability of the people due to the changing environment and people's approach towards new and more developed societies. In this globalized world each and every individual wants to come up with more and better living of standard and in order to fulfil their desires and wishes human 's are neglecting the nature and its absorbing capacity and as a result haphazard construction and uncontrollable developments are taking place ignoring the type of areas and its resisting capacities. Many works has been done on earthquakes hazards taking place in the Himalayan regions but in doing so communities are often neglected in this of the region. Their vulnerability and ability to cope in a disaster is always unknown and if their traditional way of battling with these kind of disasters are being followed than the chances of damage will be reduced. Communities' participation in the governmental organisation is very important so that their local ideas can be adopted and applied on the ground level. The paper contributes in the field of importance of traditional knowledge in controlling the damages and aftermaths in an earthquake and tried to show the difference of construction work to resist any sort of disaster taking place in this region.

The North-East Himalaya has a complex geology. Seismic activities in this region are due to the tri-junction of three mountain belts that are Himalayan range, Mishmi Hills and Naga Patkoi range. "The huge oil reservoirs and hydroelectric power projects in this area prove its techno-economic importance and requirement for detailed seismic hazard assessment". (Kapil, Joshi and Patel 2008)

Sikkim Himalaya, situated in the north-eastern part of India, lies in one of the most seismically active zones of the world primarily attributable to the convergence of Indian plate with Eurasia at a rate of approximately 46 mm per year towards the north-northeast. As stated earlier the young fold Himalayan Mountain was created by collision of Indian plate and Asian plate 60 million years ago. The region between MCT (Main Central Thrust) and MBT (Main Boundary Thrust) is presently characterized by tectonic movements, deformation and widespread exposure of post-collisional and also high grade metamorphic rock which implies long term, large scale vertical movements also.

All these factors combine to contribute for steep slopes which are highly susceptible to weathering, mass wasting and erosion. The intense rain during monsoon along with these factor cause extensive soil erosion and also heavy loss soil nutrients through leaching. In the past 35 years there have been 18 earthquakes in this region of magnitude 5 or greater. No doubt there will be many more in the future. Some will be along the strike slip faults & others may be along the major thrust faults like the Main Central Thrust.

India's earthquake Sept. 18 was likely the result of two seismic events striking at nearly the same time, according to the U.S. Geological Survey (USGS). It was a shallow focus earthquake measuring 6.9 in Ritcher scale with its epicenter near the India-Nepal border (27.730N, 88.080E, 68 km NW of Gangtok, Sikkim, India) which shook the Northeast and large parts of northern and eastern India. According to Indian Metrological Department (IMD), the state experienced three aftershocks since the earthquake, occurring at magnitudes of 5.7, 5.1, and 4.6 within 30 minutes of the initial earthquake. At least 20 aftershocks back-to-back throughout the night were recorded.

This, in turn, calls for a multi- disciplinary effort on the part of scientists, social scientist and engineers to create a seismic micro-zonation map and vulnerability map. Hence, earthquake vulnerability is a complex problem without clear scientific and political solutions. It's an issue with major political, economic, socio-cultural, psychological, and ethical implications, which must be understood by the policy makers and wider society in order to respond effectively.

Earthquake in the Mountain Areas

The record of earthquakes in India is patchy prior to 1800. Only two earthquakes of the dozens of known historical events have resulted in surface ruptures (1st Sept. 1803 of magnitude 8.09 & August 1833 0f magnitude 7.9 near Kathmandu). Damage from large Himalayan earthquakes recorded in Tibet and in Northern India suggests that earthquakes may attain Magnitude 8.2. According to Bilham (2004) "Seismic gaps along two-thirds of the Himalaya that have developed in the past five centuries, when combined with geodetic convergence rates of approximately 1.8 m/cy, suggests that one or more magnitude 8 earthquakes may be overdue. The mechanisms of recent earthquakes in Peninsular India are consistent with stresses induced in the Indian plate flexed by its collision with Tibet. A region of abnormally high seismicity in western India appears to be caused by local convergence across the Rann of Kachchh and possibly other rift zones of India. Since the plate itself deforms little, this deformation may be related to incipient plate fragmentation in Sindh or over a larger region of NW India".

The Sikkim Himalaya are part of tectonically active region of the "Alpine-Himalayan global seismic belt", with four great earthquakes of the world of magnitude 8.0 and above occurring in this part of the world (1897 Shillong earthquake of magnitude 8.0, 1905 Kangra earthquake of magnitude 7.8 to 8.0, 1934 Bihar-Nepal earthquake of magnitude 8.1, and 1950 Assam earthquake of magnitude 8.5).

The magnitude 6.9 earthquake occurred inland on 18 September 2011 at a shallow depth of 19.7 km (12.2 mi) has also left an imprint for the researchers to think that what may be the scenario of damage from the earthquakes occurring in the Himalayas from past to till now. At its location, the continental Indian and Eurasian Plates converge with one another along a tectonic boundary beneath the mountainous region of northeast India near the Nepalese border.

Although earthquakes in this region are usually inter-plate in nature, preliminary data suggests the Sikkim earthquake was triggered by shallow strike-slip faulting from an intra-plate source within the over-riding Eurasian Plate. Initial analyses also indicate a complex origin, with the perceived tremor likely being a result of two separate events occurring close together in time at similar focal depth.

Earthquakes as a Natural Hazard

A natural disaster is the effect of the earth's natural hazard for e.g. earthquake, landslide etc. They can lead to financial, environmental or human losses. The resulting loss depends on the vulnerability of the affected population to resist the hazard, also called their resilience.

If these disasters continue it would be a great danger for the earth. Disasters occur when hazards meet vulnerability. Thus a natural hazard will not result in a natural disaster in areas without vulnerability, e.g. strong earthquakes in uninhabited areas.

The entire Himalayan region is a 2,500 km-long belt from Kashmir in the west to Arunachal Pradesh in the east. "It can be divided into several siesmo-tectonic blocks, including Darjeeling-Sikkim, where numerous moderate magnitude earthquakes (M C 5.0) had been recorded" (Pal, et al. 2007). The whole Himalayan arc is a seismically active region in the Indian subcontinent which has given rise to many earthquakes of Magnitude greater than 8.0 since the Great Assam earthquake of 1897 in the North East. Maximum seismic activity has been seen between the Main Boundary Thrust (MBT) and the Main Central Thrust (MCT). Thrust faults are oriented in the East–West direction in the Himalayan region, which suggests that the Indian plate is moving underneath the Eurasian plate in North to NNE-SSW direction.

The eastern India–Nepal Himalayan zone has been seismically active with major earthquakes occurring in the north of the MBT. In the Sikkim Himalayas, the MBT and MCT are not parallel, with the MCT arching to form a culmination, an exceptional geologic feature which is believed to be a controlling factor for earthquakes in the region. Three other moderate earthquakes that have hit the region in recent times are the M 5.9, M 6.0 and M 5.3 events in 1965, 1980 and 2006 respectively. Events of 1965 and 1980 were caused by strike-slip movements, suggesting the presence of transverse tectonics in the region.

The Sikkim region is located in the earthquake-prone territory of the eastern Himalaya along Darjeeling-Sikkim tract, where fast and unplanned urbanization is still active with the record of a good number of moderate earthquakes in this terrain. Most workers in this field of research have divided the Himalayas into a series of longitudinal tectono-stratigraphic domains such as:

1. Sub Himalayas
2. Lesser Himalayas,
3. Higher Himalayas, and
4. Tethys Himalayas

The Sikkim Himalayan territory is characterized by intense micro-seismic activity. The earthquakes of magnitude 3.0–5.6 recorded by Sikkim Strong Motion Array (SSMA) during 1999–2002 for a span of 3 years have been presented on the IRS-1C LISS III map of the Sikkim region as shown in fig 3.2(a) below. It is evident that the earthquakes have distributed occurrences, but the hypocentral depths are reasonably well constrained in the eastern and southern Sikkim Himalaya. They are generally shallower than 35 km but exhibit a clustering within the depth range of 10–25 km as depicted in the N–S depth section of Fig 3.2(b). (Pal, et al. 2007).

According to (Ives 2004) in the Himalayan region three specific facets of mountain hazards needs to be identified:

- "The first is that- one form of catastrophic process often triggers another. Thus landslides, rock falls and avalanches are frequently initiated by earthquakes and these secondary factors may be responsible for much more damage than the initiating agent."

- "The second facet to be considered is the location of people and their habitations in relation to unstable slopes and other dangerous sites. Vulnerability is often coincided with poverty and it is the poor who frequently live in badly constructed homes located in less secure sites and among the mountain population there is high proportion of poverty."

- "The third facet is closely related to the second. Following a mountain disaster poor weather may combine with difficulty of access so that rescue and relief responses may be greatly delayed or obstructed. Distance from major population centres, the primary locations for search and rescue and supply of relief materials, or poor communications that are a common feature of mountains or both, inhibit timely response."

And hence all the problems related to social (housing etc.), political agendas and vulnerability of communities to the natural hazards increases due to improper communication and unavailability of safe places where the effected and vulnerable people can shift through.

Earthquake and Unpredictability

The unpredictability of earthquake is another one of the major factor which leads to high number of damage from the disasters like earthquake or it can be said that it one the problem that tremors of the earthquake and its time cannot be predicted as it is the need of the time, which is being demanded from the researchers to find a solution for this which is till now considered as one of the impossible thing which can be solved.

The regions of greatest seismic activity are clearly defined and although there are scientific theories on what causes earthquakes, but it is very rarely possible to forecast the time and place of a destructive earthquake. Moreover, even if such forecasting were possible, although it would reduce the number of lives lost, it would not prevent property damage.

However it is being said that one cannot predict an earthquake but according to one of the recent report of April 2012, quake occurred in Sumatra was expected by the scientists but it was also mentioned that according to their estimation it occurred a little earlier – Arun Bapat[1] especially mentioned it.

Here begins the main issue of the article related to the vulnerability of the areas, the danger and haphazard construction of building in which they are settled down. This will be discussed in the next sub-

---

[1] An Indian seismologist & Associate scientists of the newly formed International Earthquake and Volcano Prediction Centre (IEVPC), IN Orlando, Florida in the United States.

section vulnerability assessment.

(a) Vulnerability Assessment:

"Social Vulnerability is one dimension of vulnerability to multiple stressors and shocks, including abuse, social exclusion and natural hazards. Social vulnerability refers to the inability of people, organizations, and societies to withstand adverse impacts from multiple stressors to which they are exposed". (Wikipedia)

These impacts are due in part to characteristics inherent in social interactions, institutions, and systems of cultural values. Because it is most apparent when calamity occurs, many studies of social vulnerability are found in risk management literature (Peacock and Ragsdale 1997; Anderson and Wood row 1998; Alwang, Siegel et al. 2001; Conway and Norton 2002). However, social vulnerability is a pre-existing condition that affects a society's ability to prepare for and recover from a disruptive event.

"A vulnerability assessment is the process of identifying, quantifying, and prioritizing (or ranking) the vulnerabilities in a system. Vulnerability from the perspective of disaster management means assessing the threats from potential hazards to the population and to infrastructure. It may be conducted in the political, social, economic or environmental fields."

This section basically deals with the assessment of vulnerable areas, human sufferings and the building in which they are living which gives the overall picture of the various types of construction in this part of the Himalaya especially in the study area Chungthang and Gangtok area (Northern & Eastern Sikkim) in the eastern Himalaya. Here vulnerability in general deals with the social vulnerability in the area, the communities, their losses, preparedness and the capacity of the communities to cope up or deal with during a disaster or a hazard.

Figure Showing Structural Type

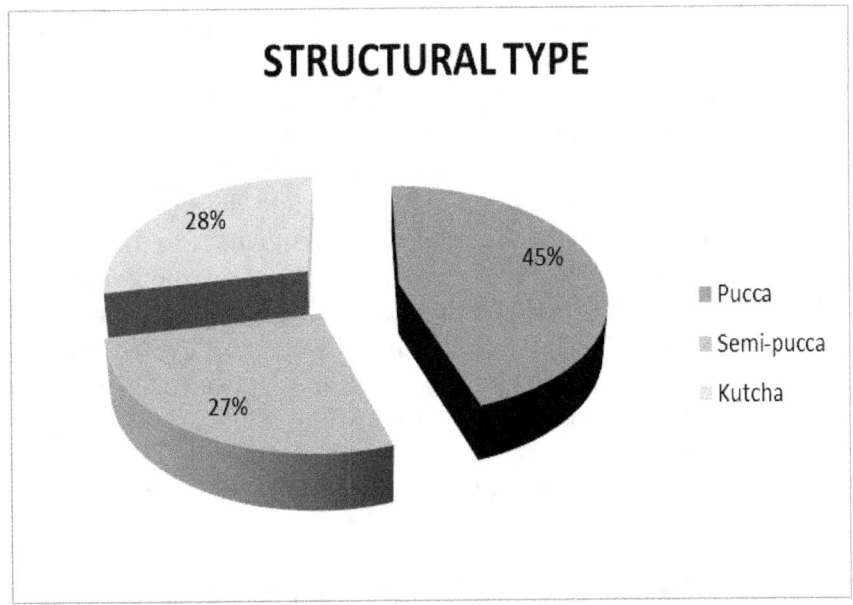

*Showing percentage type of house structure in the study area
(Source: Survey Dec. 2011)*

The above pie-diagram shows the total percentage of different types of structures in the study area which basically includes the area of Chungthang and Gangtok. The data gives a clear picture of the type which is common in the area and is widely used by the people of these areas i.e. Pucca houses are built mostly by the people over there, instead of the fact that the area is at very high altitude and a small tremor can damage a lot in the area and is also prone to earthquakes as compared to other areas. It cannot be said that pucca houses should not be constructed or any kind of development should be hindered but the level of construction i.e. building multi-storey should not be preferred to high level. Among the 200 houses surveyed total pucca houses were around 90 and 56 kutcha houses were there. This generally means that the proportion of damage is also very high in the pucca houses. In these areas high proportion of construction of multi-storeys is being preferred according to the survey which risks the life of the residents and increases the vulnerability for them and for the infrastructure and properties.

The earthquake of 18th September 2011 in Sikkim gives a clear and best example of this fact that pucca houses are damaged mostly and people are suffered or suffering more in these houses in comparisons to others. Some of the damaged houses in the recent earthquake of 2011 in and around study area, the photograph 3.2 below show the structures are made in such a way that it is rendered in state of imbalance with even slight stress in the building during quake. The unplanned structure of the building creates havoc for the people residing in it. In such a seismic zone this type of construction should not be allowed to minimize the damage and loss of life & injuries. The below picture clearly explains that increasing development in cities and with time in villages also creates or push them towards more risk in a hazard event.

Showing Damage to house and to School Building (R) due to Earthquake

Earthquakes damaged house in Singtam, Gangtok

A damaged school in the recent earthquake 2011, Chungthang, North Sikkim

(Source: Survey, Sept. 2011)

Figure Showing Damage of a five-storey building, Gangtok
(Source: Survey, Sept. 2011)

If the same thing is compared with the earlier earthquake of Sikkim occurred on 14th Feb. 2006 of magnitude 5.7 on Richter scale was not greater in size and the damage occurred due to this quake was disproportionate to the size of the earthquake and this also establishes the high level of seismic vulnerability of the region. These damages are the consequences of poor design and construction practices in an inadequate professional environment that is also challenged by the lack of trained human resources in the state. "There is consensus in the scientific world that Sikkim and its adjoining areas will likely witness major earthquakes in the future. This, combined with the poor construction practices prevalent in the area, spells tremendous risk for the population of this region" (Kaushik, et al. 2006).

Solution to this problem may lies in opting safer construction through appropriate construction system, good building materials and control in their poor quality and involving more skilled manpower for design and construction and their supervision is very necessary in this region of India where damage due to earthquake is very high. These things are important to be remembered in the mountainous Himalayas as almost all of the Himalaya falls under the high seismic zone.

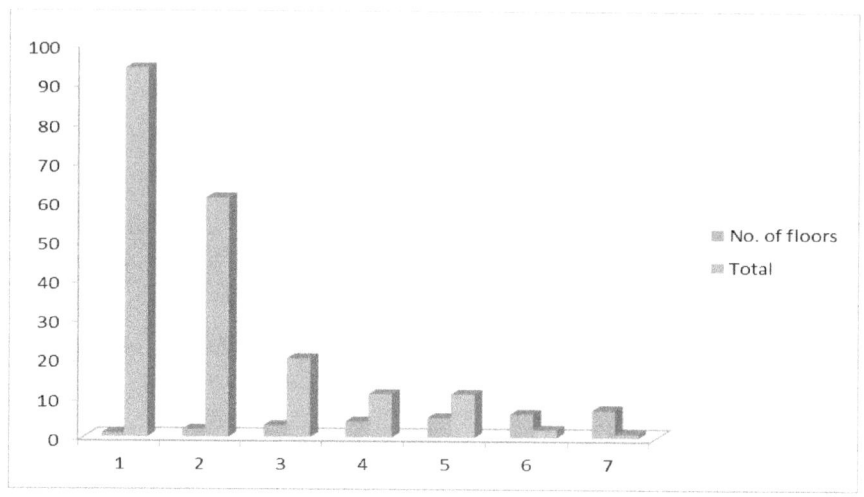

Figure Showing Number of floors and their total in the study area (Source: Survey Dec. 2011)

The above graph shows the construction of floors in the surveyed area ranging from 1 to 7th floor, however the graph shows that highest number of floor which is constructed is 1 which is around 94 in total and the lowest is 7th floor which is only 1 in number. This data is recently taken after the earthquake of 2011 and if the building height is not so high than what is reason for its collapse, it is poor constructions and unavailability of materials. The construction of 7 storey building is found in the Gangtok area and in Chungthang the highest construction is found around 5 storey, which means people in this high altitude is still constructing high buildings because of lack of awareness and lack of knowledge about the consequences and ill-effects of the earthquakes.

After 2006 earthquake the construction of multi-storeyed buildings was not stopped and its affect was again seen after 2011 earthquake. One of the measure factors may be governing for the ban of multi-storey buildings is government policy for the state seeing its necessity. However the region has the policy not to build multi-storey but it was not followed by its people because of lack of implementation policies of the government and also lack of awareness among the people or in the society.

Figure Showing Development of Cities

(Source: Survey July 2013)
Photo Plate Showing Haphazard Construction of Buildings

(Source: Survey July 2013)

Aftermath of earthquake is mainly the effects on the community or individual due to collapse of building. Most of the injuries and deaths are due to collapsing of buildings and it includes other factors. It is also being observed that most of the cracks are in the governmental building. The case of collapse is not there in the government buildings but cracks occurred in these buildings are in high proportion and this arises a question in front of the government about the construction material and design and also planning of disaster preparedness in the region.

A different type of house constructions has different effects on house damage, so the loss of life and property will also be different. It will differ from concrete house to bamboo and wooden houses. The damage will be more in the concrete houses than that of the bamboo one. These were in a one way traditional way of reducing damage extent by constructing traditional houses. It is being said that wooden houses can minimize the casualties during earthquake. No cracks were observed in the entire structure & a bit crack on the ground floor due to irregular surface or loose binding of rock and soil and there was no casualties or severe injury to most of the people living in these type of houses.

One of the respondent aged 92 Years, stated that construction of these wooden houses they have learned it from their forefathers and they first used to choose the woods which are more durable and less fungi affecting. The main disadvantage with wooden houses is that it easily attack by decay fungi during the monsoon season. But plastic coating material over the roof and plastic paint on the wall can minimize the decay fungal attack.

(b) Dimension of earthquake resistance households and damages

The extent of damage also depends on the awareness among the people and their behaviour towards it because most of the time being known and familiar to some of the facts many people don't follow it. The present chapter is going to focus on the awareness factor and their preparedness for these kinds of disasters and the total number of damage in and around the study area.

Figure Showing Earthquake resistance housing

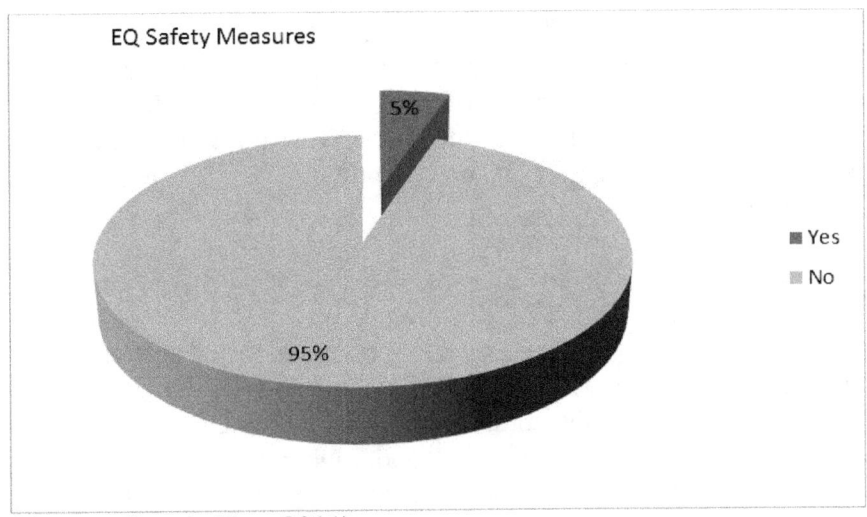

(Source: Survey Dec. 2011)

Figure Showing Houses damaged

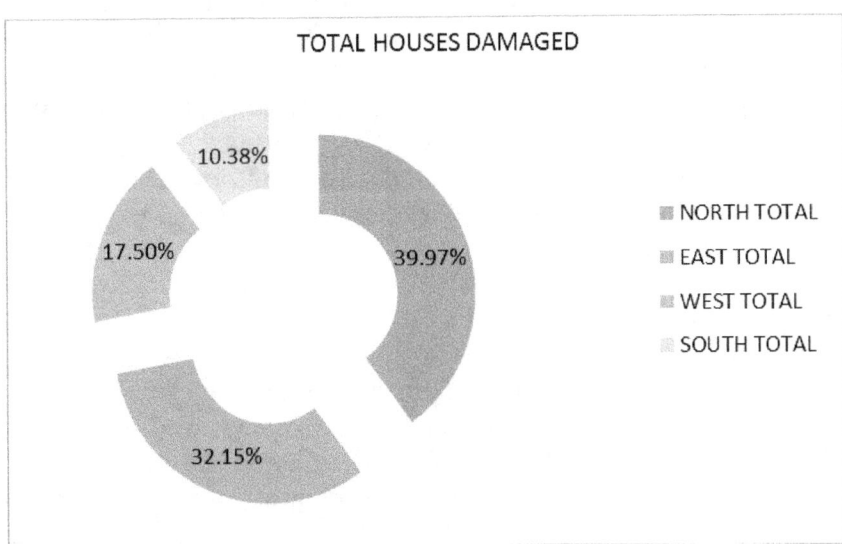

(Source: Sikkim Express, 30th April, 2012)

The total damages across the four different districts of Sikkim shows a vast difference in the data. North district has the highest percentage of damaged houses 39.97% as seen in the figure 3.7, which is almost 40 %, followed by the East district. Lowest damage was registered in south district. One of the reasons behind the high damage in the northern part is the nearness to the epicentre of the earthquake. As it is depicted from the figure the area is prone to hazard and the north happens to be the most susceptible part.

Amount of damage many a times also depends on type of house constructed. While surveying it is noticed that most of the damage is occurred in the modern type of houses constructed with the use of bricks, cement, stones materials and using pillars in the houses and which also presents high in stature while traditional houses are not much damaged because of use of wood, mud, and bamboo materials for construction. Even if there is damage of traditional house no injuries noticed to the people who lived in these types of houses.

Of the total 200 houses surveyed, about 39 % were modern and around 27.50 % were mixed type i.e its construction plan consisted of both modern as well as traditional. On the other hand 33.50 % houses were traditional. It is clear that the highest percentage of construction is modern type of houses followed by traditional and then mixed construction. However, the percentage of traditional houses is not much less but it less from point of view of modern & mixed type of construction. Altogether it has high proportion of modern houses in which very few peoples made their houses earthquake resistant and most of them do not have any knowledge about these things.

With the newly constructed modern houses problem of dampness also starts. However in the study area the percentage of dampness in the houses is not high but around 26.50% of houses has the problem of dampness whereas 73.50% of people reported in negative about the dampness of their houses. These problems occur many times due to unavailability of good raw materials, using the raw materials properly for the construction and also lack of skilled labour.

Conclusion

From the above description it clear that people of these places have not much idea of constructing earthquake resistant housing. The level of education is just divided into the literates and illiterates. The percentage of literate people were high almost around 76.50 % and the people who have never studied before, their percentage is around 23.50 %. But here the main fact is, being the higher percentage of literates it can solve the problem because of the fact that the literacy is mainly primary and so in the area many peoples have no idea about earthquake resistant house which can resist long and even if damage occur the loss will not be much and chances of injuries decreases in these type of situation.

The level of education is basic but important indicator to understand the societal well-being and their awareness. It can be seen from the figure 3.12 that most of the people are literate but their level of education also matters in many ways. Most to the people are educated only up to primary level and may not appreciably understand its effect and what would be the prudent steps during these disasters. It is also found that very few people know about the organizations or NGO's in the nearby areas. The percentage is around 13.50 % among which the information about the organization or social groups exists and this shows that the area is not much developed or connected to outside world.

From the above discussion it can be said that these some of the variables which explain the people's awareness about the construction of earthquake resistance house and the percentage of people used it (fig. 3.4), and the type of house constructed by the people with the changing and developing world also force others to change with time. Some of the respondents also mentioned that in this century and with capitalisation & modernization people are preferring bamboo or wooden houses. They think that it saves money and time and cheap labours are available which doesn't cost much to them. Many people think the family is poor or low who lives in these types of houses. But these should not be preferred much because construction differs from one place to another and area to area and it should be done by observing the place and area and its danger to the disaster and hazards.

Post-earthquake scenario is basically the result of the works in this field and the scenario of the study area existing after the earthquake. The pressure on the communities and their socio-economic life always become worse after an earthquake.

It includes the people's participation in different groups and their awareness about earthquake and its aftermaths and number of peoples involved in any organisation because by knowing these things one can estimate the preparedness and the scenario of the whole area can be predicted to some extent. As people are not much familiar with the different organization or never get any training in any activity obviously their level of knowledge will be less and the preparedness level will go down automatically.

The first-hand experience & information of the conditions and aftermaths of the earthquake right after the occurrence of the incident which shows the ground reality that whether in authenticity it is true to say that high building construction in the unfavourable environment really effects the society and its people highly or it is just for the say. The study gives the clear picture that height of the building and construction material differs from one place to other and its affects make them more vulnerable to such kind of hazards.

The study has certain limitations of time and access to some of the areas was not possible where more affected people and their vulnerability can be better studied. Due to the shock of the hazard which took place in the society it was very difficult for the people of those areas to communicate in a better way. The study in short indicates that awareness among people about the respective disaster which can take place in the areas is very necessary so that they can take proper precautions and can help each other during calamity. Lack of proper education and information can affect the individual and whole community in many different ways which always makes them more vulnerable to any kind of disaster. To cope with the disaster community's help and proper understanding is also very necessary.

References

Journal Papers:
1. Kapil, M., A. Joshi, and R.C Patel. "The assessment of seismic hazard in two seismically active regions in Himalayas using deterministic approach." J. Ind. Geophysics. Union 12, no. 3 (2008): 97-107.
2. Bilham, R.,. "Earthquakes in India and the Himalaya: Tectonics, Geodesy and History." ANNALS OF GEOPHYSICS 47, no. 2/3 (April/June 2004): 839-858.
3. Pal, I., et al. "Earthquake hazard zonation of Sikkim Himalaya using a GIS platform." Springer Science+ Business Media B.V, 2007: 333-377.
4. Ives, J.D. Himalayan Perceptions- Environmental change and the Well-being of Mountain People. Oxon, 2004.
5. Kaushik, H.B., K Dasgupta, D R Sahoo, and G Kharel. Sikkim Earthquake of 14 February 2006. Reconnaissance, Tata Steel Limited, 2006.
6. Cutter, Susan L. J. Bryan Boruff, and W. Lynn Shirley. "Social Vulnerability to Environmental Hazards." SOCIAL SCIENCE QUATERLY 84, no. 2 (2003): 242-261.

Chapter-IV

Spatial and Transportation Concerns for Climate Change- Issues and options for Hill Areas

Ashwani Luthra*

Abstract

Climate Change has been a cause of concern of almost all the sections of the society nationally and globally because of its negative impacts. Increment in greenhouse gases, especially Carbon Dioxide (CO_2) is responsible for Global Climate Change, whose share is estimated to have increased by 30% since pre-industrial times. Consequently, there has been general consensus that the global temperature has increased to the tune of 2°C and transport has been a major greenhouse gas emitting sector. Unplanned urban growth, greater dependence on private vehicles in the absence of energy efficient mass public transport systems and poor fuel technology are some of the glaring reasons for increasing CO_2 share in the atmosphere. International and national efforts have begun in different sectors to control the climatic changes with a view to save the human settlements and mankind from its adverse impacts. Sustainable spatial and transportation planning options have been suggested as mitigating options to climate change impacts. The present paper attempts to take a stock of the changing global climate and identify the mitigation measures especially concerning the spatial planning and transportation sector to control climate change with special reference to hill areas.

Key words: Spatial Transportation, Carbon Dioxide, Fuel, Climate Change, Hills

* *Faculty, Guru Ramdas School of Planning, Guru Nanak Dev University, Amritsar*

Introduction

Since the beginning of industrial revolution, human activities have led to unprecedented changes in chemical composition of earth's atmosphere. The global atmospheric concentration of carbon dioxide, a greenhouse gas (GHG) largely responsible for global warming, has increased from a pre-industrial value of about 280 ppm to 379 ppm in 2005. Similarly, the global atmospheric concentration of methane and nitrous oxides, other important GHGs, has also increased considerably [Ministry of Environment & Forests, 2010].2 Unprecedented spatial spread of urban settlements to house increased population, whimsical increment in industrial units, and high reliance on private transport are the major contributors to changes in chemical composition. These chemical changes have been recognized to have led to global climate change. A study conducted by U.S. Environmental Protection Agency [2008] reveals that electric power, transport and industry contribute about 88% of the carbon emissions in the air. Transport sector alone contributes to about 23% of the total carbon emissions.3 Hilly areas are no exceptions to these trends and patterns as green hills are coming bald to meet the increased housing needs. Number of private transport modes is increasing day by day to meet the increased travel needs in the absence of public transport facilities.

Density of traffic is increasing due to lack of matching increment in road length/ widening. Consequently, the combined impact has been on increasing micro temperature and environmental degradation of the urban settlements in hilly terrains. National Appropriate Mitigation Actions (NAMA) for climate change have proposed for application of land-use planning principles to reduce energy consumption and limit urban sprawl. Consequently, role of spatial planner has become multi-fold to make efforts to plan sustainable human communities and different systems within them as counter measures to reduce the impacts of climate change.

---

2   Climate Change and India: A 4x4 Assessment (A Sectoral and Regional Analysis for 2030s), INCCA: Indian Network for Climate Change Assessment, Ministry of Environment & Forests, Government of India, November 2010.

3   U.S. Environmental Protection Agency, Inventory of Greenhouse Gas Emissions and Sinks: 1990-6006, April 2008

Climate Change: Concept, State of Art

According to Ministry of Environment & Forests [2010], climate change is recognized as a significant manmade global environmental challenge.4 'Global Climate Change', 'Global Warming', 'Green House Gas Emissions' and the like terms have caught attractions of policy makers, technocrats, scientists and researchers in the middle of 20th century. Increment in Green House Gases (GHGs) in the atmosphere is responsible for global climate change [Luthra, Ashwani, 2010].5 Climate change refers to changes in long-term trends in average temperature. Man's efforts to cater to his needs have been primarily responsible for climate change.

Since past few decades researchers have noticed that the global temperature has been rising continuously. It has been agreed in general that the global temperature has increased to the tune of 2°C [While, 2008] and it is expected to rise by 1.5° to 3.5° C by 2100.6 Citing International Penal on Climate Change AR4, Ministry of Environment & Forests, 2010 mentioned that rise in temperature by the end of the century with respect to 1980-1999 levels would range from 0.6°C to 4.0°C and the sea level may rise by 0.18 m to 0.59 m during the same period. The all-India maximum temperatures show an increase in temperature by 0.71°C per 100 year and all-India mean annual minimum temperature has significantly increased by 0.27°C per 100 years during the period 1901-2007 [Ministry of Environment & Forests, 2010].7

Urban areas have born the impacts of climate change the most. According to working paper on 'Cities, Climate Change and

---

4   Climate Change and India: A 4x4 Assessment (A Sectoral and Regional Analysis for 2030s), INCCA: Indian Network for Climate Change Assessment, Ministry of Environment & Forests, Government of India, November 2010

5   Luthra, Ashwani (2010)

6   http://www.enotes.com/public-health-encyclopedia/climate-change-human-health

7   Climate Change and India: A 4x4 Assessment (A Sectoral and Regional Analysis for 2030s), INCCA: Indian Network for Climate Change Assessment, Ministry of Environment & Forests, Government of India, November 2010

Multilevel Governance'8, climate change is expected to impact the cities and their regions through increased intensity of heat waves, directly affecting the human health; increases in intense rainfall events, increasing the risk of inland flooding; retreat of mountain glaciers, impacting water availability and its quality; and an increased risk of drought and water shortage in already dry regions [OECD Environmental Working Papers N°14,2009]. Urban centres may also be particularly vulnerable to some of the distributive impacts of climate change. Climate change is expected to have physical and economic consequences across numerous and diverse human activities.

Tourism acts as an engine of growth for the hill regions/settlements by benefiting them through increased employment, income, infrastructural facilities, etc. It accounts for 40-60% of international tourism (as per UN and WTO estimates) and its global value has been estimated to be as high as 1 trillion [Luthra, Ashwani, 2003].9 Tourist traffic to Himachal Pradesh has increased to 5.10 million in 2002 out of which 0.14 million have been the foreigners. Shimla, the Capital of the State, is the most important tourist town of the State, which attracted about 1.74 lac tourists in 2011 and is expected to attract 20.45 lac tourists by 2025 [City Development Plan Shimla, 2025].10 As a result of increased tourism lot of land is developed for hotels, shopping areas, roads and man-made tourist spots, which consume large chunks of land for these purposes. Other towns and cities of hill areas are no exceptions to such trends.

Increased population in a hill town has direct bearing on demand for space for housing, which leads to expansion of urban space and reduction in tree cover. It is evident that the urban requirements are consuming the green cover rapidly, hence contributing to adverse effects of climate change. Reduction in rainfall, lesser snow cover and smaller duration of snow are some of the glaring effects in hill areas in past few decades. It has impacted the farm production adversely and the economy of the city and the region is under losses.

8   OECD Environmental Working Papers N° 14 (2009)
9   Luthra, Ashwani, 2003

10   City Development Plan Shimla, 2025

On account of tourism whereas there have been economic gains, losses are yet more severe ecologically and socio-culturally. Unprecedented spatial growth and other environmental hazards when clubbed with climate change have outranging physical, physiographic, socio-economic and health impacts on the residents of the hill settlements.

Transportation Profile

Sprawling spatial pattern is partly responsible for higher emissions in urban areas and other forms of environmental stresses. Himachal being an important tourist destination, urban development along its major roads, even in difficult terrain is a bitter reality. Such unplanned urban sprawl has led to unprecedented increase in highway traffic and traffic at the tourist destinations (towns) as well. Ironically, vehicles are increasing but road width is decreasing due to encroachments and unauthorized constructions as well as on account of on road parking. During the peak hours, there is an enormous rush in buses. Traffic load on roads has increased manifold, witnessing chronic problems of bottlenecks, traffic jams and delays. Number of accidents has also increased considerably. The chronic traffic chaos is frequent on the major motorable roads of the city. High traffic volume on narrow roads of the city, bottlenecks and jams are cause of high levels of vehicular pollution especially during peak hours.

Increased vehicular pollution is directly associated with climate change proposition as CO_2 emitted by the vehicles is a greenhouse gas that impacts the climate change to a great extent.

Issues in Hill Areas

To accommodate the rising population in the urban settlements huge parcels of land are put to urban uses, which reduce the green cover. Speculative tendencies of the individuals have also led to converting natural green cover into urban uses. Except for central area, hill towns generally witness low density development, that too in patches at times. Thus, a huge green cover is lost that could absorb large quantum of CO^2 emission. Consequently, loss of green cover directly impacts the climatic conditions in a region in particular and global climate change in general.

Not only high consumption of land for urban uses but the way it is put to various uses is a cause of concern in hilly areas. Sporadic development of urban uses on the peripheries of the towns increases trip lengths, which leads to the use of automobiles to perform different activities in the centre and other parts of the settlement. The outcome of such developments is addition of CO_2 to the environment and hence to climate change.

Generally, hill areas are characterized by mono-nucleated commercial development where the settlement has grown around/along a commercial area. Such development leads to uni-directional flow of traffic to the centre for various reasons. High traffic volume in the centre and on major arteries of the city radiating to the centre cause high CO_2 emission levels.

Also, the tourists reach the tourist spots at specific places by their own vehicles in large quantum, resulting in high traffic density at those spots and result in increased demand for parking. High traffic density leads to high concentration of CO_2 emissions and high parking demand leads to requirement of parcels of land for parking such vehicles that disturb the green cover at times. Both situations impact the global climate change adversely and also do not present conducive conditions for hill environment.

High land values in the central areas of cities has led to over exploitation of natural resources and denser development. Loss of green cover on one hand and higher use of energy products (air conditioners) to counter heat on the other hand lead to higher micro temperature in the area. The composite consequence of such developments has been adverse impact on climate and higher demand for energy in the region.

The corridor type urban development is no way desirable because it results in development of housing nodes along the highways. Whereas such developments disturb the ecology of the hill areas, the fumes of highway traffic impact the residents of these developments.

Research reveals that size of any settlement has direct bearing on its transport demand. Studies also reveal that due to various reasons the increased travel demand in the cities is not catered by the public transport system these cities have. Therefore, because of inadequate supply of mass transport services nearly 60% to 70% of the travel needs are met by the private modes. The transport scene on the urban roads being chaotic ultimately leads to high proportion of CO_2 emission, thus adding to climate change.

Transport system management (TSM) measures are either non-existent or inappropriate in most of the cases. Barring few cities, neither the authorities nor the public at large are having concern for meeting the travel needs in a planned manner. The impact has been chaotic traffic scenes, frequent jams, conflicts, accidents, etc. The net outcome of all these conditions has been increased vehicular emissions. The central areas are worst effected by such conditions. The intersections are usually the most affected areas from environmental point of view as occurrence of traffic jams, conflicts, congestion, etc. are frequent at these spots. It leads to frequent stopping and start of the vehicles and even longer halts of traffic, thus resulting in high emissions.

Large number of old vehicles and their seldom maintenance result in reduced operational efficiency of such vehicles and increased emissions levels. The public transport vehicles used in hill rears are no different from such inefficiencies. Hence, their contribution to different types of GHGs, especially CO_2, is quite high.

Heterogeneous traffic conditions, improper traffic management, high traffic congestion and frequent stop & go system by different vehicles, etc. lead to differentials in the quantities of emissions. Vehicles under stop/start conditions use up to three times more fuel and cause three times more emissions than those in free flow traffic. The hydrocarbon emission at idling for petrol driven vehicles is 750 PPM compared to 300 PPM at cruising and 4000 at deceleration. Similar is the case with respect to CO_2. Therefore, the fluctuations in the movement of a vehicle lead to high air pollution levels.

As a consequence of climate mean changes the temperature in the hills has been increasing in terms of intensity and duration. The tourists visiting hill towns are not realizing the charm of the climate hills usually have. Therefore, the tourists are trying to find new avenues and spots at higher ranges, resulting in reduction in tourism related activities in the lower ranges. Consequently, the less touched hill places are targeted by the tourists. Tourism being the backbone of the economy of the hill regions, the government is also encouraging the development of remote tourist places for potential tourism. Thus, germs of haphazard urban sprawl reach such places as well and green cover is further reduced in the region. Such an activity is in no way good from climate change point of view because in the longer run it is going to affect the future generations adversely in numerous ways, be it health, productivity or damage to eco-system.

Increased temperature in hills has led to increased energy consumption due to heating. Air conditioners are used in the lower ranges. The heat emitted by the air conditioners further increases the temperature in the area hence adding to climate change in the area.
It has been observed that the snow fall in the hill regions has been starting late since a long time in north India. Also, its duration has been less. This has impacted the agricultural production of staple crops of the hill areas to a great extent in different regions.

Climate change affects the worker's productively adversely, leading to less production and lesser growth of the total production of the region. Hill areas are no way different. Lower productivity of the workers has a strong bearing on long-term economic development.
There are chances of increased mortality and morbidity from, e.g. development of vector borne diseases due to increase in global mean temperature. Number of deaths may rise because of more frequent heat wave and thermal stress.

Loss of economic activity due to lesser tourism leads to cultural losses and migration. Workers migrate to planes or nearby areas in search job to feed their families. There have been many areas in lower ranges of hills from where the working man power migrates to other urban areas.

Spatio-Transport options for Hill Areas

It is evident that there is an urgent need to undertake some policy measures to control and regulate the development and GHG emissions for the sustainable growth of future communities in the hill regions. Following spatio-transport mitigation measures are suggested to head for India's commitment to reduce CO_2 emissions by 25% by 2020.

Spatial planning measures and controls should be adopted and implemented at the earliest possible. Master Plans and Zonal Development Plans must be prepared on priority basis for all the hill towns and cities. It is strongly recommended that Regional Planning Approach should be followed while preparing the Master Plans as it will help in analysing the potentials of different geographic areas and micro regions and plan for the same for their development in future. In no way any development should be allowed to come up which is not in consensus with the provisions of Master Plans.

Principle of land use-transport integration should govern the preparation of Master Plans for the hill towns and regions. Decentralized distribution of activities will reduce travel by private transport to a large extent as the trip length will reduce remarkably. Location of major centres of housing, shopping, employment and recreation should be put closer to each other to minimize the number & length of trips and hence result in reduced pollution. Also, the amount of energy consumption will be lower. A study by RITES indicates that with a reduction in trip lengths, pollution level will decrease by 20% (Mishra, S, 1998).

Planning should be done to avoid low density development so that spread of the town is reduced and green cover is saved. Also, public transport, when introduced, can be operated economically. Development of self-contained integrated communities will result in more dependence on non-motorised transport (NMT) modes like walking, thus reducing the vehicular emissions to a great extent.

Hill towns, especially the bigger towns, should be developed on the principle of decentralized planning. The activity areas should be suitably distributed so that the settlements develop on sustainable environment basis. Such efforts shall help in avoiding the uni-directional flow and unnecessary concentration of traffic in central areas of the towns.

Hill areas can save the climate change to a large extent. Therefore, strict, stringent and rigid zoning regulations should be prepared for different zones and implemented religiously to save the environment of hill regions. The core/ central areas of the hill towns should be given special attention as they are most vulnerable to exploitation. As far as possible concentration of activities should be avoided in them so that unidirectional movements to them can be avoided. They should not be developed as high density commercial or any other activity areas.

Special regulations and controls should be prepared and implemented for heritage zones and any such special areas. Such areas should be planned as pedestrian precincts/ zones and in no way vehicles should be allowed to enter these zones. Peripheral parking provisions should be made for the tourist vehicles visiting such zones without disturbing the natural environment of the parking sites.

There is an urgent need that the hill towns should have world class public transport system to suit the needs and requirements of the tourists visiting them and for the local residents. The popular tourist spots should be connected by well-designed and appropriate public transport system. Mass public transport will play a vital role in decongesting the roads and reduce CO_2 emission to a great extent. Electricity based mass transport system is advocated for the hill towns. Possibilities should be worked out for efficient ropeway system to popular tourist spots on difficult terrain.

Well thought of transport system management (TSM) measures will help in reducing the air pollution level in the city in total and congested areas particularly.

Following are some of the TSM measures suggested to reduce air pollution in the cities:
- Introduce road pricing or area licensing scheme for congested routes during peak hours in the city with a view to decongest

the route/area.

- A progressive road pricing policy i.e. increase in route charges in critical areas during peak hours, will induce lesser vehicles to use roads of these roads, especially by their own vehicles.

- A well planned parking policy will help in reducing the air pollution by about 20-30%. On street parking should be strictly banned on major arterials. Progressive parking charges for parking lots around the central area and popular tourist spots should be implemented to optimum use of the parking lots.

- Removed traffic bottlenecks by improvements in road geometry, traffic signs and signal, etc. will supplement the cause of the efforts made. It is estimated that air pollution load shall reduce by about 10% if the traffic is able to move at teh design speed of the road.

- Restrictions on the movement of heavy vehicles during peak hours or day time will reduce traffic volume on main arteries of the town to a large extent resulting in reduction in the traffic problems due to through traffic and improvement in the air environment as well.

- Use of catalytic converters should be made mandatory in the petrol driven vehicles. Catalytic converters remove the bulk of hydrocarbons and carbon monoxide but little of nitrogen oxides. Use of catalytic converters in petrol driven cars can reduce CO_2 and HC levels by more than 70%.

- Proper maintenance of in-use vehicles can reduce exhaust smoke by 30-50%. The competent authority should conduct pollution checkups more frequently at specific points on the main roads and near central areas so to control the pollution levels in the town.

- Fuel composition and its characteristics play an important role in emission performance. Petrol and diesel are the commonly used fuel used in automobiles. But the pollution generated by them is affecting the climate adversely. Therefore, it is high time to use alternative fuels like electricity, solar energy, compressed natural gas (CNG), liquefied petroleum gas (LPG), methanol, ethanol, vegetable oils, hydrogen and synthetic liquid fuels derived from hydrogenation of coal as they have been proved to be less air polluting. It is proposed that the CNG operated smaller vehicles should be introduced in the central area or popular tourist spots to facilitate the tourists and the local inhabitants. Such an effort will help in reducing the air pollution levels down significantly.

- Heavy penalties should be imposed on the polluters so that the hill towns/ regions do not contribute to global climate change.

Conclusion

Hill areas are sensitive to global climate change. Their spatio-transport conditions impact the local temperature conditions in particular and global climate in general. Unplanned and haphazard spatial development of the hill towns has led to huge loss of green cover on the one side and poor traffic and transport conditions on the other side have adversely impacted the environment of hill towns. Rise in CO_2 emission levels have added to GHGs and hence climate change. The suggested spatio-transport measures can help in reducing the climate change impacts to a great extent.

References

1. Corfee-Morlot J. et. al. (2009). Cities, climate change and multilevel governance, OECD Environmental Working Papers N° 14, OECD.
2. Luthra, Ashwani. (2003). Guidelines for eco-tourism in Himachal Pradesh- a case of Shimla, proceedings of 52nd NTPC, Institute of Town Planners India, New Delhi.
3. Luthra, Ashwani. (2010). Role of transport in climate change: reasons and mitigation measures, paper presented at International Seminar on Climate Change: Spatial Concerns and Mitigation Measures, Institute of Spatial Planning and Environment Research, India, Panchkula 16-18 December.
4. Sankhyan, A. R. (2003). Revitalization and rejuvenation of Shimla, proceedings of 52nd NTPC, Institute of Town Planners India, New Delhi.
5. Sankhyan, A. R. (2009). Concerns of tourism infrastructure in Himachal Pradesh, paper presented at workshop on Integrated Infrastructure and Planning – Contemporary Best Practices, Guru Ramdas School of Planning, Guru Nanak Dev University, Amritsar, 13-14 March.
6. Sankhyan, A. R. (2010). State transport network plan –a case of Himachal Pradesh, paper presented at National Seminar on Sustainable Lifelines: Transportation Planning and Management, Guru Ramdas School of Planning, Guru Nanak Dev University, Amritsar, 12–13 March.
7. Environmental Protection Agency. (2008). Inventory of greenhouse gas emissions and sinks, U.S., 1990-6006, April.
8. Ministry of Environment & Forests. (2010). Climate change and India: a 4x4 assessment (a sectoral and regional analysis for 2030s), INCCA: Indian Network for Climate Change Assessment, Government of India, November.
9. Shimla Municipal Corporation. (2005). City Development Plan Shimla, 2025, Government of Himachal Pradesh.

Chapter-V

Impacts of Climate Change on Rivers: A Case Study of Lower Tapi basin

Paresha M. Baria and Dr. S.M. Yadav*

Abstract

Ample scientific evidence is available to verify that the global climate is changing. Increase in global average temperature, rise in sea levels and change in precipitation patterns are the major factors reflecting the climate change effects. To control the threats from extreme precipitation events will be a critical component of climate change adaptation. The present study is an attempt to find out trend of extreme events in context of climate change. The study of extreme events is important in the stochastic behaviour of rainfall pattern. Trend is simply defined as the rate and direction to which the individual data of a time series is changing. There are many methods for trend analysis in the main category of Parametric and non-parametric trend analysis. Parametric trend analysis is carried out when distribution of the time series is known. Graphical method and least square methods are the examples of parametric trend analysis. Non-Parametric trend analysis are carried out when distribution of time series is unknown. Mann-Kendall method and Sen's test are the examples of non-parametric trend analysis. Trend analysis is carried out to know the phenomenon becoming "worst or good". For example if series of observations has been made, using these data one can interpret whether the phenomenon is changing in due course of time or stable. In statistical terms this is a determination of whether the probability distribution from which they arise has changed over time.

Key words - Climate change, Extreme precipitation events, Kakrapar rain gauging station, Tapi River

* Research Scholar and Professor in the Civil Engineering Department, Sardar Vallabhbhai National Institute of Technology, Surat, India

Introduction

Adequate scientific evidence (e.g., IPCC, 2007) exists to show that the global climate is changing. The variation in climate is perhaps greater than any other area of similar size in the world. Change in precipitation patterns is one of the prominent signals of climate change. More extreme precipitation events observed due to the effect of global climate change (Min et al. 2011; Reiss and Thomas 2007, Willems, P.2013).It has direct impact on river runoff.

Likewise, changes in the regional precipitation pattern also have a direct impact on magnitude and frequency of floods, droughts and water availability. Changes in precipitation patterns and frequencies of extreme precipitation events will affect runoff and river discharges at various time scales from sub-daily peak flows to annual variations. Due to effect of flooding events massive socio-economic and environmental damage occurs. Floods are the most commonly hazardous events caused by extreme rainfall because of the threat to human life and the great expense required to construct and maintain hydraulic flood control structures (Climate central 2013). The knowledge of changes in extreme precipitation patterns helps to use strong, suitable and accurate techniques for projections of flood frequencies and magnitudes under climate change, development of flood protection measures by adopting the impact of climate changes. It also helps in revising reservoir policies to overcome flood damages. Long term data has been used by various researchers for the study of climate change (Dessens and Bucher, 1995; Serra et al., 2001; Marengo, 2004). Study of different time series data have proved that trend is either decreasing or increasing. Storm magnitudes have been increased over time in the South East portion of Kansas as a result of growing effects of global climate change (Vahid Rahmani, S.M.ASCE1 et. al.2014).

Trend of Extreme rainfall events and flooding have been increased during the last century and expected to continue in Midwestern United State (Pryor Sara C. et. al., 2013). There is a large variation in the amounts of rainfall received at different locations. Analysis of one-day extreme rainfall series has shown that the intensity of extreme rainfall has been increased over Coastal Andhra Pradesh and adjoining areas, Saurashtra and Kutch, Orissa, West Bengal, parts of northeast India, east Rajasthan (National Climate Centre Research Report 2010).

The extreme events studies are one of the interesting fields of natural sciences. The purpose of extreme value analysis is to measure the stochastic behaviour of a process at unusually high or low levels. The stochastic behaviour of extreme events can be studied by their probability distribution function. The statistical frequency analysis of extreme rainfall can be understood as a normalization procedure allowing site-to-site comparison. A very large variation of the frequency can be caused by the random variation in time of rainfall intensities (Vaes, G. et. al., 2001). Therefore, several applications relay on rainfall frequencies, such as the design of Civil engineering projects (bridge, dyke and dam) or climate change studies and variable climate trends analysis. (Kharin and Zwiers 2005; Zwiers and Kharin 1998).

The southwest (SW) monsoon, which brings about 80% of the total precipitation over the India is critical for the availability of freshwater for drinking and irrigation. Changes in climate over the Indian region, particularly the SW monsoon, would have a significant impact on agricultural production, water resources management and overall economy of the country. Changes in rainfall due to global warming will influence the hydrological cycle and the pattern of stream-flows and demands (particularly agricultural) requiring a review of hydrologic design and management practices (Jain and Kumar 2012).The frequency analysis methods are widely used to relate the magnitude of extreme events such as heavy rainfall and floods to a probability of occurrence (Stedinger et al. 1993) in the context of climate change.

Analyses of extreme events are also used for areas like finance and insurances, urban drainage, hydrology and climate (Kyoung et al. 2011). Rainfall patterns are liable to change significantly as a result of climate change (Madsen et. al.2009). Trends in recent decades indicate an increasing frequency of extreme precipitation events in many regions (Cuevas 2011; Mehrotra and Sharma 2011). Improved knowledge of the frequency and magnitude of rainfall events is necessary for the design of effective and economical hydraulic control structures to reduce the risk of property damage and loss of life.

Due to the scenario of changing climate it is expected to have considerable impacts on the rainfall-runoff processes attributable to increasing or decreasing trends in hydro meteorological time series (floods, droughts, heat waves, etc.). Future replicates of the extreme rainfall events are no more statistically identical from the historical counterparts as these impacts can no longer be assumed to be stationary. If the effect of climate change on changing patterns of precipitation events is not taken into account then such changes or variability can lead to under estimation/ over estimation of parameters for the design and operation of water infrastructures, water shortages, water stresses, and agricultural failures (Zekai Şen, technical note, 2012).

Study Area

The Tapi is the second largest westward draining interstate river basin. It covers a large area in the State of Maharashtra besides areas in the states of Madhya Pradesh and Gujarat. An ogee shaped masonry pickup weir has been constructed across the Tapi river near kakrapar in surat district in Gujarat. Kakrapar lies between 21°16'7"N latitude 73°21'52"E longitude. Kakrapar water resources project has catchment area of 1875 km2. Mean annual rainfall in the catchment area is 786mm. The weir was constructed at a cost of Rs.20.61 crores. The weir is 621 m long and 14m high. Two canals take off from either bank to irrigate an area of 2.28 lakh ha. This project was commissioned in the year 1954 as stage - I of the Ukai project.

Figure Showing Tapi River Basin

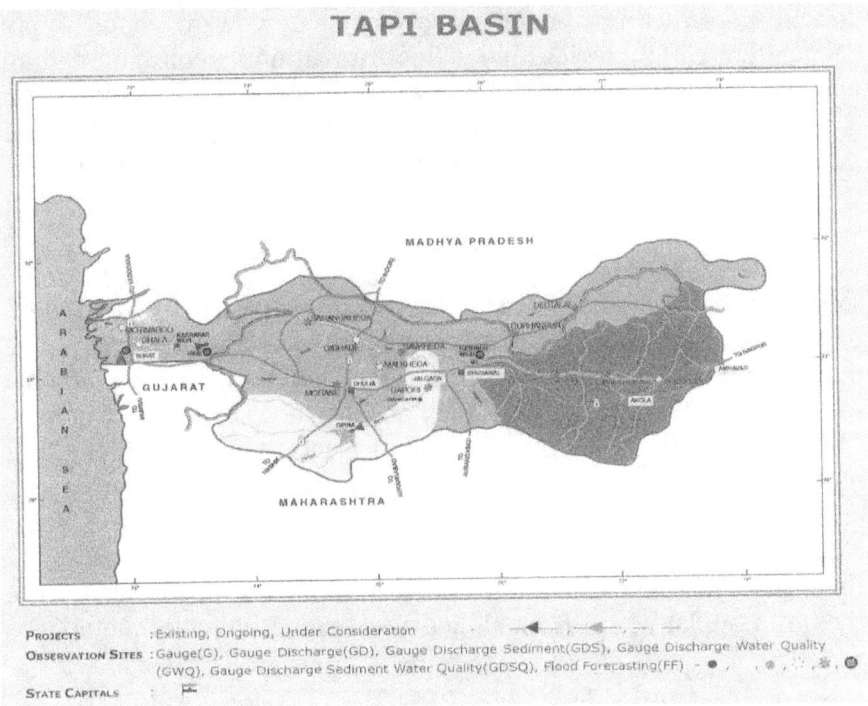

Trend Analyses

Arrangement of statistical data in accordance with occurrence of time is known as time series. It enables us to study the past behaviour of the phenomenon under consideration, compare the actual situation on the basis of past record and analyse the causes of such variation, compare the changes in the values of different phenomenon at different times or places and predict the behaviour of the phenomenon in future. Trend means the general tendency of the data to increase or decrease during a long period of time. If rainfall data of particular area is collected and plotted on a graph one can easily visualise the pattern of rainfall, whether rainfall is increasing or decreasing. Such studies referred as trend analysis. The trend analysis may be general, smooth, long-term, average tendency. It may be possible the overall tendency may be upward, downward or stable. Such tendencies are the result of the changes which are more or less, constant for a long time or which changes very gradually and continuously over a long period of time. It should not be inferred that all the series must show an upward or downward trend. It may happen that certain series values fluctuate around a constant reading which does not change with time. If the time series values plotted on graph paper cluster more or less, around a straight line, then the trend exhibited by the time series is termed as linear otherwise is known as non-linear trend. The term long period of time is a relative term and cannot be defined exactly.

Trend analysis methods are categorised as parametric and non-parametric methods. Parametric trend analysis is carried out when distribution of time series is known. Trend can be studied by Graphic (or free hand curve fitting) method, Method of semi averages, Method of curve fitting by principle of least squares and Method of moving averages.

Non-parametric trend analysis is carried out when distribution of time series is unknown. Non-parametric trend analysis is carried out by most popular Mann-Kendall and Sen's slope estimator method.

Parametric Methods

Graphic Method

A free- hand smooth curve obtained on plotting the values Yt against 't'. This gives an idea about the general 'trend' of the series. Smoothing of the curve eliminates other components like regular and irregular fluctuations. This method doesn't involve any complex mathematical techniques and can be used to describe the all kind of trends, linear or nonlinear. It is very simple method to study trend analysis and it is also easy to draw trend. Sometimes the trend line drawn by the experienced statistician for computing trend may be considered better than a trend line fitted by the use of a mathematical formula. This method is very subjective and curve varies from person to person who draws it. The work should be attempted by skilled and experienced people. Since the method is subjective, the prediction may not be reliable.

Method of Semi Averages

In this method the whole data is divided in two equal parts with respect to time. For example if the given data are from 1961 to 1972 i.e. over a period of 12 years the two equal parts will be first six years i.e. from 1961 to 1966 and 1967 to 1972. In case of odd number of years like 9, 13, 17 etc. two equal parts can be made simply by omitting the middle year. For example if the data are given for 13 years from 1961 to 1973 the two equal parts would be from 1961 to 1966 and from 1968 to 1973, the middle year 1967 will be omitted. An average (arithmetic mean) of each part is obtained after the data have been divided into two parts. We thus get two points. Each point is plotted against the mid-year of the each part. Then these two points are joined by a straight line which gives us the trend line. The line can be extended downwards or upwards to get intermediate values or to predict future values. Advantage of this method is that irrespective of any person who is drawing the trend line it gives same trend line, which was the dis- advantage of graphical method. This method is simple to understand as compare to moving average method and method of least squares. The method assumes linear relationship between the plotted points irrespective of the fact whether that relationship exists or not. The main problem of this method is if we add some more data to the original data then whole calculation is to be done again for the new data to get the trend values and the trend line also changes. As the arithmetic mean of each half is calculated, an extreme value in any half will greatly affect the points and hence trend calculated through these points may not be precise enough for forecasting the future.

Method of Least Squares

The principle of lest square is most popular and widely used method of fitting mathematical functions to a given set of data. Method yields very correct results if correct mathematical function is used. An examination of plotted data often provides an adequate basis for deciding upon the type of trend to be used apart from usual Arithmetic scales, semi-log or log-log scales may be used for graphical representation of the data. The various types of curves that may be used to describe the given data practice are (if Yt is value of the variable corresponding t and a, b, c are the coefficients) showing as follows:

1. A straight line:	$Yt=a+bt$	(1)
2. Second Degree of parabola:	$Yt=a+bt+ct2$	(2)
3. Kth degree-polynomial:	$Yt=a0+a1t+a2t2+aktK$	(3)
4. Exponential curves:	$Yt=abt$	(4)
5. Modified Exponential curve:	$Yt= a + bct$	(5)

Deciding type of trend to be fitted on the given data:

1. A straight line: When the time series is increasing or decreasing by equal absolute amounts.
2. Second Degree of parabola: when simple graph is plotted looks like curve type variation in the data.
3. Exponential curves: when series is increasing or decreasing by constant percentage rather than constant absolute amount. In this case when the data is plotted on semi-log paper gives straight line.

This method completely eliminates the part of subjective judgement, enables us to compute the trend values for all the given time periods in the series and the forecast values are also quite reliable. Though the method is most popular and widely used it is tedious and time consuming as compared with other methods. Addition of a new observation requires all calculation to be repeated. Future predictions are based on the long term variation ignoring the cyclical, seasonal and irregular fluctuations. Determination of the type of the trend curve to be fitted is the main limitation of this method.

Method of Moving Average

It is a method for computing trend values in a time series which eliminates the short term and random fluctuations from the time series by means of moving average. Moving average of a period m is a series of successive arithmetic means of m terms at a time starting with 1st, 2nd, 3rd and so on. The first average is the mean of first m terms; the second average is the mean of 2nd term to (m+1)th term and 3rd average is the mean of 3rd term to (m+2)th term and so on. If m is odd then the moving average is placed against the mid value of the time interval it covers. But if m is even then the moving average lies between the two middle periods which does not correspond to any time period. So further steps has to be taken to place the moving average to a particular period of time. For that we take 2-yearly moving average of the moving averages which correspond to a particular time period. The resultant moving averages are the trend values. This method is simple to understand and easy to execute. It has the flexibility in application in the sense that if we add data for a few more time periods to the original data, the previous calculations are not affected and we get a few more trend values. It gives a correct picture of the long term trend if the trend is linear. If the fluctuations are regular and periodic then the moving average completely eliminates the oscillatory movements, provided the period of moving average is exactly equal to the period of oscillation and trend is linear. For a moving average of $2m+1$, one does not get trend values for first m and last m periods. As the trend path does not correspond to any mathematical function, it cannot be used for forecasting or predicting values for future periods. If the trend is not linear, the trend values calculated through moving averages may not show the true tendency   of data. The choice of the period is sometimes left to the human judgment and hence may carry the effect of human bias.

Non-parametric Methods

Mann-Kendall Test

This test, which is usually known as Kendall's statistic, has been widely used to test for randomness against trend in hydrology and climatology. It is a rank-based procedure, which is robust to the influence of extremes and good for use with skewed variables. One of the problems in detecting and interpreting trends in hydrologic data is then confounding effect of serial dependence. Specifically, if there is a positive serial correlation (persistence) in the time series, then the non-parametric test will suggest a significant trend in a time series that is, in fact, random more often than specified by the significance level (Kulkarni and Van Storch, 1995). For this, H. Von Storch and Navarra (1995) suggest that the time series should be 'pre-whitened' to eliminate the effect of serial correlation before applying the Mann–Kendall test. Before applying the Mann-Kendall test, possible statistically significant trends in a precipitation observations (x1, x2, ., xn) are examined using the following procedures:

1. Compute the lag-1 serial correlation coefficient (designated by r1).
2. If the calculated r1 is not significant at the 5% level, then the Mann–Kendall test is applied to original values of the time series.
3. If the calculated r1 is significant, prior to application of the Mann–Kendall test, then the 'pre-whitened' time series may be obtained as (x2- r1x1, x3-r1x2, . . ., xn - r1xn-1).

This method is useful since missing values are allowed and the data need not conform to any particular distribution. In this test the relative magnitudes of the data is used rather than their measured values.

Sen's Slope Estimator Method

It is distribution free and not affected by seasonal fluctuations. This technique involves in arranging the collected data in the rank wise and scatter plotting and then calculating the median of those data. Based on that median the data type of trend is decided. Sen's method is not greatly affected by gross data errors or outliers, and it can be computed when data are missing. Sen's estimator is closely related to the Mann-Kendall test.

Frequency Distribution Method

Changes in heavy and extreme precipitation events were first documented by Iwashima and Yamamoto (1993), who used the data from scores of stations in Japan and the United States. Easterling et al. (2000) have found that changes in mean precipitation are insignificant while changes in heavy/very heavy precipitation are statistically significant. Frequency distribution method is used for the study of extreme events. The occurrence of extreme rainfall events has large amount of variability in rainfall data. Frequency distribution method of extreme rainfall events was carried out on the basis of daily rainfall amount. As per the classifications by IMD the rainfall events are divided into six different categories from 'light' to 'exceptionally heavy' depending on the amount of rainfall in a day (Table 1). This classification used by IMD is for the station rainfall data.

Table Showing Classification of rainfall events based on one day rainfall

Broad categories used in this study	IMD classifications of rainfall event	Rainfall (R) in a day (mm)
Category I (Low)	Light	$0.0 < R \leq 10.0$
	Moderate	$10.0 < R \leq 35.5$
	Rather heavy	$35.5 < R \leq 64.4$
Category II (Medium)	Heavy	$64.4 < R \leq 124.4$
Category III (Extreme)	Very heavy	$124.4 < R \leq 244.4$
	Exceptionally heavy	$R > 244.4$

Innovative Method

Low, medium and high values of a parameter are very important issues in climatological, meteorological and hydrological events. Furthermore these values are used to decide various design parameters based on scientific aspects and real applications everywhere in the world (Ozgur Kisi and Murat Ay 2014). Even though there are commonly used trend identification techniques, such as parametric and non-parametric methods, their validity is possible under a set of restrictive assumptions, such as independent structure of the time series, normality of the distribution, and length of data. It is also not possible to calculate trend magnitude (slope) except through regression approach. This brings additional assumptions for the theoretical validation in practical applications.

With this concept, a new trend method recently proposed by Şen is innovative method. Which is based on the basis of subsection time series plots derived from a given time series on a Cartesian coordinate system. Trend free time series subsections appear along the 45° straight line in such a graph. Increasing (decreasing) trends occupy upper (lower) triangular areas of the square area defined by the variation field of the variable concerned. The validity of this new approach is recognized through a set of Monte Carlo simulations by taking into consideration independent and dependent processes (Zekâi Şen, technical note, 2012). In this new approach, all the aforementioned assumptions in the parametric and non-parametric methods are avoided, and moreover it is possible to calculate trend magnitude from square area plots. Low, medium and high values of the parameters were graphically evaluated by this method. It was found that the Şen trend test compared with the MK trend test had several advantages. The results also revealed that the Şen trend test could be successfully used for trend analysis of water parameters (Ozgur Kisi and Murat Ay 2014).

Data and Methodology

As per the water resources information system of India (WRIS), using the SRTM DEM (Shuttle Radar Topography Mission (SRTM) Digital Elevation Models) data of NASA, having a spatial resolution of 90 meters, the basin and sub-basin boundaries for the Indian subcontinent have been delineated. As per this information, the country has been divided into 25 major river basins and 103 sub-basins. All major river basins and many medium river basins are inter-state in nature which covers about 81% of the geographical area of the country. An understanding of the spatial and temporal distribution and changing patterns in rainfall is a basic and important requirement for the planning and management of water resources (Jain and Kumar 2012). To understand any phenomenon it is important to collect the data pertaining to that phenomenon. Once data is collected over a period of time suitable analysis has been done by calculation and plotting graph to find trend analysis which gives the idea about the behaviour of phenomenon.

For present study the daily rainfall data are collected for kakrapar rain gauge station. Kakrapar rain guage station is a part of Tapi river basin. The daily rainfall data are collected from state water data center, Gandhinagar, Gujarat. The daily rainfall data are collected for a period of 1962 to 2010.

In the present study, following methods are used for extreme rainfall trend analysis:

  a. Frequency Distribution Method
  b. Innovative Method of Trend Analysis

Frequency Distribution Method

In this method an attempt has been made to find the long term trend of changing patterns of extreme precipitation events under three broad categories of rainfall events classified by IMD as per (Table 1).As exceptionally heavy rainfall events (>244.4 mm in a day) are not very common over the entire region of India, the rainfall categories of very heavy and exceptionally heavy rainfall events are further regrouped to make the 'extreme' rainfall events 'Category iii' in the present study (>124.4 mm in a day) in the broad classification (Table 1). Similarly, the rainfall categories of 'light', 'moderate' and 'rather heavy' of IMD classifications are also regrouped into one broad category, Category i (low) in the present study with ≤64.4 mm rainfall in a day, whereas heavy rainfall events with rainfall >64.4 and ≤124.4 mm in a day remained as one broad category of 'medium' rainfall or Category ii in the present study (Attri and Tyagi 2010, Pattanaik and Rajeevan 2010). In this study category I, II and III are identified by class 1, class 2 and class 3.

Innovative Method of Trend Analysis

If two time series are identical to each other, their plot against each other shows scatter of points   along 1:1 (45°) line on the Cartesian coordinate system. Whatever the time series are whether trend free or with monotonic trends, all fall on the 1:1 line when plotted and data values sort themselves in ascending (or descending) order along the 1:1 line.

To identify weather the existing trend in a given time series with respect to the idea of 1: 1 line is positive or negative a plot of the first half of the time series against the second half is plotted by considering two halves and the sorting procedure. It becomes obvious that monotone increasing (decreasing) trend in the given time series fall above (below) the 1:1 line. This idea can be used in any engineering hydro meteorological or hydro climatic time series trend identifications. It is also possible to have time series with half plots in which there are scatter of points on both sides of 1:1 line. Like low (high) values are more (less) in the first half than the next half, or the opposite situation may occurs. These cases correspond to non-monotonic trends where within the same time series there are increasing and decreasing trends at different scales even hidden ones (Zekai Sen, technical note, 2012). In this method the annual maximum time series is used for the analysis. In actual situations a mixture of the all cases explained in this paragraph appears, and accordingly, the necessary interpretations must be done to better understand the composition of the time series structure.

Results and Discussion

Frequency based extreme rainfall events
The result analysis by frequency distribution method of Kakrapar rain guage station for the data period 1962 to 2010 shows that the frequency of light to rather heavy rainfall (0 < R ≤ 64.4 mm) has slightly decreasing trend (Fig.2) during south-west monsoon season from June to September. The frequency of heavy rainfall (64.4< R ≤ 124.4 mm) shows an overall increasing trend (Fig.3) over the basin. The frequency of extreme rainfall (Rainfall ≥ 124.4 mm) shows decreasing trend (Fig.4) during south-west monsoon season from June to September.

Figure Showing Light to rather heavy rainfall (0 < R ≤ 64.4 mm)

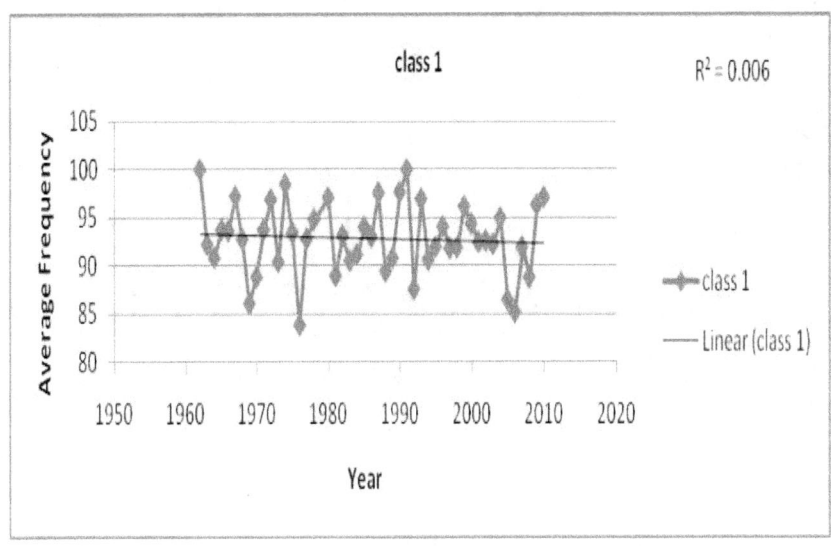

Figure Showing Very heavy to exceptionally heavy rainfall (R > 124.4 mm)

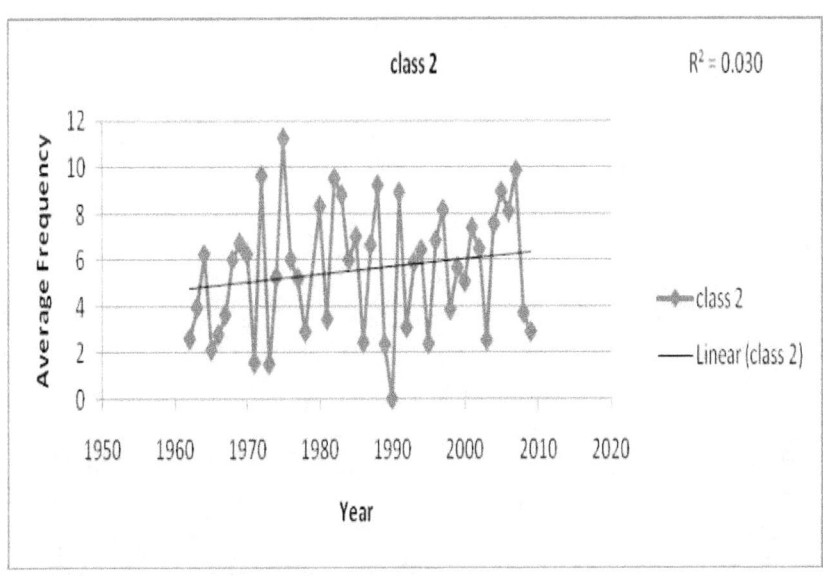

(a) Showing Heavy Rainfall

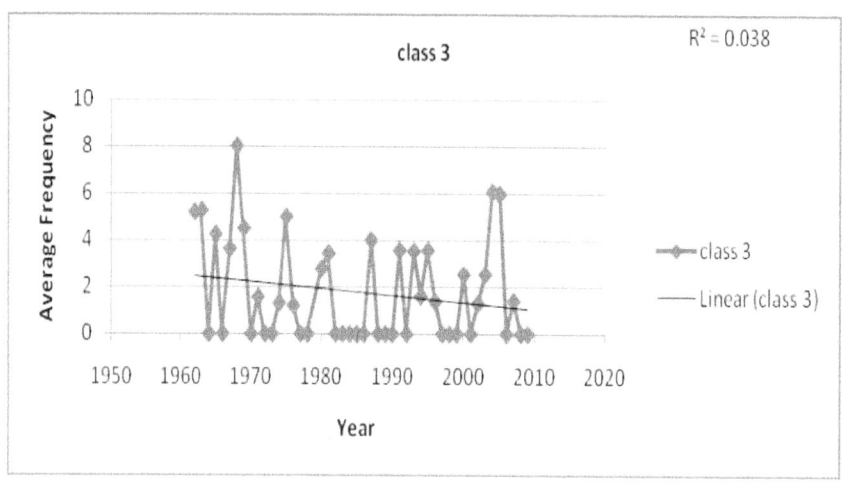

Innovative Trend Analysis Method

Result analysis by innovative trend analysis (Fig.5) shows that in heavy rainfall category no trend is observed and in very heavy rainfall category decreasing trend is observed.

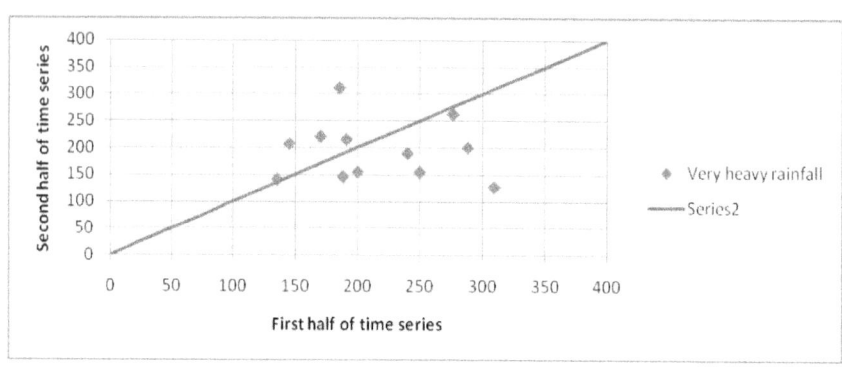

(b)

Figure Showing plots for (a) Heavy rainfall, (b) very heavy rainfall

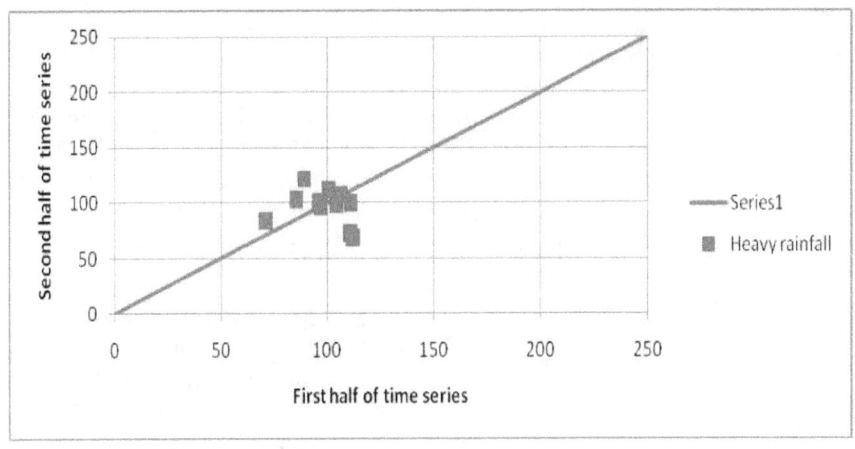

Table Showing Interpretation of Results

Sr. No.	Methods	Categories	
		Heavy rainfall	Very heavy rainfall
1	Frequency distribution method	Slight Increasing trend	Decreasing trend
2	Innovative trend	No trend	Decreasing trend

Conclusions

An attempt was made to study the extreme rainfall trend using frequency distribution method and innovative trend analysis methods. From the analysis, the frequency based method has shown increasing rainfall events trend in class 2 ($64.4 < R \leq 124.4$ mm) and decreasing rainfall trend in class 3 ($R > 124.4$ mm) with coefficient of determination ($R2$) value 0.0063 and 0.0303 respectively. Where as in innovative trend analysis method in case of heavy rainfall the scatter points are closer to the 1:1 line means the trend magnitude (slope) is weak. In very heavy rainfall category the more scatter points fall onto the lower triangular area of the scatter region which shows decreasing trend. In the frequency distribution method as $R2$ values very small they are unable to give information about the positive or negative trend. Where as in innovative method it gives fair good information.

References

[1] Min S.K., Zhang, X., Zwiers, F.W., and Hegerl, G.C. (2011), Human contribution to more-intense precipitation extremes, Nature, 470, 378–381.

[2] Reiss, R., and Thomas, M. (2007), Statistical analysis of extreme values: With applications to insurance, finance, hydrology and other fields, 3rd ed., Birkhauser, Basel.

[3] Willems, P., Olsson, J., Arnbjerg-Nielsen, K., Beecham, S., Pathirana, A., Gregersen, I., Madsen, H., and Nguyen, V. (2013), Climate Change Impacts on Rainfall Extremes and Urban Drainage: a State-of-the-Art Review, World Environmental and Water Resources Congress 2013: pp. 1131-1135.

[4] Central, xtreme Precipitation Events are on the Rise, Published: Jul 9th, 2013(http://www. climatecentral.org/ gallery/maps/extreme-precipitation-events-are-on-the-rise)

[5] Dessens J. and Bucher A. (1995), Changes in minimum and maximum temperatures at the Pic du Midi relation with humidity and cloudiness, 1882–1984, Atmospheric Research 37, 147–162.

[6] Serra C. Burgueno A. Lana X. (2001), Analysis of maximum and minimum daily temperatures recorded at Fabra observatory (Barcelona, NE Spain), in the period 1917–1998, International Journal of Climatology 21, 617–636.

[7] Marengo JA. (2004), Inter decadal variability and trends of rainfall across the Amazon basin, Theoretical and Applied Climatology 78, 79–96.

[8] Vahid Rahmani, S.M.ASCE1; Stacy L. Hutchinson2; J. M. Shawn Hutchinson3; and Aavudai Anandhi4, Extreme Daily Rainfall Event Distribution Patterns in Kansas, Journal of Hydrologic engineering © ASCE / April 2014.19:707-716

[9] National Climate Centre Research Report No: 3/2010), Changes in extreme rainfall events and flood risk in India.

[10] Vaes, G., Willems, P., and Berlamont, J. (2001), Trend Analysis on 100 Years of Rainfall Data, Urban Drainage Modeling: pp. 922-923.

[11] Kharin, V., and Zwiers, F. (2005), Estimating extremes in transient climate change simulations, J. Clim., 18, 1156–1173.

[12] Zwiers, F.W., and Kharin, V.V. (1998), Changes in the extremes of the climate simulated by CCC CGM2 under CO^2 doubling, J. Clim., 11, 2200–2222.

[13] Jain, S.K., and Kumar, V. (2012). Trend analysis of rainfall and temperature data for India, Current Science, 102(1), 37–49.

[14] Kyoung, M., Kim, H., Sivakumar, B., Singh, V., and Ahn, K. (2011). Dynamic characteristics of monthly rainfall in the Korean Peninsula under climate change, Stochastic Environ. Res. Risk Assess, 25(4), 613–625.

[15] Madsen, H., Arnbjerg-Nielsen, K., and Mikkelsen, P. S. (2009).Update of regional intensity–duration–frequency curves in Denmark: Tendency towards increased storm intensities, Atmos. Res., 92(3), 343–349.

[16] Cuevas, S. C. (2011). Climate change, vulnerability, and risk linkages.Int. J. Clim. Change Strategies Manage, 3(1), 29–60.

[17] Mehrotra, R., and Sharma, A. (2011), Impact of atmospheric moisture in a rainfall downscaling framework for catchment-scale climate change impact assessment. Int. J. Climatol., 31(3), 431–450.

[18] Zekâi Şen, technical note on, Innovative Trend Analysis Methodology is part of the Journal of Hydrologic Engineering, Vol. 17, No. 9, September 1, 2012. © ASCE, ISSN 1084-0699/2012/9-1042-1046

[19] Kulkarni, A., and H. von Storch, 1995, Monte Carlo experiments on the effect of serial correlation on the Mann-Kendall-test of trends, Meteorologische Zeitschrift 4 NF 82-85

[20] H. von Storch and A. Navarra , Analysis of climate variability,Springer. 1995. 4. 334.

[21] Iwashima T, Yamamoto R. 1993, A statistical analysis of the extreme events: Long-term trend of heavy daily precipitation, Journal of Meteorological Society of Japan 71: 637–640.

[22] Easterling DR, Evans JL, Groisman PY, Karl TR, Kunkel KE, Ambenje P. 2000, Observed variability and trends in extreme climate events: a brief review, Bulletin of the American Meteorological Society 81: 417–425.

[23] Ozgur Kisi and Murat Ay, Comparison of Mann–Kendall and innovative trend method for water quality parameters of the Kizilirmak River, Turkey, Journal Of hydrology, Volume 513, 26 May 2014, Pages 362–375.

[24] Attri, S.D., and Tyagi, A. (2010), Climate profile of India, Indian Meteorological Department, New Delhi.

[25] Pattanaik, D.R., and Rajeevan, M. (2010), Variability of extreme rainfall events over India during southwest monsoon season. Meteorol. Appl., 17, 88–104.

[26] Pryor Sara C., et.al, The impact of climate change on United States, now and in the future, Chapter18.Midwest, V.11, Jan 2013.

[27] Stedinger, J.R., Vogel, R.M., and Foufoula-Georgiou, E. (1993), Frequency analysis of extreme events, Handbook of hydrology, D.R. Maidment, ed., Chap. 18, McGraw-Hill, New York.

Chapter-VI

Cities and Climate Change: Dichotomy of Modern and Traditional City Planning in Kathmandu Valley

Bishwodev Bhattarai*

Abstract

Climate Change has become a most discussed topic from the beginning of this millennia. From past few decades, the impact of Global warming and climate change has been clearly felt. The discourse of Climate Change comes parallel with energy use and carbon dioxide emission. Cities are one of the major sector contributing CO^2 emission and energy use. City comprises of buildings and buildings requires energy for construction and operation. Kathmandu valley, suited well in the lap of mountains, dates back to early 4th century A.D. The valley comprised of several traditional towns around has been infested by haphazardly constructed modern buildings. The traditional system of planning based on Vedic principles was sustainable and appraised by every foreign scholar who visited. The focus was on urban sustainability and each town within the valley were self-sustained in terms of food, daily needs, urban services and so. The valley has a record of several major earthquake hit, and the materials used were such that, they could be reused. Use of timber, mud and adobe brick construction, it was not only climate adaptive but also resource efficient. Today, the traditional planning has been abandoned and modern construction and planning system have invaded the traditional technology and process. Kathmandu today emits nearly 1.1 million tons of CO^2 annually and this figure is increasing. The growing buildings and resource consumption is making the city unsustainable. Today, we are after huge constructions and our system of planning is diverted into competitive market. Use of materials with high embodied energies and technology which demand high operational energy have changed our attitude of sustainable livelihood.

Key Words: Climate Change, Embodied Energy, City Planning, Urbanization, Carbon Emission

* Department of Architecture and Urban Planning, Institute of Engineering, Tribhuwan University, Pulchowk, Lalitpur, Nepal

Introduction

Climate change has become focal issue of this millennia on which notable researches have been conducted and still undergoing. The trend shows, considerable part of world's economy accounts climate change and global warming related research & study. The widespread concern of climate change is an outcome of the massive industrial revolution of 18th and 19th century in the west and its impact have caused substantial rise in GHG's. Asian countries, specifically South Asian's are the most vulnerable to climate change impacts, deliberately seen in agriculture and bio-diversity (Brömmelhörster 2009, 1). Industrial revolution accounted to rapid urbanization and huge energy consumption. That was the time when world's rural population started urban migration resulting aggressive tension in urban life. Until then, the cities of Nepal were unknown of industrialization & urban transition, as almost 98% of total population lived in rural areas (CBS 2012) and majority of urban residents were relying on agriculture.

Kathmandu, city which dates back to 4th century A.D, have even older existed history, house more than 50% of Nepal's Urban Population. Today, Nepal's total official urban population is 17%, (CBS 2012) but it is expected to be more than 20%. The world's urban population today is 53% and consumes more than 90% total world's resources (WHO N A). City consumes huge, goods, services and energy but together it has high productive value. Urban sector in Nepal contributes 62% total country's GDP (Muzzini and Aparicio 2013, 1) and the figure is growing.

In recent years, Nepal's urban population is increasing with annual average of 4% (Muzzini and Aparicio 2013, 19) and astonishingly Kathmandu is one of the most migrated city out of 58 other municipalities in the country. The city is well known for its traditional settlements and called as City of Temples. In recent days, Kathmandu is being invaded with modern buildings and structures and lacks basic city planning. The haphazard urbanization and insensible use of technology and materials have posed threat in urban environment. The mounting conversion of urban land into housing plots and decreasing urban forest and agriculture lands have affixed hinterland with Kathmandu city. Increase in urban area and population indicates increase in resource and energy consumption. Until today, valley depends on imported fossil fuel which accounts major foreign import and demand of which is increasing day by day. On one side, city is expanding and on the other, there's increased energy demand. Unlike traditional cities of Nepal, which were resource efficient, self-contained and self-sufficient, today's modern cities are consuming more and more energies. The dense mixed settlement in the midst of farmland contained whatever a city dweller needed, from earthy materials to heavenly spiritualism. Even few decades earlier, the township was a mixture of rural and urban life, which today's planner conceptualize as a Rurban, an ideal urban space.

The chapter describe about the traditional settlement planning of the valley, which were supposed to be sustainable and resource efficient. It is evident that, modern technology although inevitable have created lots of problem in ecology and environment. In verge of meeting demand and need of a city, lots of industries and innovations have been made. Today, people of Kathmandu have nearly forgotten the traditional way of building & planning. The argument is that, are we really moving on the right direction? Or is this the time to rethink? We had never contributed in global warming and at this moment, Kathmandu is heading in such a way that it is most consuming city of Nepal. Coming section will highlight on the modern and traditional planning of Kathmandu valley, in terms of its technology, materials, energy and sustainability aspects.

Climate Change: Role of Cities

City and Climate Change

City is a complex whole of different systems, composed of various sub-systems of which people are in its central foci. Fundamentally, city has three components, People, Built Space and Open Space and all are equally important. City is dynamic space where trade, commerce, industry interact with people, composed of dwellings, recreation, entertainment etc. A city is assumed to be self- contained and people enter city in a hope of getting better services and facilities.

Climate change is the resultant of global warming, a phenomenon in which greenhouse gases like carbon dioxide prohibit heat from escaping into space as a result of which the temperature of earth is increased (Subba 2011). It results in the rise of temperature subsequently increasing sea level as a resultant of melting of snow

Table: Global Sector Wise CO_2 Emission

Sector	2003 Emissions (Gt CO_2)	% of total
Electricity	9.9	41%
Fuel Conversion	1.7	7%
Industry	4.5	18%
Transport	5.1	21%
Buildings	3.2	13%

Source: (WEC 2007)

and glaciers. The impact has been seen in Maldives with rise in sea level (Quiret 2011) where the highest point of land is just 2.4 m from sea level. Other part of the world is also facing uneven monsoon and extreme climatic condition.

It is thus important to know how cities and climate change is inter-related. Yes, indeed a city has everything within and the consumption of city is very high whether it be energy or resources. Consumption requires production and production requires resources and energy. Energy is directly associated with GHG and Cities are often blamed for contributing disproportionately to global climate change. Numerous sources state that cities are responsible for 75–80 percent of all human caused greenhouse gases (GHGs), although the scientific basis for these figures is unclear (Satterthwaite and Dodman 2009). Even though it is fact that contribution of cities in climate change is immensely high.

In search of energy, human have extracted fossil fuels and extreme use of it to fill the energy demand have lead changing climate through global warming. The table shows global CO_2 emission sector wise and electricity sector contributes highest. The per capita energy use of India in 2004 was 0.58 tons of oil Equivalent11 (15 times more in USA) whereas per capita CO^2 emission is 1.02 tones/ year (19 times more in USA) (WEC 2007, 30), which is even less in

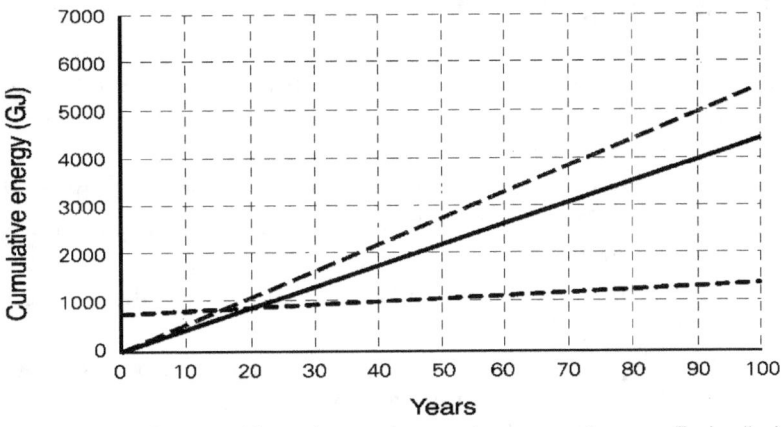

High operating ━ ▪Normal operating ━━Low operating ━ ━Embodied

Fig: Cumulative comparison of operating energy and embodied energy

case of Nepal. Energy consumption of so called developed world is higher and CO^2 emission is even higher, and it is obvious that the contribution of least developed Asian countries in climate change is far less. Coming into Nepal, per capita energy use in kg of oil equivalent is just 314 (IEA NA), and this average is more in urban areas. Kathmandu which consumes highest percentage of energy imports have population of 2.5 million which is very less in context of global cities. In fact we shall not overlook its energy consumption and carbon emission pattern because we can easily manage to keep ourselves away from the actors of global climate change. In recent years, the consumption pattern of Kathmandu have raised significantly and towering energy demand and growing urban area

---

11 **Kilogram of Oil Equivalent** is the total energy consumed in terms of petroleum oil equivalent. It is a normalized unit of energy. By convention it is equivalent to the approximate amount of energy that can be extracted from one kilogram of crude oil.

have increased carbon emission. The increased buildings and infrastructures may have accounted very less in global climate change but has clearly impacted on its local climate.

Building, Energy & Climate Change

The concern of this paper is built space of a city and coming section will deal on it with specific example of Kathmandu Valley. City composed of buildings and buildings rises through its constituent building materials. Building and energy is interrelated and a study shows that building sector consumes 40% of total global energy consumption (UNEP NA). But actually, building doesn't consume energy, people does and it depends how people build their buildings.

Traditional Nepali society spent their energy in Cooking, Baking Bricks & Tiles, and Molding metals. Although their dependency was totally in firewood and the rational use of firewood along with symbiotic human-nature relationship lead towards sustainable society. The household energy use for heating and ventilation was nearly zero and still same outside Kathmandu valley, in rural community. Traditional settlements had everything within a town boundary and salt & gold were mere imports. In contrast to traditional lifestyle, today's town heavily rely on numerous energy sources for various activities. Cooking, Washing, HVAC, Travel, Recreation, Sports & Entertainment, Lighting, Using Electrical Appliances etc. are some common energy use sectors and this accounts operational energy of a building. Besides this, construction of building requires building materials and every materials have its embodied energy12. A normal modern residential building construction requires 30% of its total lifecycle energy if we consider age of building to be 50 years (Milne and Chris 2013). Any building thus have its embodied energy and runs through operational energy.

---

12 **Embodied Energy:** It is the sum total of energy required to produce any goods or services, considered as if that energy was incorporated or 'embodied' in the product itself. The energy from production to reach its final destination is counted. The more is the embodied energy of a product, more it is supposed to emit carbon. Here, the concept of it is important because every product have contributed CO_2 emission during its manufacture.

Summarizing the concept, we can conclude that building is unified structure developed from constituent building materials and building materials are outcome of resource and energy. Energy consumption indicates CO^2 and GHG's emission, which are elements of climate change. More over urban buildings are more energy consuming compared to rural vernacular buildings.

Kathmandu and it's City Planning

Kathmandu City is a capital of glory. Although it's inscribed record is only 4th century old, its history dates back to Gopala Period. The great Bagmati civilization started soon after the Manjushree from Tibet, dried the Valley which was previously a Lake, channeling water to the South of Kathmandu by cutting Chovar Gorge. The valley had a fertile soil and settlement started from its Western side. After the down fall of Kirata, Lichhavi ruled the valley, which was an era of urban development in Kathmandu. It was the time when art, architecture and township of valley was flourished. Lichhivi reign came into the end by beginning of 13th century and Malla dynasty started ruling Kathmandu Valley. The art, Architecture and Planning gained a new elevation and the traditional building technology and lifestyle remained unchanged until the beginning of Rana Regime. Then after, western classical and neo-classical architecture entered and later on, after first motorable road constructed joining Terai and valley in late 1950's, modern construction and development began.

Today, more than 95% of valley's buildings are concrete built. The entire planning for physical infrastructure and services are modern. Government's policies are also prioritizing modern development which in fact could be avoidable in case of residential building. Today, tension between modern and traditional settlements is visible and even though, there are several benefits of traditional houses, people are attracted in modern buildings. This section of paper deals with Traditional and Modern Township, the material and technology, sustainable practices and energy outlook.

Traditional Planning

The traditional planning was based on Vedic philosophy, following ancient doctrine of Vaastusastra. Chanakya, in his popular Aarthasastra have explained some basics of Vedic Township. Most of the traditional cities and satellite towns of Nepal and India were based on Chanakya's town planning principles (Deshkar 2010). These towns had 3 major streets running either side of the cardinal direction. On the center there is a temple and Palace and on the periphery, so called lower hierarchical community resides.

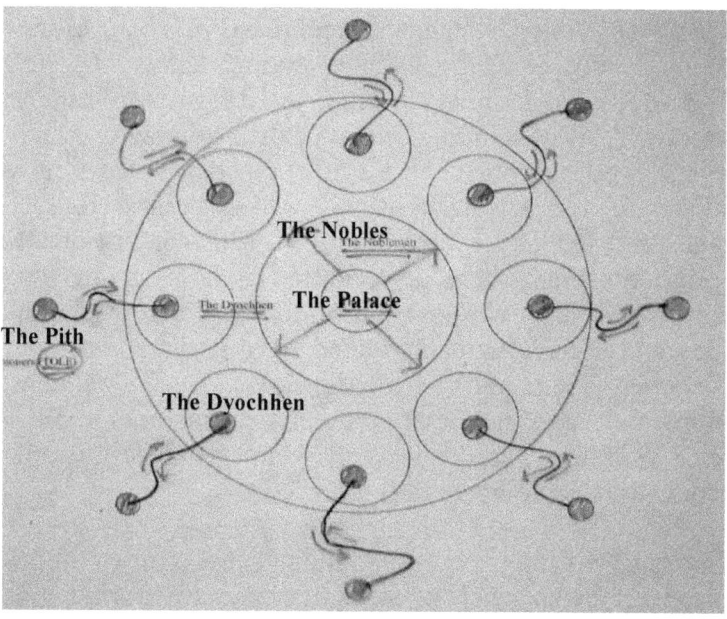

Fig: Traditional City Pattern, Source: (Tiwari NA)

The city were surrounded by farmland and besides agriculture, people were engaged on business and production of goods like carpet, textiles, oil, earthen pots, metal works, wood works etc. Traditional settlement of valley had continuous source of water supply through water spout (Hiti), nowhere found in other part of the world. Proper street connectivity for festivals and day to day travel, proper provision of Solid Waste Management through traditional compost pit called Saga. The human excreta were used in Farmland as a fertilizer and virtually, there was no such thing like waste. The popular proverb "Peta ko Khetama Kheta ko Petama" unanimously indicating the farm products is for human stomach and by product of it, human excreta is for farmland.

The symbiotic relation between human and nature gave rise to god of city and god of nature. City god, Aastamatrika, Tole Ganesha, and Kul Deta (clan god and goddess) were liable to protect city dwellers and in return, people worshipped them with full faith. The nature god, Pith away from settlement were worshipped as protector of nature. The settlement were such that, they were on highland, called Pringa, Dole were sloppy unsuitable for settlements and Farmlands were on Tala, a lowland. A concentric planning based on caste zoning kept priest and ministers near to the Palace, whereas, farmers and cleaners were at the periphery, near to the farmland.

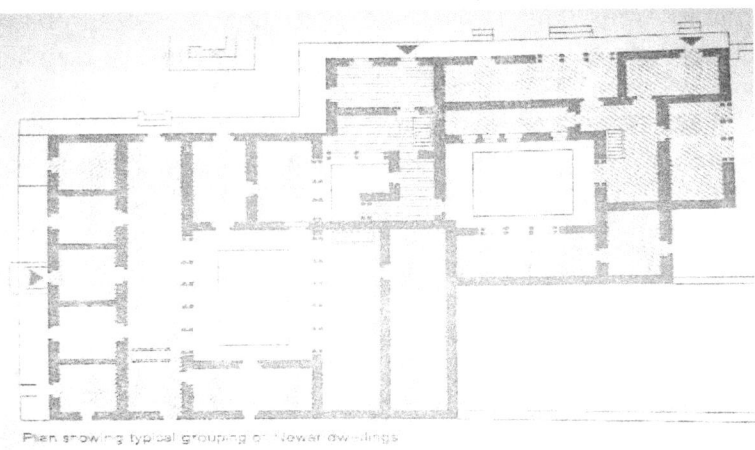

Plan showing typical grouping of Newar dwellings

Fig: Ko Bahal Tole Patan (Typical Newari Courtyard)
Source: (Korn 2007)

The residential buildings had a courtyard, a central open space often used as a social space. These space were used to dry grains and agro-products and also provide socio-cultural space. The buildings around courtyard were owned by people of same clan and often contain a temple or Monastry in its center. The city elements of traditional society were the temples, the houses, the open spaces (Pati, Dabali, Hiti, Palace Squares, Chowks), the Palace and the Streets. These were in perfect harmony and city had functioned well to cater need of people at that time.

Material and Technology

The Kathmandu valley was frequented with earthquake hit and technology was developed so that it could respond to the disaster that comes time and again. Disaster is one of the major issue in today's climate change discourse. Disaster leads to massive reconstruction. The water from river through pit conduits was supplying water to the people of city through stone spouts and community wells. Those water after household use goes to farmland or kitchen garden. The streets were paved using bricks which is porous and absorb water. Destruction and for reconstruction it need huge materials which again comes from burning carbons. The traditional societies of Kathmandu were well aware of earthquake and they used light construction materials. The Bricks, the Mud and the Timber. Except bricks, embodied energy for mud and timber is literally zero. Also, the forest around the valley supplied timber for the construction and were wisely used. Bricks were also reused and no such dump yard found so far in the valley which had used brick pieces. This suggests that even after earthquake, all those bricks were used for

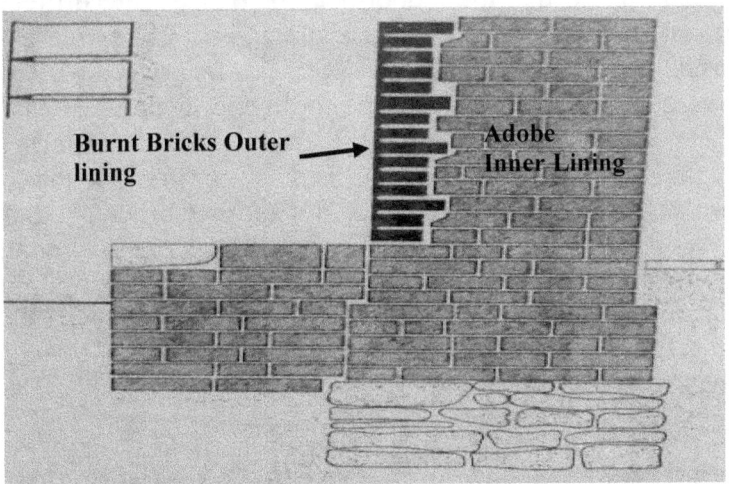

Fig: Typical Wall Section
Source: (Korn 2007)

The long overhanging tiled (Jhingati) roof protecting the wall from splash of monsoon rain is yet another feature of the buildings. The wall consisted of two layer of brick, outer burnt brick (Dachi Appa), often smooth, protects rain to penetrate and a layer of adobe on its inner part, which makes the internal environment climate responsive. Coming on the technology, the masons were highly skilled. The residential building were built through support of community and neighborhood through mutual exchange of service. People were aware of earthquake, so structures were strengthened using timber members. The massive & high plinth of the building were constructed so as to minimize the effect of earthquake. The use of mud mortar and timber member makes easy to reconstruct the building even if it gets collapsed due to its easy workability. It is said that during great earthquake of 1943, Prime Minister Juddha S.J.B Rana refused to take foreign aid and whole city was recovered through the sole effort of peoples of Kathmandu. Imagining this, if same thing happens in Kathmandu today, it would be a worst nightmare. Imagine how much energy would be wasted to reconstruct whole city and how much it contribute in global carbon emission.

Energy Outlook

It has been found that the indoor/outdoor temperature difference of traditional building is 5°C less in summer and 5°C more in winter, whereas this is only 2°C for a RCC framed structured building (Bajracharya 2013) and this is due to double layer of Bricks, outer burnt and inner adobe. This literally indicates, the indoor environment of traditional building is more comfortable than that of modern buildings. This fact concludes that, traditional building is energy conserving both in construction and operation. Adoption of this will certainly contribute in energy conservation and minimizing carbon emission.

Modern Planning

Modern Urban Planning in Kathmandu started when first piped water supply, Bir Dhara came into operation in 1895 (DWSS NA). Then in 1911, Pharping Hydropower, claimed as first hydropower in

South Asia, supplied electricity in Palaces of Kathmandu Valley.

The first motorable road in Kathmandu Valley was constructed in 1924 (Situla 2009). The modern urban planning come into existence only after formal initiation of Periodic Planning. Today, Kathmandu valley comprises of a metropolitan city, a sub-metropolitan city, three municipalities and 49 urbanizing villages. The valley covers 665 Sq.Km of total area and encloses the entire area of Bhaktapur district, 85% of The Kathmandu valley alone has more than 600,000 buildings out 1,045,575 of national total urban houses (CBS 2012). The increasing buildings in Kathmandu valley have not only created urban congestion but also diminishing open spaces and green surfaces. Yearly, some 10,000 buildings are newly constructed in the valley and more than that, nearly 200 hectare of land converted into hard surface and prevents rain water from ground recharge (Pokharel 2014). The valley's total road covers 13-14 % of its total area, which is more than 838 KM and this figures is increasing annually. Huge portion of total country's capital investment is being invested in Kathmandu Valley. The qualitative knowhow indicates that major construction work is concentrated in Kathmandu valley, both from private sector and public sector.

Significant change in land use of Kathmandu valley has been seen from past 80 years, and a chart shown here indicates, residential buildings are dramatically increasing with loss of agriculture lands. Material and technology

Today's construction and production industry consumes huge amount of fossil fuels. Kathmandu valley alone consumes 31% of total national petroleum imports. The materials used for construction are all manufactured burning carbon contained fuels. Despite of Nepal' huge hydropower potential, we are facing sever power cut-offs and more than 800MW of electricity is deficient to meet current electricity demand.

Use of materials like, Cement, Bricks, Steel, Composite Panels, Ceramic Tiles, Aluminum, Glass, with very high embodied energy is increasing day by day. Materials like bitumen, asphalt, aggregates with relatively less embodied energy is being used in infrastructure sector to seal earth surface in the name or road, drainage, canals, and so. The materials we are using today have very high embodied energy and come in expense of huge carbon emission.

Energy Outlook

Metaphorically, a modern city requires energy even to breathe. This means, people are using energy in every activities. A normal household requires energy for cooking, heating, ventilating, Operating electrical appliances, lighting, travel, etc. Besides this, there is huge waste generation from building sector. Nearly 350 tons of wastes are landfilled daily and energy used in production to landfilling is beyond the calculation. The hazardous methane that generates on due decomposition have 23 times more GHG effect than CO^2. A modern building is using materials with high embodied energy and also spending very high energy on its operation. The planning of the town is aslo such that very huge energy is spent on meeting travel demand of public.

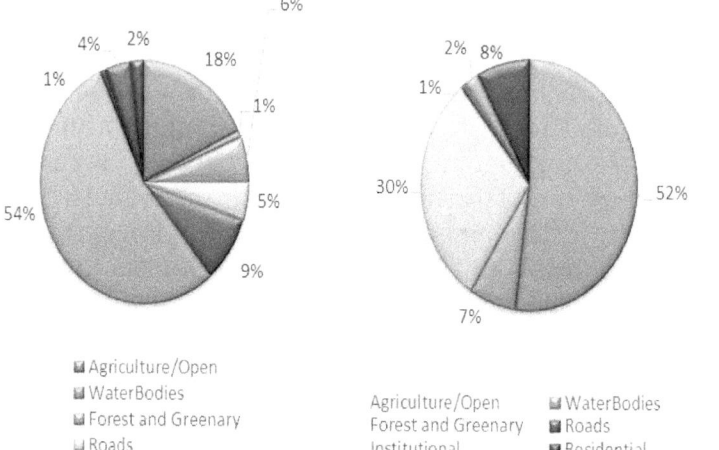

Land Use of Kathmandu Valley 2003   Land Use of Kathmandu Valley 1920

Source: (Maharjan 2013)

Energy is required from cradle to grave but the pattern of use is indicating dreary future of Kathmandu. Energy comes out with expense of CO_2 and we can consider modern township of Kathmandu valley is not energy efficient as it used to be.

Present Kathmandu: Energy and Emission

So far, we are clear about modern and traditional building and planning process. Modern society is demanding more energy and are consumption if towering. In this section, general overview of carbon emission has been shown,

General Considerations

Energy and Carbon Equivalent (As per Australian Govt.)
 1 GJ energy = 0.098 Ton of CO_2
 1 Ltr. of Petroleum Burning = 2 Kg of CO_2 (Avg.)
 1 Unit of Hydropower (KWH) = 15 gram (Avg.) of CO_2
 (EDF NA)
 Average embodied energy of normal residential building of age 50 years = 1000 GJ

Now considering 600,000 total buildings in valley at present, we can assume that 600 Million GJ of energy has already been used whose carbon equivalent is 58.8 million tons of CO^2. Here, operating energy has not been assessed. This means that, we have spent 58.8 million tons of CO^2 in constructing buildings of our city.

Considering 10000 new buildings being built every year, 10 Million GJ of energy are being used and 0.98 Million Tons of CO^2 every year being emitted?

The more we are urbanizing, the more we are consuming and the consumption pattern study of Nepal's Central bank shows following figures, considering the table aside, Kathmandu is Using 142,184,720.71 ltr of petroleum yearly and emitting 284.37 Million Kg of CO^2 every year. From hydropower, consumed solely by Kathmandu, yearly 10523.252 tons of CO^2 is being emitted.

Table: Consumption of Kathmandu Valley

Sr. No.	Consumption	Unit	National Share (%)	Remarks
1.	Electricity	701550133.3	29.2	Kwhr
2.	Petroleum products	24.075749	30.7	Billion Rupees
	2.1 LPG	4044411	60	KG
	2.2 Petrol	57773761.54	45.5	Ltr.
	2.3 Diesel	67531715.69	15.5	Ltr.
	2.4 Kerosene	12834832.49	37.6	Ltr.

Source: (NRB 2012)

Now coming into Per Capita CO^2 emission, Nepal falls under the bottom line. This figure is highest in Washington which is 19.7 Tons/ Capita, where as in Kolkata, it is only 1.83 Tons. For Kathmandu it is only 0.42 Ton CO^2 per capita per year (Devkota 2012) and if we come across 2.5 Million population, we are emitting, 1.075 Million tons of CO^2 yearly.

Analysis and Elucidations

We are entering in the age of globalization and consumption pattern of people have changed significantly over past decades. The sustainable life style of the past is changing and city life is becoming more complex. Although, we are glad that we hadn't had much role in global climate change and global share of Nepal is very negligible, the changing lifestyle and living pattern is taking us towards untenable future.

We are adopting modern construction and planning system to meet current need. We are deliberately urbanizing and our cities are growing. As we are growing, our energy demand is also growing which ultimately increases GHG and CO^2 emission. Kathmandu, which was Rurban few decades back is changing its morphology and is Nepal's primate city today.
The Kathmandu is facing severe water scarcity. Surface water from the Bagmati River is extremely polluted and ground water sources are almost exhausted. We are countered by uneven monsoon and extreme temperature with fluctuating local climate. Malaria and dengue which were seen only plains of Nepal are occurring occasionally in the valley. These are some general scene of today's Kathmandu valley and very few people are aware of these facts. The planning of Kathmandu has to be reconsidered to tackle these challenges and this doesn't mean we have to bounce back to the history, but can adhere basics of traditional planning.

Way Forward

It is clear that he city's role in CO^2 and GHG gasses emission is very prominent. The role of cities is therefore cannot be kept aside in countering effect of climate change. Although we are on midway of distress, it is never late to step forward to minimize carbon emission and energy use. Our forefather lived in an era where there was no facilities that we have today and their livelihood was simple. Still our rural community, almost 80% of total national population is residing the same pattern of life that our ancestors lives.

Kathmandu consumes almost 31% of total country's petroleum import had hosts 60 % of total urban buildings. The per capita energy demand and CO^2 emission is increasing. The changing life style and city's growth are indicating need of quick intervention. Government has not given much focus on issue of Climate Change and have failed to manage city's expansion and haphazard growth. We lack policy for sustainable city. The use of modern materials and technology has been associated with social prestige and people are desperate in using those.

The city seeks concentration of global community. City is a productive sector, it generates ideas and knowledge but at the same time pose threat to the environment. Managing cities ultimately manages issues of climate change and more. Kathmandu, although stands far beyond other global cities, it is major consuming city of Nepal. The difference seen today between modern and traditional planning clearly suggest that we are leading towards uncertain future.

Energy and climate change is intricately interrelated. The sustainable livelihood and lifestyle is nothing more than one's attitude. Few changes in behavior of people can help to tackle challenges of Climate change. Although Katmandu's contribution in global scene in negligible, we can set an example. Adopting few technologies like mud mortar and timber construction, porous paving, habit of reusing or reducing material rather than recycling, managing organic wastes for composting, minimizing use of unnecessary resource consumption can largely help cities to tackle climate change. A traditional living style with modern mind is what we need and what Indian PM Narendra Modi visualized in Gujrat. And this can give a better urban future, which today's planner need to realize at the earliest.

References

1. Bajracharya, Sushil Bahadur. 2013. A study on thermal performance of traditional residential buildings in Kathmandu valley. Lalitpur: Institute of Engineering, Tribhuwan University.
2. Brömmelhörster, Jörn. 2009. The economics of climate change in Southeast Asia: A regional review. Jakarta: Asian Development Bank.
3. CBS. 2012. Nepal Demographic Report. Kathmandu: Central Bureau of Statstics.
4. Deshkar, Sameer M. 2010. "Kautilya Arthashastra and its relevance to Urban Planning Studies." Institute of Town Planners, India Journal 7 (1): 87-95.
5. Devkota, Kalanidhi. 2012. "UCLG ASPAC Members: Towards Low Carbon Cities." Jakarta: NA.
6. DWSS. NA. http://www.dwss.gov.np/. Accessed July 7, 2014. http://www.dwss.gov.np/.
7. EDF, Energy. NA. http://www.edfenergy.com/. Accessed July 7, 2014. http://www.edfenergy.com/ energyfuture/energy-gap-climate-change/hydro-marine-and-the-energy-gap-climate-change.
8. IEA. NA. www.iea.org. Accessed July 7, 2014. http://www.iea.org/stats/index.asp.
9. Ives, J.D. 2004. Himalayan Perceptions- Environmental change and the Well-being of Mountain People. Oxon.
10. Kapil, M., A. Joshi, and R.C Patel. 2008. "The assessment of seismic hazard in two seismically active regions in Himalayas using deterministic approach." J. Ind. Geophys. Union 12 (3): 97-107.
11. Korn, Wolfgang. 2007. Traditional Architecture of the Kathmandu Valley. Second. Kathmandu: Ratna Pustak Bhandar.
12. Maharjan, Pratap. 2013. http://tunza.eco-generation.org/. Accessed July 7, 2014. http://tunza.eco-generation.org/ambassadorReportView.jsp?viewI D= 3804&searchType=title&searchName=Is%20 the%20urban%20development%20of%20Nepal %20environmentally%20sustainable?%20&page Number=1.
13. Milne, Chris. 2013. "Embodied energy." Materials Embodied Energy, NA NA: 205-209.

14. Muzzini, Elisa, and Gabriela Aparicio. 2013. Urban Growth and Spatial Transistion in Nepal. First. Wasignton DC: World Bank.
15. NRB. 2012. The Share of Kathmandu Valley in National Economy. Kathmandu: Nepal Rastra Bank.
16. Pal, I., S. K Nath, K. Shukla, D. K. Pal, A. Raj, K.K.S Thingbaijam, and B.K Bansal. 2007. "Earthquake hazard zonation of Sikkim Himalaya using a GIS platform." Spainger Science+ Business Media B.V 333-377.
17. Pant, Dongol. 2009. "Kathmandu Valley Profile, Briefing Paper." Kathmandu: Kathmandu Metropolitan City.
18. Quiret, Matthieu. 2011. http://content.time.com/. Accessed July 7, 2014. http://content.time.com/time/world /article /0,8599, 2097119,00.html.
19. Rayamajhi, Nistha. 2013. "Kathmandu Valley's road construction: The rationale behind the Hold up." The Republica, December 13: Online.
20. Satterthwaite, David, and David Dodman. 2009. "The Role of Cities in Climate Change." In State of the world: Into a WarmingWorld, edited by NA, 75-77. Washington: World Watch Institute.
21. Situla, Tulsi Prasad. 2009. "Infrastructure Development in Nepal: Opportunities." Kathmandu: SCAEF.
22. Subba, Mahendra. 2011. "Cities and Climate Change." Kathmandu: N/A.

23. Tiwari, Sudarshan. NA. "Eco-city: Time To Act Now." Kathmandu: NA.
24. UNEP. NA. United Nations Environment Program. Accessed July 5, 2014.http://www.unep.org/sbci/AboutSBCI /Background.asp.
25. WEC. 2007. Energy and Climate Change. First. London: World Energy Council (WEC).
26. WHO. N A. World Health Organization. Accessed July 6, 2014.http://www.who.int/gho/urban_health/ situation_trends/urban_population_growth_text/en

Chapter-VII

Some Reflections on Food Security, Poverty, Inequality & Marginalization

Jitender Prasad*

At the outset it would be pertinent to spell out the main objectives of the paper. The paper tries to cover the dimensions of one of the major theme relating to the challenges and socio-economic dimensions in food security. The main issue of the seminar Reorienting Agricultural Research to ensure food security is indeed quite relevant but the implicit in it is the socioeconomic dimensions of development. That would mean issues of resource conservation, eco-friendly plant protection, organic food grain production; preserving biodiversity through integrated farming system must be in harmony with nature, environment and ecology for sustainable development. Therefore, while incorporating the provisions of food security, its politics both at the national level and global level acquires importance. Rightly observed M.S. Swminathan, on the eve of completing twenty five years of NDTV celebration meet to which he was invited, "Future belongs to nations with food grains not guns."

Viewed in this context the present paper proposes to discuss the challenges and socio-economic dimensions of food security in three parts. The first deliberates upon issues relating to the global aspects of food security. The second deals with the provision of the food security Bill 20013 that was recently passed in the parliament and the third part deals with the analysis of the perspectives on development discourse.

Global Nature of Inequality and Deprivations

Social inequality has been recognised as one of the major theme in social science. In Sociology the classical sociologists recognised

* Professor of Sociology, M.D. University, Rohtak

inequality of class, status and power. It generally meant studying the internal processes of socio-economic differences that produced inequality, disadvantage and exclusion. In a diverse country like India caste, class, gender, ethnicity, minority and constitutionally recognised groups such as scheduled castes, scheduled tribes and OBC suffer from multiple deprivations. The Indian State has devised several schemes to help them improve their socio economic conditions. All types of social stratification- caste and class based inequality, social status distinctions and socioeconomic factors that cause hierarchical divisions reducing the life chances of some have been the focus of the study in major disciplines.

Economic inequality is recognised as the major source of the world's problems with poverty, hunger and health and for that reason the issue of food security for poor countries forms the central focus of the social scientists' study. The Gross Domestic Product (GDP-it is made up of all the goods and services on record as produced by a country's economy per year) and Gross National Income(GDI- it refers to income earned by individuals or corporations outside the country) continues to be the two globally recognised parameters of development . On these two counts World Bank i.e., internationally recognised lending organisations put countries into various categories as high income, upper middle income and lower middle income or low income. The high income countries are generally advanced industrial nations (starting first with UK and later joined by US, European countries, Canada and Japan) that arose about two and half century ago. They account for 15 per cent of world population and claim about 79 per cent of world's wealth. The availability of food, good housing conditions, state drinking water and material comforts that they enjoy are not available to middle income or low income countries. The middle income countries includes, Eastern and South Eastern Countries, oil rich countries, the middle east and North Africa and the Latin American countries which have 45 per cent of world population but account for just 18 per cent of annual wealth produced. Finally, China with 1.3 billion populations has 22 Per cent of world population and has acquired rapid economic growth but its per capita income was reported to be $1100 per year in 2003 which is close to the per capita income of low income countries of $ 766. The low income countries include, much of Eastern, Western, Sub-Saharan Africa; Vietnam, Cambodia,

Indonesia, India, Nepal, Bangladesh and Pakistan- all these were predominantly had agricultural economies and began to industrialise about a century ago. In 1999 they constituted 40 per cent of world population and produced about 3 per cent of World's production.

The extent of hunger and undernourishment is one of the scourges of world today. According to the estimate of the United Nations World food programme (UNWFP-2001) 830 million people go hungry every day, 95 percent of them are found in developing countries like India. Hunger is defined as a diet of 1800 or lower calories per day. It is considered insufficient to provide adults with the nutrient required for the active healthy lives. According to UNWFP 200 of worlds hungry comprise of children below 5 years of age who are reported malnourished and under weight. Every year an estimated 12 million children die due to hunger. The irony of the situation is that the amount the US population spends on pet food each year is about $13 billion which could eradicate much of the world's human hunger (Giddens: 535). Drought alone affects an estimated 100 million population in World today. In fact the combination of drought and internal warfare has devastated production of food causing million's of people's death. In Latin America 11 Per cent of people, 33 per cent in Sub-Saharan Africa and 17 per cent in Asia were reported malnourished. The countries affected by famine and starvation are too poor to afford technologies required for food production and nor they have means to purchase it. Paradoxically while the world hunger continues food production continues to increase. Needless to add the growth of food production is not evenly distributed around the world.

The socioeconomic dimension of food security problem that the underdeveloped countries faced earlier has now acquired global character. The developed, underdeveloped and developing countries are equally concerned about devising mechanism to link it with the development discourse. The paradox of the situation is that recently the 9th ministerial conference that was held at Bali concluded in December did not fully endorse the provisions of food security Act that was meant to discuss the matter relating to farm subsidies. In the proposed meeting a tough and tricky negotiations were advanced to get its farm subsidy programme into the WTO framework. The support from other developing countries with similar programme will have crucial bearing and this was also realised by the Director General of WTO Roberto Azevedo. Thus the WTO which was founded in 1995 would assume important role if the issue of food security is resolved within its ambit. Negotiations with other countries and regional groupings that involves the US, Japan and the European Union may have positive results on the issue of food security as was contemplated in the food security bill that was passed in the monsoon session of the parliament that concluded in December 2013, more out of compulsion than out of the realistic assessment of alleviating the sufferings of the people who live in under the perennial conditions of shortage of food in the third world countries. India's stand in the international forum with regard to the food subsidies is well known to the members of the developed countries. Commenting on the recently concluded 9th WTO ministerial conference in December at Bali a leading news paper's editorial observed, "The interim mechanism devised as via–media will allow India to continue with its agricultural support price programme undisturbed until a final solution is negotiated. ... Indeed from a larger perspective, the agreement at Bali is just the beginning."(The Hindu, Dec 13, 2013).

A background of the available food scenario may be visualised when we were informed that at the global level in developed countries there has been a phenomenal growth. It is further reported that shops in western countries are overflowing with consumer goods and same is the situation in our country's government storehouses where huge piles of food grains are kept in open to rot. In spite of the Supreme Court's directive the food grains which are kept in open are not distributed among the poor and the needy making the poor suffer from malnourishment. Even the farmers who borrow money from the informal sources find it difficult to clear the debt due to not receiving the adequate price for producing food grains. No wonder the reports of farmers being forced to commit suicide is reported not only from the drought prone areas of Vidarbha and Orissa but even from the prosperous districts of Punjab and Haryana as well there has been the reported incidents of farmers resorting to suicide to avoid the pains and ignominy of facing perpetual indebtedness.

The southern regions of Karnataka, Tamil Nadu, and Andhra Pradesh and even from the prosperous Northern regions there has been large scale reported incidents of farmers committing suicides. Needless to add the media has also reported the incidents of starvation death. The irony of the fact is that this entire precarious situation has been witnessed at the time when the govt's go downs and granaries have plenty of food grains so much so that their Safe storage has become a great problem. In want of sufficient storage facility the food grains rot. And furthermore in order to earn foreign exchange the country continues to export the food grains. What is worrying is the fact instead of offering the grains to the poor districts the grains are exported and sold at the subsidised price.

Some of the well- known economist has worked out statistical details about the food grain availability and food grain absorption from govt statistics in our country for nearly a century. Utsa Patnaik's calculations based on the available official statistics suggest that in the period between early 90s and 2001, food grain absorption dropped to levels lower than during the years of World War II. In order to tide over the situation and provide relief to the vast population of the hungry and deprived sections of the country the govt decided to prepare a food security bill which was passed in the monsoon session of the parliament in December 20013.

Provisions of Food Security Bill

It would be pertinent to examine some of the provisions of the bill that was subsequently passed and became an act. A little examination of the provisions of the food security act will put the development perspective into proper perspective. To examine the socio-economic dimension of the food security it is prudent to analyse the food security and institutional arrangement of that promises to ensure the supply of the improved quality of food grains through Public distribution scheme and the mid day meal scheme. The food security bill is committed, "to Provide for food and security in human life cycle approach by ensuring access to adequate quantity of quality food at affordable prices to people to live a life with dignity and for matters connected there with or incidental thereto."(The Food Security Bill 2013: 1).

As per the provision of the security bill, "every person belonging to priority households shall be entitle to five kilogram's of food grains (i.e., rice, wheat or coarse grains or any combination thereof conforming to such quality norms as may be determined by the Govt.) per person per month at subsidised prices." The concerned Govt.'s public distribution system will be entrusted to supply the food grain. The eligible households under the Antodya Anna Yojana will be specified by the state Government. The entitlements of persons belonging to the eligible household shall extend up to seventy five percent of the rural population and up to fifty per cent of the urban population. The act further spells out that pregnant women and lactating mother and children shall be entitled to the following, (4.a) meal, free of charge, during pregnancy and six months after the child birth, through the local anganwadi so as to meet the nutritional standards.... (5.1a) in case of children in the age group of six months to six years, age appropriate meal, free of charge, through the local anganwadi so as to meet the nutritional standards...(b) in the case of children, up to class viii or within the age group of six to fourteen years, whichever is applicable, one mid-day meal, free of charge every day except on school holidays, in all schools run by local bodies, govt and govt aided schools so as to meet the nutritional standards...."(5.2) Every school, referred to in clause(b) of sub section (1) and anganwadi shall have facilities for cooking meals, drinking water and sanitation. (6) The state govt shall, through the local anganwadi identify and provide meals, free of charge, to children who suffer from malnutrition so as to meet the nutritional standards. (See the National Food Security bill, 2013).

Development Discourse

Since the paper is directed to incorporate perspectives on the socio-economic dimensions of food security a focussed discussion on the development discourse needs to be highlighted while discussing the problems of food security it would be pertinent base the debate on the issues relating to the elimination of poverty and hunger. It would be pertinent to debate issues relating to development and widespread problems of hunger and undernourishment that affect the life of those who suffer when famines occur. In the ensuring debate on development approach a certain level of GDP- centric perspective on economic growth was witnessed. By 1970s the critics of economic growth model dismissed the logic of its rationality. Some questioned the economic growth by raising the issue of its impact on people's quality of life index (QLI.). While dealing with the QLI experts suggested factors like health, education and living standards of people to be included in understanding development. Some other critics pointed out the issue of equity among individuals, groups or regions. Thus it was during the decades of 1970s and 1980s alternative paradigms of development based not only on economic centric aspect of growth begun to gain importance.

In the decades of 1990s in development discourse a paradigm shift from economy to people centric model of development was advanced by the social scientists. The accomplished professional economists of global repute while advancing their ideas of development exhibited responsiveness to prevailing social realities. Poverty, deprivation, starvation, hunger, education and health were not treated as individual attributes of certain third world countries such as India alone. They were considered global phenomena covering different countries of human world. Therefore, the shortage of food and people's entitlement to reduce poverty and hunger were considered products of historically evolved social realities.

Keeping in tune with the human dimension of development Mahbubul Haq, the great Pakistani economists' own account innovative departure can be found in his reflections on human development (New York; OUP, 1995). The book has thrown systematic light on the actual lives lived by people especially by the relatively deprived. He took initiative to shift focus from national income accounting to human wellbeing by developing some new indicators to measure the process of change. The concept of human development was adopted by the United Nations Development Programme (UNDP) for all countries of the world. Three substantive measures that were marked out included (a) life expectancy at birth, which is the outcome health conditions (b) adult literacy and gross enrolment ratio at primary, secondary, college and university level and (c) the gross domestic product (GDP) per capita which reflected economic conditions of people. It was considered to be a vital component and significant contribution in development discourse. It has a crucial bearing on human wellbeing such as health and education. Besides, it suggested a new procedure of identifying levels of human development with measurable indicators. It is in this context Human development index (HDI) was evolved as a universally acknowledged category. Using the measurable indicators mentioned above it was possible to accordingly rank countries, states within countries, states within countries and even districts and regions within it. The additions of gender development index and gender empowerment measurement since 1995 have further enhanced the value of measuring development in precise terms. That parameter of development discourse has been backed up by United Nations (UN) and professional groups whose ideas influenced policies of several governments.

Two arguments of those who contest the HDR criteria belong to two opposite ends of spectrum. The first consider economic growth to be vital ingredients of development and at the other end of spectrum one finds those who argue HDR to be inadequate measure of understanding actual social conditions. It is in this context that the concept of development as freedom was advanced by the noted noble laureate Amartya Sen. He observed, "Development is… a process of expanding the real freedoms that people enjoy."(2000:3). He further observed, "Development requires the removal of major sources no freedom, poverty as well as tyranny, poor economic opportunities as well as systematic social deprivation neglect of public facilities as well as intolerances or over activity of repressive states." According to Sen, "Sometimes the lack of substantive freedom relates directly to economic poverty, which robs people of the freedom to satisfy hunger or to achieve sufficient nutrition or to obtain remedies for treatable, illness or the opportunity to be adequately clothed or sheltered or to enjoy clean water or sanitary facilities." Highlighting the elements of development he considered freedom as central to the process of development because of first, evaluative reasons to judge whether the freedoms that people have are enhanced or not and second, the effectiveness reason i.e., achievement of development is thoroughly dependent on the free agency of people. Illustrating the idea of development as freedom Sen has identified five different types of freedom which include the instrumental perspective that consists of (a) Political freedom (b) economic facilities (c) social opportunities (d) Transparency Guarantees and (e) Protective Security. The instrumental freedoms link with each other and with the ends of enhancement of human freedom in general.

What Amartya Sen considered crucial in analysing hunger is the substantive freedom of the individual and the family to establish ownership over an adequate amount of food which can be done either by growing food or by buying it in the market. It is possible for a person to suffer from starvation even when there is food available in plenty but has loss of income due to unemployment or loss of purchasing capacity due to drought or famine.

Conclusion

Thus hunger relates not only to food production and agricultural expansion but also to the functioning of the entire economy. The operation of the political and the social arrangements may influence people's ability to acquire food. Sen rightly points out that the sensible govt policy is required for the efficient functioning of economic and social institutions. Undernourishment, starvation and famine are influenced by the working of the entire economy and society- not with just the food production and agricultural activities. In case the poverty, education, good health and nourishment is not possible through the charitable distribution of food supplied to the people living below poverty line in the poor households- what is important is increasing and raising the capability and people's ability to acquire food. And for that the entitlement right that a person enjoys is vital; in other words, the commodities over which a person has entitlement or ownership or command. Thus the facts that determines family entitlement to food depends on first, whether there is endowment i.e., the ownership over productive resources are there or not. Second, an important influence consists of production possibilities and their use. The ownership of technology and its availability would also determine the production possibility. Third important aspect relates to the exchange conditions- the ability to sell and buy goods. The equilibrium of survival is sustained by this exchange especially when economic crisis arises due to famine. For example, during the 1943 Bengal famine, the exchange rates between food and the products of particular types altered radically (Sen, 200:262-64).

Chapter-VIII

Impact of Climate Change on Traditional Farming Systems in Himachal Pradesh

Tilak Raj*

Abstract

The world is now facing a new era of climate change. Over the past 50 years, humans have changed ecosystems more rapidly and extensively than in any comparable period of time in human history. At every point of production, agriculture influences and is influenced by ecosystems, biodiversity, climate and the economy. The agricultural growth could be severely affected by changes in key climatic variables (i.e., rainfall and temperature). Global temperature is increasing; the sea level is rising while storm surges, floods, droughts and heat waves are becoming more frequent. Subsequently, agricultural production is decreasing. The hill State of Himachal Pradesh has diverse agro-climatic conditions. The agriculture in the State is characterized by traditional cropping pattern and methods of cultivation. The large dependence on rains makes the farming less remunerative and unviable especially for marginal and small farmers. These sections of farmers are facing economic hardships due to poor resource position. They have very little surplus capital to invest on purchases of inputs required by modern agriculture. The climate change may manifest significantly in the State through warming and rainfall changes. The impact potentially significant to small farm production is loss of soil organic matter due to soil warming. Higher air temperatures are likely to speed the natural decomposition of organic matter thereby affecting fertility. The focus of the present study is to examine the impact of climate change on traditional farming systems. Descriptive research design is followed and the present study is solely based on secondary sources of data.

Key Words: Agriculture, Climate change, Cropping pattern, Small farms, Traditional Farming

* Assistant Professor, University Business School, Panjab University, Chandigarh, India

Introduction

The world is now facing a new era of climate change. Over the past 50 years, humans have changed ecosystems more rapidly and extensively than in any comparable period of time in human history. At every point of production, agriculture influences and is influenced by ecosystems, biodiversity, climate and the economy. The threat of climate change has caused concern among scientists and researchers. The agricultural growth could be severely affected by changes in key climatic variables (i.e., rainfall and temperature). Global temperature is increasing; the sea level is rising while storm surges, floods, droughts and heat waves are becoming more frequent. Subsequently, agricultural production is decreasing. Agricultural productivity also affected by climate change in two ways: first, directly, due to changes in temperature, precipitation and/or CO^2 levels and second, indirectly, through changes in soil, distribution and frequency of infestation by pests, insects, diseases or weeds.

Agricultural activities have both beneficial and harmful effects on environment through changing the quality or quantity of soil, water, air natural habitats, biodiversity and landscapes. The extent of these environmental impacts depends on the effects of farming practices on ecosystems at the local, regional, national and international levels. While some of the environmental effects of the agriculture occur at the farm, it can sometimes be difficult to attribute impacts to specific farms. One of the salient features of the traditional farming systems is their high degree of biodiversity, in particular the plant diversity in the form of polycultures and/or agroforestry patterns. This strategy of minimizing risk by planting several species and varieties of crops is more adaptable to weather events, climate variability and change and resistant to adverse effects of pests and diseases, and at the same time stabilizes yields over the long term, promotes diet diversity and maximizes returns even with low levels of technology and limited resources.

The main stay of the people in Himachal Pradesh is agriculture. The topography being hilly, the cultivation is generally on terraced fields. The farming is done on sloping and fragmented lands. Agriculture in the Tribal area is still traditional and primitive. Traditional agriculture represents the original method of farming that developed through the interaction of social and environmental systems. This method involves the intensive use of local knowledge and natural resources supporting biological diversity by means of alternating practices (various farming methods and crop rotation). The large dependence on rains makes the farming less remunerative and unviable especially for marginal and small farmers. The number and holdings under marginal and small categories of holdings has been continuously increasing over the time. As a result about 86.4 percent of the farmers in the state have holdings of less than two hectares. Such holding are worst affected by erratic rainfall and other vagaries of weather. The majority of small and marginal farmers in Himachal Pradesh are poor and in the clutches of a vicious circle of poverty arising out of low production with consequentially low income, low saving and low investment. A large proportion of their family labour remains unemployed even during the peak agricultural season. The labour forces of the marginal and small farmers have to depend on casual wage employment as supplementary source of income for making both ends meet. Due to poor economic conditions the small and marginal farmer families are subjected to malnutrition, under nutrition and also hunger.

Climate Change and Agriculture

Climate is the long term pattern of weather conditions for a given area. Climate change refers to a statistically significant variation in either the mean state of the climate or its variability, persisting for an extended period. The rapid rise in the world's population and our ever-growing dependence on fossil fuel-based modes of production has played a considerable role in the growing concentration of greenhouse gases (GHG) in the atmosphere. As a result, global temperatures are increasing, the sea level is rising and precipitation patterns are changing. Agricultural production is decreasing, freshwater is becoming scarcer, infectious diseases are on the rise, local livelihoods are being degraded and human well-being is diminishing. Higher air temperatures are likely to speed the natural decomposition of organic matter and to increase the rates of other soil processes that affect fertility. Under drier soil conditions, root growth and decomposition of organic matter are significantly suppressed, and as soil cover diminishes, vulnerability to wind erosion increases, especially if winds intensify. In some areas, an expected increase in convective rainfall – caused by stronger gradients of temperature and pressure and more atmospheric moisture – may result in heavier rainfall, which can cause severe soil erosion.

An unexpected change in the monsoon could precipitate a major crisis, triggering more frequent droughts as well as greater flooding in large parts of State. Dry years are expected to be drier and wet years wetter. Improvements in hydro-meteorological systems for weather forecasting and the installation of flood warning systems can help people move out of harm's way before a weather-related disaster strikes. Investments in R&D for the development of drought-resistant crops can help reduce some of the negative impacts. The acceleration of environmental degradation and climate change has direct effects on agricultural productivity and food security. Climate change is the most important global environmental challenge facing humanity with implications for natural ecosystems, agriculture & health. Changes in temperature and precipitation could have a significant impact on more than 9.14 lakh people who are dependent on agriculture in the State.

In some areas, an expected increase in convective rainfall - caused by stronger gradients of temperature and pressure and more atmospheric moisture - may result in heavier rainfall, which can cause severe soil erosion. Conditions are usually more favourable for the proliferation of insect pests in warmer climates. Longer growing seasons may enable a number of insect pest species to complete a greater number of reproductive cycles during the spring, summer, and autumn. Warmer winter temperatures may also allow larvae to winter-over in areas where they are now limited by cold, thus causing greater infestation during the following crop season. Most studies have concluded that insect pests will generally become more abundant as temperatures increase, through a number of inter-related processes, including range extensions and phenological changes, as well as increased rates of population development, growth, migration and over-wintering. Migrant pests are expected to respond more quickly to climate change than plants, and may be able to colonise newly available crops/habitats. The possible increases in pest and disease infestations may bring about greater use of chemical pesticides to control them, a situation that may enhance production costs and also increase environmental problems associated with agrochemical use.

Strategies for Facing the Climate Challenge

A variety of issues need to be considered, including land-use planning, watershed management, disaster vulnerability assessment and the various programmes countries use to encourage or control production, limit food prices, and manage resource inputs to agriculture. The study suggests following measures to tackle the fast emerging negative impact of climate change on the agriculture sector in the area under study are:

- Awareness generation about the impact of climate change on the agriculture sector is prime importance.
- Improved training and general education of populations dependent on agriculture is required.
- Research on new variety development, incorporating various traits such as heat and drought tolerant, salt and pest resistant should be given prime importance.
- Emphasis should be given on the use of environmental friendly organic inputs such as organic manures bio-pesticides and bio fertilizers.
- Use of crop diversification strategies (intercropping, agroforestry, crop-sequencing, etc.) and integration with other farming activities such as livestock raring etc. are required.
- Infrastructure facilities like transportation, distribution and market need to be improved.
- Effective steps are required towards forest conservation and tree plantation programmes. Agro-forestry and social forestry need to be given a big push. Trees improve soil structure and reduce soil erosion.
- More efficient water use, and improved soil management practices, together with the development of drought-resistant crops can help reduce some of the negative impacts of climate change.

- Effective steps are required towards forest conservation and tree plantation programmes. Agro-forestry and social forestry need to be given a big push.
- There is no need to build huge dams, which may have their long term negative effects. Instead of one big dam, a number of small dams and check dams can be constructed.
- In the rural area the efficient and environment-friendly technologies should be given preferences. The technology that can recycle, re-use of waste from agriculture, horticulture, dairying, mining should be promoted.

Setting-up of Regional Weather Stations are required

Farmers should be encouraged to prepare and use manure in a scientific manner. They can be given training to prepare farmyard manure, composite manure and green manure.

Conclusions

Climate change is an integrated system of several atmospheric phenomena and their products. At the surface, concentrations of greenhouse or radioactive gases such as carbon dioxide, chlorofluorocarbons, methane and nitrous oxide have clearly increased since the onset of the industrial revolution. During the recent past the climate of all over the world are changing and Himachal Pradesh (HP) is no exception. It has been put additional stress on the ecological and socio-economic systems in general and on the agriculture sector in particular. It will have an economic impact on agriculture, including changes in farm profitability, prices, and supply. The small and marginal farmers are the most vulnerable and are being affected maximum due to climate change. The specific climate variables viz. increased temperature, extreme events like flood, drought and storms are very important. Wet and dry spells cause significant impact on standing crops, physiology and loss of economic products (cash drops). Climate change having a direct impact on the vegetation, natural and cultivated, as also on the availability of water in the rivers and streams. Farmer should prepare for climate change, minimizing crop failure through increased use of drought- tolerant local varieties, water harvesting, extensive planting, mixed cropping, agroforestry and a series of other traditional farming system techniques.

References

1. Altieri, M.A. and C.I. Nicholls, (Biodiversity and Pest Management in Agroecosystems), 2nd edition, Haworth Press, New York, 2004.
2. Jones, P.G. and P.K. Thornton, The Potential Impacts of Climate Change on Maize Production in Africa and Latin America in 2055, Global Environmental Change, 2003.
3. Kavi Kumar, K.S., Shyamasundar, P. and Nambi, A.A., Economics of Climate Change Adaptation in India, Economic and Political Weekly, XLV (18), 2010.
4. Kumar K and Parikh J. Climate Change Impacts on Indian agriculture: the Ricardian approach, In Measuring the Impact of Climate Change on Indian Agriculture, edited by A Dinar, R Mendelsohn, Everson, J Parikh, A Sanghi, K Kumar, J Mckinsey and S Lonergan, Washington, DC: The World Bank (World Bank Technical Paper No 402), 1998.
5. Mitra, S.K., Key Note Address: Consultative Meet on Impact of Climate Change on Agriculture & Farmers, Adaptation, organized by WWF, NRMC (NRMC) on 13-10-2009.
6. Miguel A Altieri and Parviz Koohafkan, Enduring Farms: Climate Change, Smallholders and Traditional Farming Communities, Third World Network Penang, Malaysia, 2008.
7. Morton, J.F., The impact of climate change on smallholder and subsistence agriculture. PNAS 104: 19697-19704, 2007.
8. Nagaraj, A., India's Climate Change: Development and Equity, Economic and Political Weekly, XLV (18), 2010.
9. Raymond Guiteras, The Impact of Climate Change on Indian Agriculture, University of Maryland, September, 2009.

10. Robert Mendelsohn and Ariel Dinar, Climate Change, Agriculture, and Developing Countries: Does Adaptation Matter? Oxford Journals, Economics & Social Sciences, World Bank Research Observer, Volume 14, (2), 1999.

11. Rosenzweig, C. and D. Hillel, Climate Change and the Global Harvest: Potential Impacts of the Greenhouse Effect on Agriculture, Oxford University Press, New York, 1998.

12. Rosenzweig, C. and D. Hillel, Climate Change and the Global Harvest: Impacts of El Nino and Other Oscillations on Agro-ecosystems, Oxford University Press, New York 2008.

13. Sarkar, S. and Padaria, R.N., Farmers' Awareness and Risk Perception about Climate Change in Coastal Ecosystem of West Bengal, Indian Research Journal of Extension Education, 10(2), (2010).

14. http://www.climatefrontlines.org/en-GB/node/525, Impact of Climate Change on Traditional Agricultural Practices: Cases from Eastern Himalayas of India.

15. http://unu.edu/publications/articles/why-traditional-knowledge -holds-the-key-to-climate-change.html

16. http://www.twnside.org.sg

Chapter-IX

Existing Municipal Solid Waste Management Scenario in Faridabad City

Kokila Yadav, S. P. Kaushik and M. L. Bansal*

Abstract

Municipal Solid Waste (MSW) is generated in Faridabad city in Haryana, India, due to its rapid economic growth, increasing population and change in living standards of city. This paper analyses critically existing municipal solid waste management in study area. At present, the total solid waste generated in Faridabad Municipality is around 618 tons/day, but the waste collected by the Municipality is about 470 tons/day, which means almost 148 tons/day of the solid waste remains uncollected. Presently, there are three dumping sites which are temporary in nature. Recently, three NGOs named Ramki (NIT), Vishal Protection Force (Old Faridabad) and International Academy (Balllabhgarh) have been awarded the work of door-to-door collection by MCF. After collecting the waste from the houses, these NGOs transfer it to the nearest collecting points. There are at present 342 collection points in the city provided with community bins, open bins, dumper bins, etc. Capacity of Compost Plant situated at Bandhwari village (Gurgaon road) is 1000TPD. It includes 600TPD for Faridabad and 400TPD for Gurgaon. Presently, 200MTP is used for making compost, fuel pallets and RDF. The wastes are being dumped in the open without any treatment. Salvage of materials with recycling potential and value by rag-pickers takes place primarily at the collection points and partly at the landfill sites. Collection and dumping of domestic and municipal wastes is a serious problem in Faridabad city because of its impact on environment and public health. This leads to the pollution of ground and surface water because of leaching. Polluted water flowing from waste disposal sites caused serious pollution of water supply.

Key Word: Municipal solid waste (MSW), New Industrial Township (NIT), National Capital Region (NCR), Tone per Day (TPD), Municipal solid waste management (MSWM)

*Research scholar, Associate Professor and Professor, Department of Geography, Kurukshetra University, Kurukshetra, India

Introduction

The 'Municipal Solid Waste' includes commercial and residential wastes generated in municipal or notified areas in either solid or semi-solid form excluding industrial hazardous wastes but including treated bio-medical wastes [1]. Solid waste is a material which can't be used beneficially without its suitable processing. It is an unwanted material left from the different processes and sometimes it may also be in usable form. One of the obvious consequences of rapid urbanization is the growing generation of solid wastes, and many civic authorities face unprecedented problems for their rapid collection and proper disposal. The sudden outburst of population in urban areas, due to shifting from rural area in search of job and modern facilities had resulted in a substantial increase in the generation of solid waste and challenged the old waste management system. Everyone try to dispose of the waste material at the earliest whenever an opportunity is available. This practice usually ends up as illegal dumps on streets, open spaces, water bodies and waste land. Solid wastes management includes all administrative, financial, legal, planning, and engineering functions [2]. The management of solid waste is one of the challenges facing most of the urban area in the world [3].

The quantity and nature of the waste generated vary with the activities and with the level of technological development in a country. "The issue of waste is not only because of the increasing quantities but also largely because of an inadequate management system [4]. The environmentally sound management of solid wastes issue had received the attention of international and national policy making bodies and citizens [5]. The improvement of solid waste management is one of the greatest challenges faced by the Indian Government. The government and the local municipal authorities have taken many initiatives towards the improvement of the current situation [6].The municipal agencies spend 5-25% of their budget on SWM, which is Rs. 75-250 per capita per year . The waste quantities are estimated to increase from 46 million tons in 2001 to 65 million tons in 2010 [7]. NEERI [8] has conducted extensive studies on quantum of waste generation in various cities. Studies have revealed that quantum of waste generation varies between 0.2-0.4 kg/capita/day in the urban centers and it goes up to 0.5 kg/capita/day in metropolitan cities. Poor SWM related problems have resulted in serious environmental and social complications [9]. The problem of managing solid waste is caused by poor waste collection, storage and disposal leading to subsequent pollution and environmental degradation [10]. Due to lack of building control, formal settlements experience housing extensions which result in the destruction of planning standards [11].

Solid waste is mainly generated from the houses, commercial and industrial areas and hospitals etc. Due to rising income and influence of western life style, the consumption of products that have shorter life spans results in higher volumes of plastic, paper, glass, rags, food items, vegetables and parts of dead animals, radio-active materials, broken and unusable plastic goods. Now-a day dumping such a large quantity of solid waste is not possible because of the very high cost of land which is required for dumping.

Moreover, land at the outskirt of the metro cities is required for residential and other purposes. Normal compositing also requires a long time and hence requires a lot of space. Therefore, we need some latest techniques which are faster and can handle easily large amount of solid wastes in an efficient manner. Artificial composting is one of such technique which can be utilized to solve the current problem of solid waste in big cities.

Objectives

The chapter aims to critically examine and evaluate existing municipal solid waste management in Faridabad city.

Study Area

Faridabad is identified as one of the Delhi Metropolitan Area (DMA)/ National Capital Region cities and accordingly it has strong linkages with Delhi. NH 2 from Delhi-Mathura passes through the length of the city and is the central axis of the city of Faridabad. Faridabad is situated on the Delhi-Mathura NH-2 at a distance of 32 km from Delhi, at 28° 25' 16" N latitude and 77° 18' 28" E longitude.

The present geographical area of Faridabad is 207.88 sq. km. The rapid urbanization, increasing commercial and industrial activities and changing life styles in Faridabad are leading to a steady increase in the generation of solid waste. MCF is responsible for the collection, transportation and disposal of all solid waste generated in the city, except the untreated bio-medical waste and hazardous industrial waste, which is taken care of by the respective generators. MCF organizes the collection and transportation of the waste through a team of its own conservancy workers and a fleet of vehicles and dumper-placers. The waste collected is disposed at various dumping yards without any treatment. Population in Faridabad city is estimated to be about 16.62 lakh in 2011. The NCR regional plan for 2021 has projected the population of Faridabad as 25 lakhs. The Faridabad Municipal Corporation consists of Old Faridabad, Ballabgarh and New Industrial Township (NIT) [12]. Solid waste of Faridabad city is increasing rapidly due to industrial growth and location in NCR (National Capital Region). The population, urbanization, higher per capita income, standard of living, and changing lifestyle is also contributing to increased solid waste. Strict rules and regulations related to solid waste disposal may bring good change in solid waste characteristics and its management. Rapid urbanization, increasing commercial and industrial activities and changing life styles in Faridabad are leading to a steady increase in the generation of solid waste. MCF is responsible for the collection, transportation and disposal of all solid waste generated in the city, except the untreated bio-medical waste and hazardous industrial waste, which is taken care of by the respective generators. MCF organizes the collection and transportation of the waste through a team of its own conservancy workers and a fleet of vehicles and dumper-placers. The waste collected is disposed at various dumping yards without any treatment.

Data and Methodology

City population data was collected from the provisional population tables, census of India, 2011. The total municipal solid waste generation and ward wise solid waste was estimated. City Development Plan has provided insight to study solid waste management in Faridabad city. The solid waste management system of the metro cities such as Mumbai, Delhi, Kolkatta and Chennai was also examined. The secondary literature review proved to be an important asset in the absence of access to information available with the Municipal Corporations Faridabad. The major source of information was the City Development Plans(2006-2012) developed for sourcing funds under the Jawaharlal Nehru National Urban Renewal Mission (JNNURM) program. Primary survey includes Collection Point Survey, dumping site / Landfill site Survey and transfer station survey for a fair idea of the different types of waste being generated in the city. Municipal solid waste samples were carried out in June and September, 2011 a period covering pre and post-monsoon. Separate two sets of samples were collected from 18 selected sites for characterization of municipal solid waste.

Result and Discussion

Table No. 1 shows that Mumbai has the highest proportion of waste generation of 5335 ton per day with 0.436 per capita (kg/ day), followed by Delhi (4000 ton per day with 0.475 per capita (kg/ day), Kolkata (3692 ton per day with 0.347 per capita (kg/ day), Chennai (3124 ton per day with 0.657 per capita (kg/ day), and Bangalore (2000 TPD with 0.484 per capita (kg/ day). On the other hand, Coimbatore has the least share of generation of municipal waste (250 ton per day with 0.429 per capita (kg/ day), followed by Visakhapatnam (300 ton per day with 0.399 per capita (kg/ day), Patna ((330 ton per day with 0.360 per capita (kg/ day), Cochin (347 ton per day with 0.518 per capita (kg/ day, Indore (350 ton per day with 0.320 per capita (kg/ day, Madurai (370 ton per day with 0.393 per capita (kg/ day), Varodara and Ludhiana (400 ton per day with 0.388/0.384 per capita (kg/ day), and Varanasi (412 ton per day with 0.400 per capita (kg/ day). Likewise, there is a wide variation in the generation of municipal waste. Chennai has highest per capita solid waste generation 0.657 (kg/ day).

There arc 35 wards in study area. The coverage of wards in three zones is as following:
- NIT zone ward no. 1 to 19
- Old Faridabad ward no. 20 to 27

- Ballabhgarh ward no 28 to 35

Solid waste management is an obligatory function of Urban Local Bodies. MCF is taking care of the solid waste management by proper cleaning of the streets on daily basis. Waste collection bins have been placed within the vicinity of the households so that they can use the same. The waste is lifted every day from the bins and proper measures are taken to avoid spilling of the solid waste in the city Recently, MCF has engaged three NGOs namely Ramki (NIT), Vishal Protection Force (Old Faridabad) and International Academy (Balllabhgarh) for door-to-door collection and transfers it to nearest collecting points. The rapid growth of urban population, industrialization and changing life style of peoples, the situation is becoming more and more critical with the passage of time.

The information and data on the nature of wastes, its composition and physical characteristics and the generation quantity are the basic need for the selection and for the analysis and design of disposal facility. Very large quantities are produced by household and industrial activity. Improper management of waste lead to environmental pollution, public health hazard, and adverse effects on an urban economy. Collection and dumping of domestic and municipal wastes is a serious problem in Faridabad city because of its impact on environment and public health.

Table Showing Status of Municipal Solid Waste Generation in Some Metro Cities

Sr. No.	Metro City	Population in the Municipal Corporation	Municipal Solid Waste Generation (tons / day)	Per Capita Solid Waste Generation (kg/ day)
1.	Mumbai	12288519	5355	0.436
2.	Delhi	8419084	4000	0.475
3.	Kolkata	10643211	3692	0.347
4.	Chennai	4572976	3124	0.657
5.	Bangalore	4130288	2000	0.484
6.	Ahmadabad	2876710	1683	0.585
7.	Hyderabad	4098734	1566	0.382
8.	Kanpur	1874409	1200	0.640
9.	Lucknow	1619115	1010	0.624
10.	Surat	1498817	900	0.600
11.	Pune	2244196	700	0.312
12.	Jaipur	1458483	580	0.398
13.	Bhopal	1062771	546	0.514
14.	Nagpur	1624752	443	0.273
15.	Varanasi	1030853	412	0.400
16.	Ludhiana	1042740	400	0.384
17.	Varodara	1031346	400	0.388
18.	Madurai	940989	370	0.393
19.	Indore	1091674	350	0.320
20.	Cochin	670009	347	0.518
21.	Patna	917243	330	0.360
22.	Visakhapatnam	752037	300	0.399
23.	Coimbatore	816321	250	0.429
	Total/ Average	66885287	30058	0.449

Source: CPCB, 2000, Status of Solid Waste Management in Metro Cities

Table 2 shows that in Faridabad, total solid waste generated was 82.50 T/ per day with per capita generation about 250 grams per capita per day in 1981. Presently, total quantity of solid waste is generated 617.60 T/ per day with per capita generation about 400 grams per capita per day. There is wide variation in the quantity of generation. The quantity of waste generation increased with the population growth. There is positive relationship between population and solid waste generation.

Table 2: Population and Solid Waste Generation

Sr. No.	Year	Population in Lacs	Population In Lacs (including 10% floating population)	Per Capita Waste Generated (g/day)	MSW Quantity Generation MT/day	MSW Quantity Generation (including 10% floating population) MT/day	MSW Quantity Generation MT/Year	MSW Quantity Generation (including 10% floating population) MT/Year
1.	1981	3.30	3.63	250	82.50	90.70	30112	33105
2.	1991	6.25	6.87	250	156.20	171.70	57031	62670
3.	2001	10.54	11.60	400	421.60	464	153884	169360
4.	2011	14.04	15.44	400	561.60	617.60	204984	225424

Municipal solid waste generation ton per day was calculated with the help of following formula:-

Population × Per Capita Waste Generated (g/day) = MSW Quantity generation T/day

For Example: 15.44 Lacs × 400 (g/day) = 617.60 TPD

There were 342 collection points in the city provided with community bins, open bins, dumper bins and the like. In all, 180 dustbins of MCF were located at specific collection points. For the purposes of primary collection, MCF has equipped its staff with 810 wheel barrows and 80 handcarts. The average spacing between the dustbins against the available road length is 1867 meters and the average area coverage per collection point is 0.40sq.km. The total staff of the conservancy department of MCF was 1212 against a sanctioned 1415 members. However, MCF has employed 750 conservancy workers on a daily wages basis. Thus on an average each conservancy worker is responsible for sweeping 621 meters of road length. Waste transportation and disposal was carried out on all days. Waste collected from various locations in the city was transported either to the transfer station or directly to the dumping yard. MCF uses its own conservancy vehicles. There was two JCBs of 3 Metric Tons (MT) capacity each to assist in secondary collection activities. The JCBs was reported to be making at least five trips per vehicle per day (City Development Plan, Municipal Corporation of Faridabad, 2002-2012).

Table 3 shows that 58 percent residential area waste, 11 percent commercial establishment waste, 8 percent vegetable and fish market waste, 6.50 percent garden and public places waste, 2.50 percent institutional waste and 14 percent street sweeping waste substance are present in MSW in Faridabad city. Residential waste generation quantity is unusually higher (58 percent) in Faridabad city.

There are about 342 municipal solid waste collection sites. All these sites are well spread in Faridabad city. Approximately, 600 MT/per day MSW is generated from these sites. The characteristics of municipal solid waste depend on the activities near waste collection point and living standard of the population in the area. In order to assess the solid waste characteristics, total 18 sampling sites were selected which are well spread over the entire city. The sampling sites were selected to cover different activities of the population as follows:

- Domestic
- Commercial
- Dairy activities
- Vegetable market
- Food grain market
- Meat market

12 sampling sites were selected in residential area (High, Middle, Low income group and Jhuggi areas) situated at Old Faridabad, Ballabhgarh and NIT area. 2 sampling sites were selected in commercial area situated at Old Faridabad, and NIT area. In order to

evaluate the characteristics of dairy activities waste, vegetable market waste, food grain market waste and meat market waste one site each was also selected during this case study. The analysis of MSW samples for 18 represented sites at Faridabad city has been done to study composition in term of waste constituents and results are given in table. Typical composition of MSW generated in Faridabad is given in this table 4. The characterization of MSW of MCF that includes 9.53 percent paper material, 16.53 percent of plastic, small quantities of metal (.46%) and glass (1.30%) and dust/ash and soil (33.65 percent). Organic matter consists of 46.78 percent and is the largest constituent.

Table 3 Showing Source Wise Waste Generation in Faridabad City

Sr. No.	Sources	Percent	Quantity MT
1.	Residential areas	58.00	360.76
2.	Commercial establishments	11.00	68.42
3.	Vegetable and Fish markets	8.00	49.76
4.	Gardens and Public places	6.50	40.43
5.	Institutional areas	2.50	15.55
6.	Street Sweeping	14.00	87.08
	Total	100.00	622.00

Source: Solid Waste Management Work- Municipal Corporation Faridabad, 2010

Table 4: Showing Average Composition of Waste in Faridabad City, 2011

Sr. No.	Major Component	Unit	Obtained value in sample (Percentage on wet weight basis)	
			Range	Average Value
1.	Paper	%	2.03 – 20.36	9.53
2.	Plastic	%	4.63 – 25.65	16.53
3.	Metal	%	ND – 3.80	0.46
4.	Glass	%	ND – 3.86	1.30
5.	Organic/Biodegradable Waste	%	31.30–71.96	46.78
6.	Dust/ Ash and Soil	%	8.32 – 40.02	25.63

Source: Field Sample Survey, 2011.

Sweeping of the roads and streets carried out daily by Safai Karamcharies in all MCF authorized area. Waste collected by sweeping and designated surface drains (up to 2 ft.) width is lifted and transported daily at designated dumping sites. The garbage transported to dumping sites is leveled by JCB machine and disinfectants are sprayed on it daily by sanitation department and covered by fresh earth by engineering department. Collection points in Faridabad city is also known secondary points and Khatha.

As per existing road length, drains and 342 collections points of garbage which are situated in existing regular areas of municipal corporation, Faridabad the requirement of sanitation staff as per norm and report of XEN. JNNURM shows that MCF is grossly under staffed (Table7).

Table 5: Showing List of Equipment and Vehicle in Faridabad City

Sr. No.	Particulars	Number/ Qty
1.	240 Ltr LLDPE Bins	500
2.	Littre Bin – 60 Ltr capacity with MS Frame	600
3.	4.5 Cum capacity M.s. Container	70
4.	1100 Ltr capacity Moble Bin	500
5.	Tri – cycle Rickshaw with 6 nos LLDPE Bin	1164
6.	140 Ltr capacity wheal Barrous	574
7.	3000 Ltr capacity water tanker with pressure jetting system	3
8.	Tripper Truck 6 cum capacity	5
9.	Refuse Collector Truck	16
10.	Dumper Placer Truck	18
11.	Haulage Truck of 16 cum capacity	9
12.	Animal Catcher Van	3
13.	JCB 3DX Exvator – Loader	7
14.	JCB 430Z Articulated front and Loader	2

Source: Solid Waste Management Work- Municipal Corporation Faridabad, 2010

Table 6: Showing Roads, Drains and Collection Points of Garbage in
Faridabad City

Sr. No.	Roads, Drains and Collection Points	Length in Kilometers
1.	Total length of roads and streets	1156.00
2.	Total length of drains	0907.84
3.	Total number of collection Points	0342.00

Source: Sanitation Department, Municipal Corporation Faridabad, 2010

Waste disposal is the most important aspect of solid waste
management. Table shows that only land dumping was used for
disposal of municipal waste in 1971. There was no other technique
for waste disposal. Afterward in 1991 about 90 percent of the
municipal solid waste was disposed in low lying area outside the
cities which had no provision of leachate, collection and treatment.
Approximately 9 percent municipal solid waste was used for
composting (Table 8).

Table 7: Showing Sanitation Staff Position of Municipal Corporation
Faridabad

Sr. No.	Name of the Post	Sanction in Budget	Existing	Vacant	Requirement as per norm and report of XEN. JNNURM
1.	Medical Officer of Health	1	1	-	-
2.	Senior Sanitary Inspector	7	4 +1 =5	3	15
3.	Sanitary Inspector	5	3	2	30
4.	Asst. Sanitary inspector	25	20	5	60
5.	Safai Daroga	62	50	12	120
6.	Safai Karamcharies	1316	1069 + 570= 1639	247	4571

Source: Sanitation Department, Municipal Corporation Faridabad, 2010

Table 8: Showing Waste Disposal Trends in India

Sr. No.	Waste Disposal Method	1971 (40cities)	1991 (23 cities)
1.	Land Dumping	Almost all	89.8%
2.	Composting	-	8.6%
3.	Others (Pelletisation, Vermi - composting	-	1.6%

Source: CPCB, 1999

At present, different type of solid waste require advance techniques and equipment related with collection, storage and disposal. Earlier, there were no use of modern technique and equipment's for collection, storage and disposal. This led to serious problems for management of MSW in Faridabad city. Proper management of solid waste is necessary for any city, for that, advance technology and equipment should invent and use. In the recent time, land is not available for dumping of solid waste. Cost of land increased day by day. Hence selection of suitable land becomes a challenge for the urban local bodies. There were five dumping sites in the city in 2001 out of which only three are in operation presently. Nangla enclave and Bhakri village sites are not in operation now. Following are the dumping sites of MCF:

- Kheri Road Basalwa dairy site, Old Faridabad
- BLB near Ucchagaon
- Near Badarpur Border behind Samshan Ghat
- Nagla Enclave, NIT
- Revenue estate near Bhakari village

Compost plant is situated at Bandhwari village (Gurgaon road). Capacity of compost plant is 1000TPD. It includes 600TPD for Faridabad and 400TPD for Gurgaon. However, only 20OTPD municipal solid waste is used for making compost; fuel pallets and RDF (refuse derived fuel) at present. It will be sufficient for next thirty years for Faridabad and Gurgaon.

About two-thirds (470TPD) of the total solid waste of 618 TPD generated in MCF is reported to be collected out of which 270 TPD is transported to landfill sites and 200 TPD for composting. Rest of the 148 TPD remains uncollected which also reflect the very serious problem of solid waste management of Faridabad city.

Conclusion

There are many problem related with solid waste management. Individual house problem is that if both husband and wife are working and children are schools going, they have to keep their waste basket in the open courtyard for collection by collector (cart person) to avoid smell nuisance in the kitchen and house. It is observed that the stray monkey, dogs and other stray animals heave waste basket before it is collected by the cart man. Secondly, if the individual household put the waste in community dustbin then cows, dogs and pigs (stray animals) litter the solid waste on the road and around the community dustbin causing foul smell and unhygienic problem. Therefore, quick and proper solid waste management facility is essential.

Municipal solid waste is being dumped in the open without any proper treatment. Presently, there is no organized door-to-door collection system. Salvage of materials with recycling potential and value by rag-pickers takes place primarily at the collection points and partly at the landfill sites. The city has failed to handle MSW in a scientific and systematic way.

There are mostly four types of solid waste i.e. biodegradable, non-biodegradable, Repair and construction materials and useless material. Biodegradable waste should be used for making compost and other products which are useful and fortunately MCF is about 200 TPD for composting. Construction waste should be used for lean concrete and land filling in low lying area. Recyclable material should be recycled in a proper manner so that they become more usefully. Left out material should be allowed incineration. Rag pickers should be banned and the segregation must be done by the MCF in order to increase the income from the recyclable waste. Separation and shredding of solid waste should be done carefully preferably at the primary source.

References

[1] Ministry of Environment and Forest (2000) Notification on Municipal Solid Waste (Management and Handling) Rules, India, 2000. pp. 3.

[2] T.V. Ramachandra, and S.K. Varghese, (2003) 'Exploring possibilities of achieving sustainability in solid waste management', Indian Journal of Environmental Health, Vol. 45, No. 4, pp.255–264.

[3] O. Zerbock, and M.S. Candidate, (2003). 'Urban solid waste management waste reductions in developing nations' school of forest resources an environment science, Master's International Program, Michigan Technological University, Working Paper 2003.

[4] E Tinmaz,.and, I. Demir (2005) Research on Solid Waste Management Systems to Improve Existing Situation in Corlu Town of Turkey, Science Direct, June 2005.

[5] K. Subramanian (2005) 'Solid Waste Management Issues in Indian cities', The Hindu, 23rd February, Chennai.

[6] The Expert Committee (2000) Manual on Municipal Solid Waste Management, The Ministry of Urban Development, The Government of India, Vols. 1–2, p.789.

[7] S. Kumar,, S.A. Gaikwad,, r, A.V. Shekda, , P.S. Kshirsagar and, R.N. Singh, (2004) "Estimation Method for National Methane Emission from Solid Waste Landfills", Atmospheric Environment, 38, pp.3481-3487.

[8] NEERI (1996) "Strategy Paper on Solid Waste Management in India", pp.1-7.

[9] M. P. Moore, and, B.S. Keary (2003) Global Urbanization and Impact on Health, International Journal of Hygiene and Environmental Health, 206 (4-5), pp. 269-278.

[10] T.V. Ramachandra and, B. Shruthi (2007). "Environmental Audit of Municipal Solid Waste Management." International Journal of Environmental Technology and Management 7, (4): pp 369 – 391.

[11] S. M. Kassim., and, A. Mansoor (2006) "Solid Waste Collection by the Private Sector: Households' Perspective — Findings from a Study in Dar e Salaam City, Tanzania", Habitat International 30, (4): pp 769–780.

[12] Jawaharlal Nehru National Urban Renewal Mission, Municipal Corporation of Faridabad, City Development Plan 2006-2012", p.58-62.

Chapter-X

Does Grameen Bank Contribute to the Socio-economic and Environmental Development of Rural Women? A Critical Analysis

Md. Aminul Islam*

Abstract

Both governmental and non-governmental organizations in many low income countries like ours started microcredit programs targeted to the poor. Many of these in maximum cases focused on women considering the notion that they are willing to bear credit risk than men. Women in these countries have still limited access to the wage labor market and in household decision-making. As they are poorer than men, Grameen Bank also gives priority to this group out of concern for equity. Rural women in Bangladesh are always active in both "income generating" and "income conserving" production13. The people have had also idea that Grameen Bank plays an important role in rural areas and it has now become a successful model for uplifting the socio-economic conditions of the rural women. Similarly, it has become a debated topic that Grameen Bank micro-credit program has more negative impact than positive and it has become totally commercial. The present study clarified the ideas related to this topic. That is, this study made an attempt to assess the contribution of Grameen Bank to the socio-economic and environmental development of rural women in Bangladesh. Social survey and observation methods have been used in this study.

Keywords: Contribution, Development, Ecological, Socio-economic, Grameen Bank

* *Assistant Professor, Department of Sociology, University of Rajshahi , Rajshahi, Bangladesh*

Introduction

Socio-economic and environmental development of rural women especially for Bangladesh is a controversial, debated, normative and relative topic of discussion. To put it another way these are the umbrella term which cover a wide variety of interrelated social , economic, and environmental factors that might tend to explain set of events closely related to every day social life. It includes education, occupation, income, housing, food habit, nutrition, health, working condition, recreation, social service, social security etc.,.14 It also appears from the study of human history that women never enjoyed absolute equality like men. "No country or society can achieve its potential without adequately investing in developing the capabilities of women and encouraging the empowerment of women"15. In everywhere inequality, discrimination and exploitation were common to their fate. When we are in a 21st century, women are not being allowed to live successfully the life of a human being16. Although half of the population of our country is women, their social status especially in rural areas remains very low17. The rural social structure is plagued with many problems such as, illiteracy, low life expectancy, and low rate of labor force participation, unemployment, high fertility and morbidity18 . NGO's central goal is empowering the power less women or helping them to bloom their hidden potentialities, that is power of thought, power of word, and power of organization, with a view to helping them to participate in the socio-economic development, for their emancipation from less human condition to more human condition[19]

---

14 Tahmina, Akhter, Mohila Unnoyon O Porikolpona: Bangladesh Prekshapot (Dhaka:Bangla Academy,1995).

15 T.V. Rao, Human Development Resources (New Delhi: Sage Publication, 1996).
16 Raj Kumer, (edited), Violence Against Women (New Delhi: Anmol Publication, 2000).
17 Md. Aminul Islam, "The Sixteen Decisions of Grameen Bank: Chit-chat and Reality," Social Science Journal, No.18, University of Rajshahi, (2013).
18 Shahnaj Parvin,"Empowerment of Rural Women in Bangladesh:A Household Level Analysis" (PhD diss.,, Bangladesh Agriculture University, 2004).
19, Rumel Halder and Rusheda Akhter "The Role of NGOs and Women's Perception of Empowerment: An Anthropological Study in a Village." (PhD diss., Jahangirnagar University. Bangladesh, 1999).

However, various NGO's in Bangladesh are trying to improve the socio-economic condition of rural women through small scale credit program side by side GO's planning and program. The Grameen Bank of Bangladesh is perhaps the best-known example of these NGOs. Dr. Muhammad Yunus, the founder Chairman of Grameen Bank awarded Nobel Prize in peace for its contribution. Besides, various studies on this issue also highlight the positive influence of Grameen Bank. But the researcher in his baseline survey found a gap between the contribution of Grameen Bank and positive socio-economic and ecological development of rural women.

Objectives of the study

The objectives of the study basically depend on the nature of research. Actually the objective refers to a statement of outcome of the study. A main objective of the study is to assess the contribution of Grammen Bank to the socio economic and environmental development of rural women. In this context the specific objectives of this study are to know the changes in quality of life through improved housing, health, education etc; and to know the changes in their status.

Methodology of the study

The study is simultaneously explorative and evaluative in nature. The research work was conducted in three villages under Gopalnagor union of Dhunat upazilla in Bogra district.110 beneficiaries from three villages that are 41 respondents out of 82 from konagaty, 38, out of 76 from Rajarampur, and 31, out of 62 from Ariamohan village were selected through simple random sampling. In this case the houses of the Grameen Bank has been numbered and chosen one house after one. In order to collect valid and reliable data from the GB women beneficiaries an interview schedule (questionnaire) was designed and used keeping the objectives in mind.

The collected data were coded, tabulated and analyzed in accordance with the objectives of the study. Various statistical measures like number, percentage distribution, tables, cross tabulation, diagrams, graphs, charts, etc also used in this study. For knowing the descriptive, explanatory and exploratory information of social phenomena, social survey method has been applied. However, for getting reliable and objective data, interview method has also been used in this study. For the sake of getting in-depth insight about the respondents what they say and what they actually do in their socio-cultural settings observation method has also been adopted. Data has been collected from primary and secondary sources. Both open and close-ended questions included to prepare the questionnaire. The information collected through baseline survey are mentioned below:

Table 1: Distribution of households, population, GB members and sample of GB members in study area

Sr. No.	Name of Village	House holds	Population			Respondents of GB	Sample respondents of GB		
			Male	Female	Total	Female	Female	Percent
1	Konaganti	683	11 76	1103	227 9	82	41	37.2 7
2	Razarampur	155	29 2	295	587	76	38	34.5 5
3	Ariamohan	93	16 5	188	353	62	31	28.1 8
Total		136 8	24 46	2414	486 0	230	110	100. 00

Source: (BBS 2012 and field data 2013)20

[20] *Bangladesh Bureau of Statistics (BBS)* "Community Report on Bogra Zila: Population and Housing Census 2011", Dhaka, Ministry of Planning, Government of the People's Republic of Bangladesh, 2012.

Limitations of Research

At the time of collecting data from the respondents it is observed that research is a very complicated task. The researcher did research on the performance of GB in changing socio-economic condition among the members involved in it. GB activities are so vast. He selected merely their role in changing the socio-economic condition of rural women. The researcher has also chosen 110 respondents. So, it is difficult to claim that it will be highly representative for the all branches of GB. That's to say it may not be applicable way of generalizing the role of GB. He also did this research by limited time and money. As a learner researcher he did not do all steps carefully. Maximum respondents were anxious about his data collection. They tried to hide their personal information. They also looked upon him as anti of GB. Again some of them desired to get something from him. In spite of these, he tried to do this research objectively.

History and Objectives of Grameen Bank

The Grameen Bank (GB) is a rural bank that organizes the rural poor around productive economic activities. It provides credit without material collateral to the rural poor particularly women, who were usually excluded from the conventional banking system. Dr. Muhammad Yunus, Professor of economics, started the Grameen Bank in 1976 as an action research project (Grameen Bank Project) with the hypothesis that providing credit to the rural poor without material collateral is not at all risky and "if financial resources are made available to the poor at reasonable terms and conditions they can generate productive self-employment without any external assistance"[21]. Initially the project started its activities with the following objectives: (i) to extend banking facilities to the poor men and women ;(ii) to eliminate the exploitation of the moneylender to create opportunities for self-employment for the vast utilized and underutilized manpower resource;

---

[21] Yunus Muhammad, *Grameen Bank: A Bank for the Poor* (Dhaka: Grameen Bank, 1986).

(ii) to bring the disadvantaged people within the folds of some organizational format, which they can understand, and operates and can find socio-political and economic strength in it through mutual support; and (iv) to reverse the age-old vicious circle of "low income, law savings, low investment, low income" into an expanding system of low income, credit, investment, more income, more credit, more investment, more income."

The project was experimented in a village called Jobra near Chittagong University in 1976.The GBP quickly demonstrated its success and by 1978, started its operation in two other villages in addition to Jobra. After three years of experiment the project extended its activities in Tangail district with financial support from Bangladesh Bank (Central Bank). By May 1982, the project was further extended to Dhaka, Rangpur and Patuakhali districts with financial assistance from international fund for Agricultural Development (IFAD). After a long struggle (i.e. from 1976 to 1983), Prof, Yunus succeeded to prove his hypothesis, as the realization of credit was almost cent percent during the period of observation. In recognition of the need for a separate development financial institution for the disadvantaged rural poor, the Grameen Bank Project ceased to be a project and became a bank in September 1983 with the Grameen Bank Ordinance 1983. The "Sixteen Decisions" of GB is considered to be a poor woman's social charter. It is believed to be the new dimension to the overall development of the poor. The credit has, thus, been an entry point and now serves as catalyst for change. It is also thought that by the management of the bank the social development finally helps members increase their productivity and thus ensures recovery of loans. The social development cemented the group spirit among the members. This has also helped to organize the networking among the poor. The crises coping capacity of the poor has also improved during the process22 . The social activities of GB have comprised of sanitation, health care, nutrition, training, distribution of seeds and seedlings, distribution of iodized salt, family planning, distribution of winter clothing and promotion of social reforms, etc.

---

[22] Atiur, Rahman, *Demand and Marketing Aspects of Grameen Bank* (Dhaka: Grameen Bank 1994).

The 16 Decisions of Grameen Bank

1. The four principles of Grameen Bank discipline, unity, courage, and hard work-we shall follow and advance in all walk of our lives.
2. Prosperity we shall bring to our families.
3. We shall not live in dilapidated houses. We shall repair our houses and work towards constructing new houses at the earliest.
4. We shall grow vegetables all the year ground. We shall eat plenty of it and sell the surplus.
5. During the plantation seasons we shall plant as many seedlings as possible.
6. We shall keep our families small and minimize our expenditures. We shall look after our health.
7. We shall educate our children and ensure that they can earn to pay for their education.
8. We shall always keep our children and the environment clean.
9. We shall build and use pit latrines.
10. We shall drink tube well water. If it is not available, we shall boil water or use alum.
11. We shall not take any dowry in our son's wedding neither shall we give from the curse of dowry; we shall not practice child marriage.
12. We shall not inflict any injustice on any one; neither shall we allow anyone to do so.
13. For higher income we shall collectively under take bigger investments.
14. We shall always be ready to help each other. If anyone is in difficulty, we shall all help him.
15. If we come to know of any breach of disciplined in any center, we shall all go there and help restoring discipline.
16. We shall introduce physical exercise in all our centers. We shall take part in all social activities collectively.

Source: *"The 16 decisions of Grameen Bank," http://www.grameen info.org/bank/the16.html (October 17, 2005).*[23]

---

[23] The 16 decisions of Grameen Bank," http://www.grameen info.org/bank/the16.html (October 17, 2005).[23]

Findings of the study

Table 2: Showing Distribution of Respondents in Study Area

Research Area	Number of member	Percentage
Konangaty	41	37.27
Rajarampur	38	34.55
Ariyamohan	31	28.18
Total	110	100.00

In this study, 110 women respondents of three villages have been selected. 40 (37.27%) women from Konagaty village have been selected. Among the three villages, Konagaty has significant proportion of women who are involved in Grameen Bank. The percentage of women of other two villages are 34.55% and 28.18%.

Table 3: Showing Age Status of the Respondents

Age (in years)	Frequency	Percentage
15-20	03	02.73
21-25	23	20.91
26-30	35	31.82
31-35	14	12.73
36-40	15	13.64
41-45	06	05.45
46-50	08	07.27
51-55	02	01.82
56-60	04	03.64
Total	110	100.00

From the age distribution of members it is understandable that the number of respondents in age group 21-40 is the highest concentration. They are neither young nor old rather than they belong to the middle position of age distribution. Of course there are 4 respondents whose are in the age group of (56-60). So, the number of middle aged women is significant. It may sociologically point out that the women, who belong to 21-40 years old, are interested in involving GB.

Table 4: Distribution of Respondents by their Educational Qualification

Type of Educational Qualification	Frequency	Percentage
Knowledge of Signature	63	57.27
Class I-V	27	24.54
Class V-X	13	11.82
S.S.C (passed)	05	04.55
H.S.C	02	01.82
Total	110	100.00

From this table it may be understood the educational qualification of the respondents. About 57.14% of the respondents only have the knowledge of signature, 24.54% have class one class five, 11.82% have class five to ten, 4.55% passed SSC and 1.82% passed HSC level of education. After joining Grameen Bank, maximum of them did able just to write down their names as it is mandatory for the members to sign for membership.

Table 5: Head of the Household

Head of the family	Frequency	Percentage
Husband	92	83.64
Self	06	05.45
Son	12	10.91
Total	110	100.00

Table above shows that 83.64% head of the family are the husbands of the respondents. Only 05.45% of women headed family and 10.91% is son. From this scenario, it can be conjectured that the women are powerless in the family as well as in the household. They are fully dependent on their husband. As they are living in a patriarchal society, so, they are not empowered at all.

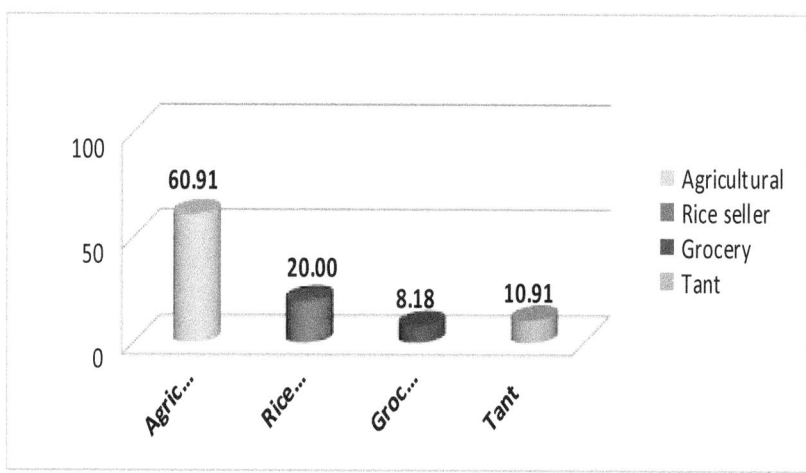

Figure Showing Distribution of the head of the household on basis of occupation

From the graph, it is easily understandable that 60.91% of the heads of the households are engaged in agricultural activities, 20.00% of them in rice selling business, 10.91% of them in Tant activities and 8.18% of them are small shopkeepers. It is an extent symptom of occupational mobility among the head of the households.

Table.6: Showing Marital status of the Respondents

Marital condition	Frequency	Percentage
Married	92	83.64
Widow	12	10.91
Divorcee	6	05.45
Total	110	100.00%

From the table placed above it appears that 83.64% of the respondents are married. That's to say they are spending their lives in their husbands' house. 10.91% of the respondents are widows and 05.45% of them are divorcee. From these it can say that Grameen Bank looks not only the married women but also the widows and divorcee.

Table 7: Showing Type of Family of the Respondents

Type of family	Frequency	Percentage
Nuclear	94	85.45
Joint	16	14.55
Total	110	100.00

From the table displayed above it can see that among 110 respondent 85.45% live in nuclear family and 14.55% women are live in joint family. In Bangladesh rural society, after 3 or 5 years of their marriage, they are to separate from their parents. But parents are not inclined to give them property before their dying. As a result they are to suffer a lot. From this suffering, the condition of women is miserable no doubt.

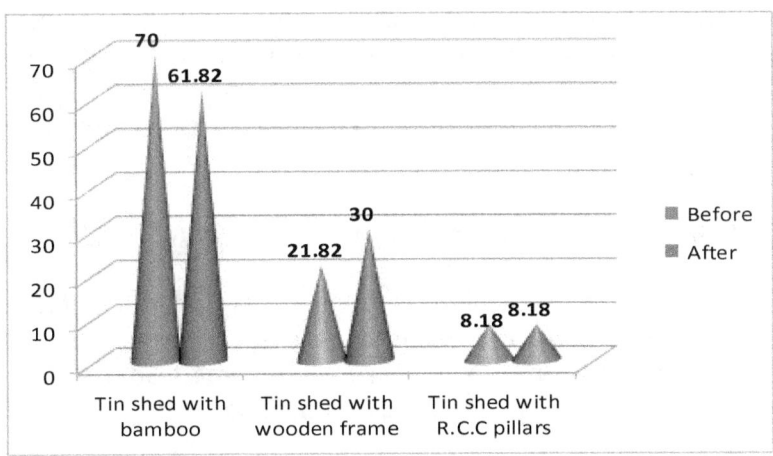

Figure Showing Housing status of the respondents before and after joining GB

The graph above clearly shows that the implementation of the housing program is extent satisfactory. The table reveals that 70.00% of the borrowers had bamboo made house before joining GB. While after joining GB the share of the bamboo made houses reduced substantially. Again, tin shed with wooden frame increased 21.82% from 30.00%. After all, the housing condition of the members improved a little bit.

Table 8: Showing Toilet Facility available to the Respondents
Before and After joining GB

Type of Toilet	Frequency (before)	Percentage	Frequency (after)	Percentage
Sanitary	55	50.00	77	70.00
Other	39	35.45	24	21.82
None	16	14.55	9	8.18
Total	110	100.00	110	100.00

Grameen Bank authority claims that they have sanitation program which is available in their sixteen decisions that is they will ensure building and using pit-latrines .Though they did not succeed, their condition improved a little bit. It is also observed that 14.55 percent of the respondent did not have any kind of latrine before joining the GB while the figure reduced to only 8.18 percent after joining. Again unhygienic latrines were used by 35.45% before joining, which went down to 21.82 percent after joining GB. It is mentionable here that, government and other NGOs have contribution side by side GB to improve this condition.

Table: 9 shows that maximum respondents have no sufficient homestead land. Nearly 47.27% of the respondents have less than 10 decimal homesteads and 26.36% have no homestead land at all. They live in their relatives' house. In village they are called refugees. But they are not truly refugees.

Table 9: Showing Ownership of Homestead land of Respondents

Amount of Homestead land (in decimal)	Frequency	Percentage
No Homestead	29	26.36
Less than 10	52	47.27
11-20	16	14.55.
21-30	10	9.09
31-40	3	2.73
41 and above	0	0.00
Total	110	100.00

It is true that they are to bow their heads to those persons under whom the respondents pass their lives. It is also evident from the table that no respondent has more than 41 decimals of homestead land.

Table 10: Showing Monthly income of the Respondents Before and after joining GB

Monthly Income	Before		After	
	Frequency distribution	Percentage	Frequency distribution	Percentage
2000-2500	20	18.18	23	20.91
2500-3000	39	35.45	35	31.82
3000-3500	25	22.73	26	23.64
3500-4000	13	11.82	15	13.64
4000-4500	7	6.36	5	4.55
4500-5000	4	3.64	3	2.73
5000 and above	2	1.82	3	2.73
Total	110	100.00	110	100.00

Table above reveals that the monthly income of the members has been decreased comparatively after joining Grameen Bank. Before joining GB 35.45 percent respondent could earn 2500-3500 in a month. After joining, it became 30.48 percent.

Table 11: Showing Monthly Expenditure of the respondents before and after joining GB

Monthly expenditure	Before		After	
	Frequency	Percentage	Frequency	Percentage
1500-2000	46	41.82	39	35.45
2000-2500	35	31.82	39	35.45
2500-3000	15	13.64	14	12.73
3000-3500	9	8.18	11	10.00
3500-4000	3	2.73	4	3.64
4000-4500	2	1.82	3	2.73
Total	110	100.00	110	100.00

From this table it also appears that the monthly expenditure among the respondents increased. About 43.81% respondents expend (1500-2000) taka in a month and 29.52% expends (2000-2500) taka in a month. After the intervention in Grameen Bank, it becomes 32.38% and 37.14%. It also may have two reasons; (i) the availability of money; (2) the high value of goods and commodity. The real fact is high value of goods and commodity.

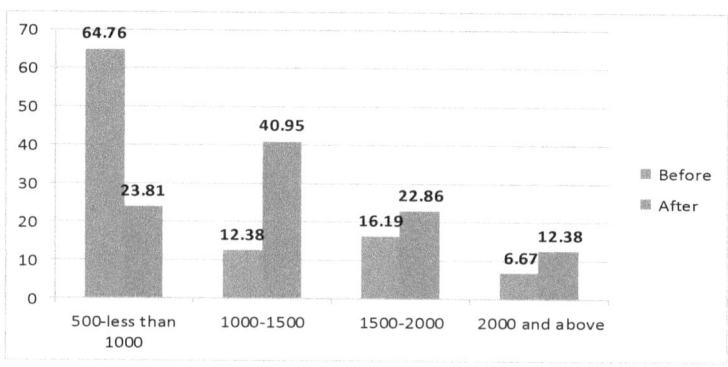

Figure Showing Yearly expenditure of respondents in taking medical care before and after joining GB

The graph placed above indicates that the expenditure in buying medicine and taking medical care increased after the intervention of Grameen Bank. Before joining it was 12.38 percent and after joining it became 40.95 percent. As they get it as cash money, they don't hesitate to use it.

Table 12: Showing Respondents' yearly expenditure in educating children before and after joining GB

Monthly expenditure	Before		After	
	Frequency	Percentage	Frequency	Percentage
No expenditure	28	25.45	8	7.27
less than 500	43	39.09	27	24.55
501-1000	22	20.00	37	33.64
1001-2000	14	12.73	26	23.64
2001 and above	3	2.73	12	10.91
Total	110	100.00	110	100.00

The table presents that yearly expenditure in educating children has increased after joining GB. GB gives them education debt, for higher degree. But it should be kept in mind that the scholarship program of government increased expenditure in education. Before scholarship program, the parents were disinterested in spending money for the education of their children.

Table 13: Showing Sources of drinking water of the respondents before and after joining GB

Source	Before		After	
	Frequency	Percentage	Frequency	Percentage
Tube well (others)	76	72.38	54	51.43
Tube well (Own)	34	27.62	56	48.57
Total	110	100.00	110	100.00

It is also a purpose of GB that they will make their members to drink tube-well water. If it is not possible, at least they will drink boil water. But it is seen that maximum respondents drink tube well water. It is noticeable that the percentage of using tube well water from their tube wells has increased. It is also mentionable here that, government and other NGOs have contribution side by side GB to improve the tube well facility of the respondents.

Table 14: Showing Distribution of the respondents by their use of contraceptives before and after of joining GB

Making Use of Contraceptives	Before		After	
	Frequency	%	Frequency	%
Yes	49	44.55	58	52.72
No	61	55.45	53	48.18
Total	110	100.00	110	100.00

The table depicts that approximately 43.81% respondents would use contraceptives before joining GB. But after joining GB it becomes (52.72%). Again, before joining GB (55.45%) did not use contraceptive. But after joining GB it becomes (48.18%). From this it can be conjectured that GB has contributed a lot in the awareness of the members about using contraceptives. But actually this is not true. The members and non-members of the GB's became aware of using contraceptives due to the media revolution and intervention of GO's Female health workers. Besides, it is related to the age structure of the respondents.

Borrower's perception of change in their economic condition after joining Grameen Bank

Questions were asked to the respondents to know their perception of change in their economic condition after the intervention of Grameen Bank. It is evident form graph that near about 18.18% respondents opined that their economic condition have improved, 32.73% opined no changes and 59.92% said that their economic condition have been deteriorated after joining Grameen Bank. The inference that can be drawn from the above analysis that majority of the borrower experiences their economic conditions have been deteriorated due to the use of loan.

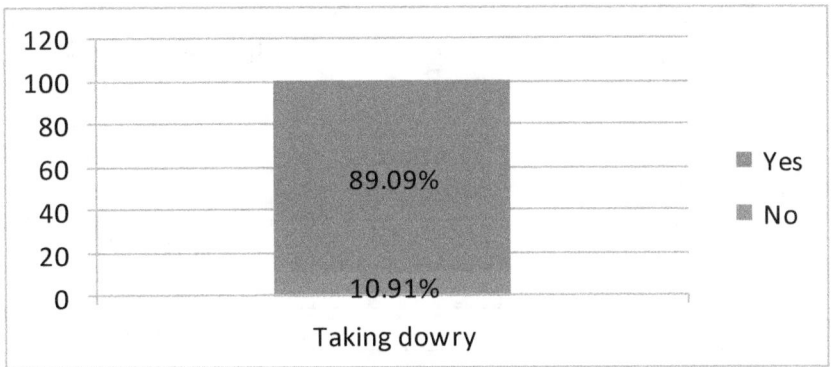

Figure Showing Attitude of the respondents towards dowry in their sons' and daughters' marriage

Questions were asked to know their attitudes towards dowry in their sons' and daughters' marriage. About 89.09% respondents said that they will take dowry. Because we can't give marry our daughters without dowry. Nearly 10.91% respondents replied that we will try to avoid this. In village there is hardly any marriage held without dowry. The respondents of the GB are not exception to this. So, GB could not make them aware about it successfully.

Table 15: Showing Capacity of Repayment of Installment

Capacity to Repay	Frequency	Percentage
Yes	80	72.73
No	30	27.27
Total	110	100.00

The table focuses that about 72.73% respondents are able to repay the installment. Because they are involved in small business, 27.27% replied that they are unable to repay and opined that, repaying installment is the cause of their familial unhappiness. As the collector of installment stays in center without taking installment, the members of the Grameen Bank sometimes think that it is against their prestige issue.

Table 16: Showing Borrowers Perception of Empowerment in the
Family after Joining GB

Condition of Empowerment	Frequency	Percentage
Empowered	17	15.45
Unchanged	68	61.82
Disempowered	22	20.00
No response	03	02.73
Total	110	100.00

The table explains that about 15.45% respondents are empowered, 61.82% replied that their condition is same to before and 20.00% said that they have been disempowered in their family. That's to say they can take part in familial decision making. Their opinions are that, after finishing loan, when they can't repay the installment, their husband behaved with them not in a friendly way. Quarrels are the common matter in family. Moreover, many of them don't consider the concept of empowerment. But as they share with their ideas with other members of the society, as they are organized, as they take part in meeting, they are empowering a little bit day-by-day.

Information on taking more credit from GB

Questions were asked among the respondents whether they are more credit or not. Nearly 86.36% replied that they need more credit whereas 13.64% answered that as we can't improve by this money, we don't want anymore. That is, sometimes it seems burden to them.

Table 17: Showing Information on Saving Capability of the
Respondents

Saving capability	Frequency	Percentage
Capable	83	75.45
Not capable	27	24.55
Total	110	100.00

Questions were also asked to the respondents whether they are capable of saving money or not. About 75.45% answered that they are capable. Again, 24.55% answered that they are not capable. The fact is that those who use the credit properly are capable of saving. On the other hand other can't it due to far behind from using this credit properly.

Table 18: Showing Knowledge of Grameen Bank's members
regarding the cleanliness of home and environment

Knowledge regarding cleanliness	Before		After	
	Number	Percentage	Number	Percentage
Yes	38	34.54	46	41.82
No	62	56.36	64	58.18
Total	110	100.00	110	100.00

The table above clearly highlights that before joining Grameen bank, 34.54 percent had knowledge regarding the cleanliness of environment. After joining it becomes 41.82 percent. Again, 56.36 percent respondents had no knowledge regarding this issue. After joining it went down 58.18 percent. The respondents were asked how did this happen? Is this the contribution of Grameen Bank? They replied that they become aware by dint of media.

Table 19: Showing Opinion on Growing More Vegetables among
the Respondents after Joining GB

Opinion	Frequency	Percentage
Increased	28	25.45
Decreased	13	11.82
Same as before	69	62.73
Total	110	100.00

It is one of the sixteen decisions that we shall grow more vegetables
all the year ground. We shall eat plenty of eat and sell the surplus.
But 62.82% respondents' condition did not change. Only 25.45
percent became able to grow more vegetables and 11.82 percent
answered that their conditions as to growing more vegetables
decreased due to the lacking of growing vegetables land.

Recommendations

To speak strictly, Bangladesh is a developing country, which is
being governed largely by patriarchy, traditional values, strong
religious tie, customs and superstitions. Women generally get less
opportunity in every sphere of life vis-à-vis men in the country. So,
merely, the contribution of Grameen Bank to contribute the socio-
economic change of rural women is not enough. In this regard it is
recommended as follows:

- The male members of the society will have to change their
  patriarchal mentality. If each and every male member
  changes his mentality and take advice in taking any decision
  it will be easy for women to be included in familial state of
  affairs.
- The GB should be flexible in not taking high interest. If they
  cling to its objectives and do not take too much interest in
  various names, the family of the respondents may be
  benefitted for that.
- The Grameen Bank authority should monitor about the
  actualization of objectives among the members who are

involved in Grameen Bank. In this regard, they can conduct workshop in every center by turns.

- They can take initiative for awareness arising programs among the members so that they can use the loan in proper sectors. In this case they can impose some conditions for the sake of actualizing their loans.
- They should conduct a training program for the members. Especially they can train up their members for small business, handicraft, small cottage and anything like these.
- They can compel the members to use their loan in buying domestic animals so that the members can change their condition from themselves by selling eggs, milk and the reproduction of these domestic animals.
- The other NGOs who are trying to empower women and alleviate poverty will have to be more conscious. They should start healthy completion for helping poor.
- The Government should take necessary steps for the rural women as development activists. As maximum people live in rural areas of Bangladesh, it is not possible to bring about development without taking them into consideration.
- The media should uphold the images of rural women by taking up various programs. Because maximum respondents belong to middle age group. They watch television. So, it is to convince them.
- The rural women also should be conscious about their rights and duties by taking education, using their time, domesticating animal, involving in other income generating sectors.

Conclusion

The objectives of Grameen Bank are doubtless helpful for rural women in developing their socio-economic and ecological conditions. Grameen Bank has no too much contribution the relation between people and environment. It needs to mention here that the activities of GB in field level do not match with these due to multifaceted problems of our rural society and highly commercial approach of this bank as well.

Because, Bangladesh is the poorest countries of the world with over population and limited per capita income as it is US $104424. UNDP Human Development Report portrays that more than half of its population lived in below the poverty line and more than 35 percent living in extreme poverty25. Mere it is not enough; women constitute half of the Bangladeshi population as stated earlier with many problems. BBS census report highlights that the rural and urban populations of Bangladesh are 76.61% and 23.39% i.e. about 77 percent of people still live in rural areas26. Among them more than half of the population is women. Gender issues and discriminatory situation between men and women remain as the core areas relating to women and development in Bangladesh. Besides, thinkers are almost agreeing that women's socio economic development is a pre-requisite for our national development[27.] Grameen Bank is one of the most important banks, which is trying to change the socio-economic and environmental conditions of rural women in Bangladesh. However in this study, it is found that the women, who belong to 21-40 years old, are interested in involving GB. About 83.64% of the respondents are married. About 57.14% of the respondents only have the knowledge of signature. After joining Grameen Bank, maximum of them did able just to write down their names as it is mandatory for the members to sign for membership. About 85.45% women live in nuclear family and near about 83.64% head of the family are the husbands of the respondents. About 70.00% of the borrowers had bamboo made house before joining GB. Again, tin shed with wooden frame increased 21.82% from 30.00%. After all, the housing condition of the members improved a little bit. Nearly 47.27% of the respondents have less than 10 decimal homesteads and 26.36% have no homestead land at all. Before joining GB 35.45 percent respondent could earn 2500-3500 in a month. After joining, it became 30.48 percent. About 43.81% respondents expend (1500-2000) taka in a month and 29.52% expends (2000-2500) taka in a

[24] *Bangladesh Economic* Survey, Economic Advisor, Economic Division, Ministry of Economic (Dhaka: The People's Republic of Bangladesh, 2013).
[25] UNDP *Human Development Report* Human Development Report, (Washington, UN,2003).
[26] BBS (*Bangladesh Bureau of Statistics*) Preliminary Report on Bangladesh population census (Dhaka: BBS, 2001)
[27] Mizanuddin, Muhammad" Gender Issues and Women and Development in Bangladesh," *Social Science Journal*, vol. 10, January (2005)

month. After the intervention in Grameen Bank, it becomes 32.38% and 37.14%. The expenditure in buying medicine and taking medical care increased after the intervention of Grameen Bank. Before joining it was 12.38 percent and after joining it became 40.95 percent. As they get it as cash money, they don't hesitate to use it. It is noticeable that the percentage of using tube well water from their tube wells has increased. One of the goals of the Grameen Bank is to ensure the use of sanitary latrines among its members; it is also observed that 14.55 percent of the respondent did not have any kind of latrine before joining the GB while the figure reduced to only 8.18 percent after joining. Again unhygienic latrines were used by 35.45% before joining, which went down to 21.82 percent after joining GB. The percentage of using sanitary latrine is 66.6% in Bangladesh28. If they need more credit approximately 86.36% replied that they need more credit whereas 13.64% answered that as we can't improve by this money, we don't want anymore. It is also revealed from the field data that 75.38% respondents became successful to create savings. And other didn't do it due to not using the credit properly. Approximately 43.81% respondents would use contraceptives before joining GB. But after joining GB it becomes (52.72%). Again, before joining GB (55.45%) did not use contraceptive. But after joining GB it becomes (48.18%).In the case of family planning the GOs programs such as media revolution and health workers became successful to make them aware about family planning than GB. Regarding the perception of change in their socio- economic condition after the intervention of Grameen Bank it is also found that near about 18.18% respondents opined that their economic condition have improved, 32.73% opined no changes and 59.92% said that their economic condition have been deteriorated after joining Grameen Bank. As to the empowerment about 15.45% respondents said they are empowered, 61.82% replied that their condition is same to before and 20.00% said that they have been disempowered in their family. Whether they are capable of repaying installment about 72.73% respondents are able to repay the installment. Because they are involved in small business, 27.27% replied that they are unable to

---

28 *Bangladesh Economic* Survey, 2013.

repay. Besides they opined that repaying installment is the curse for their familial happiness. Of course it is true that after joining Grameen Bank the village women are not seeking help from rural elite. But they seek help from money lenders and other NGOs due to not capable of repaying installment. In case of saving capacity, it is observed that about 75.45% answered that they are capable. Again, 24.55% answered that they are not capable. It is found that about 89.09% respondents said that they will take dowry. Because we can't give marry our daughters without dowry. Nearly 10.91% respondents replied that we will try to avoid this. It has already been mentioned that GB has no huge agenda regarding environmental development. In its sixteen decisions they mentioned some issues regarding ecological development. Such as: we cultivate vegetables the whole year round and sell the surplus, we see to it that our children and homes are clean, during the season for planting; we pick out as many seedlings as possible. It has also identified that before joining Grameen bank, 34.54 percent had knowledge regarding the cleanliness of environment. After joining it becomes 41.82 percent. The respondents were asked how did this happen? Is this the contribution of Grameen Bank? They replied that they become aware by dint of media. Moreover, only 25.45 percent became able to grow more vegetables. The discussions above aptly points out that GB did not yet to receive its required goal. The rural women had aspiration that they would change their socio-economic and environmental conditions involving Grameen Bank as it is available in their social charter that means in their sixteen decisions.

References

1. Chen, Mactha Alter" A Quiet Revolution: Women in Transition in Rural Bangladesh" Cambridge: Scenkhan Publishing Company, Inc. 1983.
2. Akhter, Tahmina, Mohila Unnoyon O Porikolpona: Bangladesh Prekshapot, Dhaka:Bangla Academy,1995.
3. Rao, T.V., Human Development Resources, New Delhi: Sage Publication, 1996.
4. Kumer, Raj (edited), Violence Against Women, New Delhi: Anmol Publication, 2000.
5. Islam, Md. Aminul "The Sixteen Decisions of Grameen Bank: Chit-chat and Reality," Social Science Journal, No.18, University of Rajshahi, (2013).
6. Parvin Shahnaj,"Empowerment of Rural Women in Bangladesh: A Household Level Analysis" (PhD diss.,, Bangladesh Agriculture University, 2000.
7. Halder, Rumel and Akhter Rusheda "The Role of NGOs and Women's Perception of Empowerment: An Anthropological Study in a Village." PhD diss.,Jahangirnagar University, Bangladesh, 1999.
8. Bangladesh Bureau of Statistics (BBS) "Community Report on Bogra Zila: Population and Housing Census 2011", Dhaka, Ministry of Planning, Government of the People's Republic of Bangladesh, 2012.
9. Yunus Muhammad, Grameen Bank: A Bank for the Poor, Dhaka: Grameen Bank, 1986.
10. Rahman, Atiur, Demand and Marketing Aspects of Grameen Bank Dhaka: Grameen Bank 1994.
11. "The 16 decisions of Grameen Bank," http://www.grameen info.org/bank/the16.html (October 17, 2005).
12. Bangladesh Economic Survey, Economic Advisor, Economic Division, Ministry of Economic (Dhaka: The People's Republic of Bangladesh, 2013.
13. UNDP Human Development Report Human Development Report, Washington, UN,2003.
14. BBS (Bangladesh Bureau of Statistics) Preliminary Report on Bangladesh population census Dhaka: BBS, 2001.
15. Mizanuddin , Muhammad"Gender Issues and Women and Development in Bangladesh," Social Science Journal, vol. 10, January (2005).
16. Islam, Md. Rafiqul "Socio-cultural Comparison among the Upper, Middle and Lower Class People of Dhaka City: An Anthropological Study", Social Science Journal, 11, (2005).

Chapter-XI

Comparison of Rainfall Wetness in Gujarat based on Seasonality Index of Different time Period

S. M. Yadav, Vijendra Kumar, Dr. B. K. Samtani and Priyanka Zore

Abstract

The study of rainfall wetness index is important to know mean rainfall and its variability. The present work contributes to understand the comparison of rainfall wetness in Gujarat based on seasonality index of different time period. Monthly rainfall data of Gujarat state was collected from India Meteorological Department (IMD) from ninety years. Here, first ten- ten years data are separated, second thirty- thirty years data are separated and last fourth five- fourth five years data are separated for different time period. Then monthly and seasonal scales are developed. Mean rainfall and coefficient of rainfall are studied to get the pattern and variability in rainfall based on different time period. This study will help to improve the planning and management of agriculture and water resource systems, especially during dry climate periods.

Keywords- Gujarat, Rainfall Pattern, Seasonality Index, Wetness Index, Water Resource Systems

---

* Professor, and M. Tech. students CED. SVNIT, Surat, Gujarat, India

Introduction

Throughout the world monsoon rainfall is very important for the economic development, hydrological planning and disaster management of the country [1]. From last few decades due to climate change, the spatial and temporal distribution of rainfall is having lots of variation [2]. Thus it needs to study the spatial and temporal rainfall variation. So that agriculture as well as water resource system planning and management can be improved, particularly during dry season [3]. Rainfall seasonality index is one of the methods that can be used to find out the seasonal variation in precipitation. Rainfall seasonality gives distribution pattern of rainfall on monthly basis for a defined location [4].

Numerous works have been done to find out the variation in rainfall using Rainfall seasonality index. Many investigators [4, 5, 6, 7, 8] studied the variation in rainfall pattern. [4] Studied the rainfall index in the Niger Delta Belt, Nigeria and find out that 95% of the total annual rainfall in the area is in wet season. [5] Find out the rainfall seasonality in Trinidad, West Indies using Time Series Analysis Comparing Foraminiferal Population Dynamics with Rainfall Data. [6] Carried out work for hundred years' data to find out the pattern of rainfall trends in Nigeria, the result shows that 90% of the entire pattern exhibited negative trends but only 22% showed positive levels. Using seasonality index, [7] carried out work for hundred years data to get monthly and seasonal scales variation in rainfall in Maharashtra. This study shows extreme rainfall regime in coastal area, Eastern parts and western parts indicating a rainfall regime where most rain occurs in three months or less in Maharashtra. [8] Studied the Individual seasonality index of rainfall regimes in Greece using an individual seasonality index.

Using parametric and non-parametric statistical techniques, [9] studied the trends which were used to investigate whether Indian rainfall is changing in terms of magnitude or location wise. [2] Studied the trends and spatial distribution of rainfall and rainy days over Andaman and Nicobar Islands by examining the characteristic and climatological features and found that large deviation over the northern latitudes as compared to southern latitudes of Andaman and

Nicobar Islands. Using analytical and the empirical techniques, [10] tried to find out the impact of spatial correlation in regional trends. [11]

Carried out work on daily precipitation indices in India. Study reveals that rainfall is increasing in the parts of Deccan plateau in the south and in the parts of north western Himalayas Kashmir and decreasing in the parts of Gangetic Plain and Uttaranchal. Moreover [12] studied the region wise rainfall variability in India and concluded that north India is vulnerable to droughts in the summer season. Almost same work have been done by [13] for South Africa. Result shows significant increases in the intensity of extreme rainfall events between 1931–1960 and 1961–1990 are identified over about 70% of the country except in parts of north-east, north-west and in the winter rainfall of the south west.

Therefore, in present paper, to improve the planning and management pattern of rainfall for agriculture and water resource system of region a study has been undertaken to understand the characteristics and climatological features of monthly and yearly rainfall over Gujarat state.

Study Area and Data Collection

Gujarat is a state in the western part of India and having a geographical area of 196,204 square km. Gujarat State is having 23^0 N as latitude and 72^0 E as longitude. The population of Gujarat is 62,700,003 as per 2013 census. The state of Rajasthan lies north of it, while Madhya Pradesh and Maharashtra lie on the eastern sides of Gujarat. The UT of Daman, Diu, Dadra and Nagar Haveli lie to the south of Gujarat. It is bounded by Arabian Sea on its western side. Gujarat geographical location is such that it is subjected to different types of climatic features. The state receives rainfall mainly during the southwest monsoon season (June to September). The southern parts of the state receives rainfall of 760 to 1520 mm, northern part 510 to 1020 mm, while Saurashtra region receives less than 630 mm. Gujarat is having important rivers like Narmada, Tapi and Sabarmati etc..

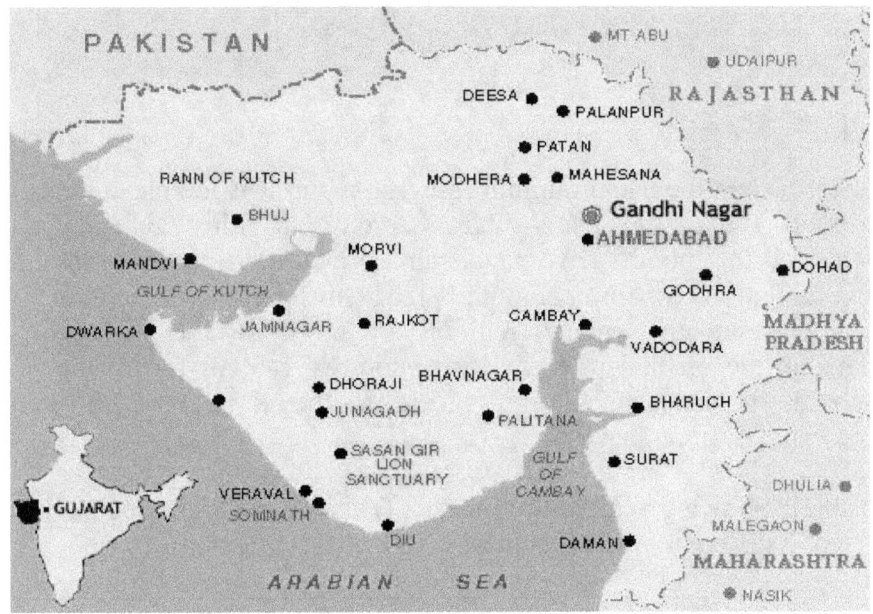

Figure 1: Showing Map of Gujarat [14]

The necessary data were collected to understand the decadal variation of rainfall pattern in Gujarat state. Monthly rainfall data of Gujarat state was collected from 1920 to 2012 National Data Centre of India Meteorological Department (IMD), Pune, India.

Methodology

The changing pattern of rainfall is investigated by computing Seasonality Index of rainfall. The understanding of seasonality pattern of precipitation and also identifying changes in seasonality index is very useful for agricultural planning. A seasonality index method has been used to find out the seasonal variation in precipitation. Rainfall seasonality gives distribution pattern of rainfall on monthly basis for a defined location [4]. The information regarding the Seasonality Index was referred from [7, 13]. Seasonality Index helps in detecting the rainfall regimes based on the monthly distribution of rainfall. Seasonal contrasts can be define as, the Seasonality Index [13], which is a function of mean monthly and annual rainfall, is computed using the following formula:

$$SI = \frac{1}{R} \sum_{N=1}^{12} \left| Xn - \frac{R}{12} \right| \quad (1)$$

Where Xn is the mean rainfall of month n and R is the mean annual rainfall. Mostly, they can vary from zero to 1.83 where zero implies when all the months have equal rainfall and 1.89 implies when all the rainfall occurs in one month [7]. The different class limits of SI and representative rainfall regimes are given in table no 1 [13]. Though the method uses the distribution of rainfall for all the 12 months, the index as table shows identifies the seasonal pattern when the value is more than 0.6.

Table1: Showing Seasonality Index (SI) classes and the associated different rainfall regime

Rainfall regime	Seasonality Index (SI)
Very equable	≤ 0.19
Equable but with a definite wetter season	0.20 -0.39
Rather seasonal with a short drier season	0.40 – 0.59
Seasonal	0.60 – 0.79
Markedly seasonal with a long drier season	0.80 – 0.99
Most rain in 3 months or less	1.00 -1.19
Extreme, almost all rain in 1- 2 months	≥ 1.20

The distribution of rainfall is important throughout the season cycle as the total annual amount of annual and monthly precipitation while evaluating its impact on hydrology, ecology, agriculture or in water use. This study aims to find the changing pattern of rainfall over Gujarat in the district scale which may have an impact on increasing extreme rainfall events and floods or drought over Gujarat. Due to climate change, greenhouse effect and unequal heating of the earth's surface over the year there is variation in rainfall. The time and duration of the seasonal rainfall is most important for the planning and management of agriculture or water management. It is very important to identify the historical changes in the mean annual precipitation.

The distribution of rainfall throughout the season or year plays an important role in ground water recharge.

Results

The average mean rainfall of Gujarat district is shown in Figure no 2. In which Kutch, Banas Kantha and Patan shows the minimum rainfall and Dangs, Narmada and Surat shows the maximum rainfall.

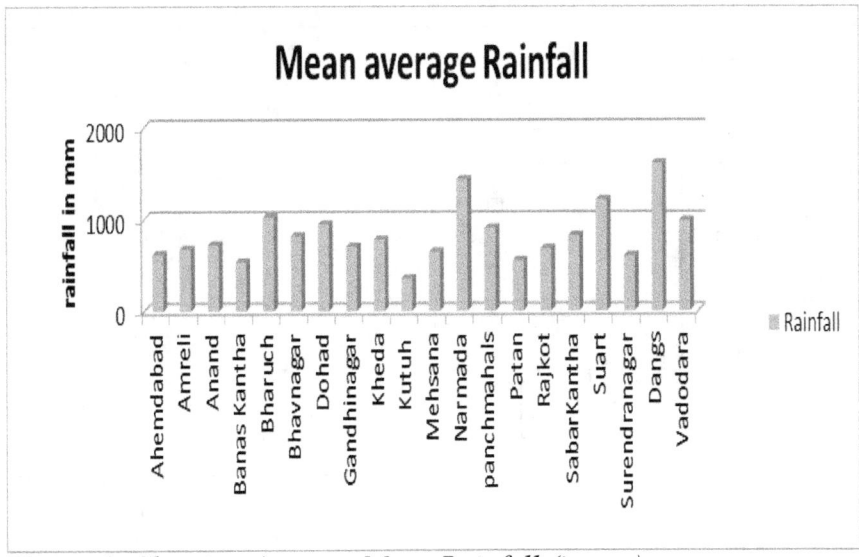

Figure 2: Showing Average Mean Rainfall (in mm)

The seasonality index has been computed for 20 major districts of Gujarat from year 1922 to 2011 dividing it into nine decadal groups showing 1922 to 1931, 1932 to 1941, 1942 to 1951 and so on and calling them 1st decade, 2nd decade and so on respectively. This will help to find out any changes in this region over the period of time. Table no 2 show the Seasonality Index of 20 district of Gujarat for nine decade. Figure no 3 gives the comparisons of Seasonality index between them in graphical form.

Table2: Seasonality Index (SI) of different district

District	1922-1931	1932-1941	1942-1951	1952-1961	1962-1971	1972-1981	1982-1991	1992-2001	2002-2011
Ahmedabad	0.1069	0.464	0.3589	1.397	0.2739	0.2378	2.0456	0.1217	1.6307
Amreli	1.382	1.766	0.2934	1.3134	0.1541	0.2717	0.9361	0.8429	1.2659
Anand	0.5625	0.385	0.3361	0.9486	0.5287	0.2381	1.8975	0.4034	2.841
Banas Kantha	0.581	0.509	0.2817	0.9694	1.9535	0.4753	1.9019	0.3921	2.2465
Bharuch	0.416	0.611	0.624	1.2246	0.0404	0.0895	0.7423	0.4084	0.9516
Bhavnagar	0.5905	0.779	0.184	1.3422	0.461	0.3411	0.6187	0.801	1.73
Dohad	0.1237	0.926	0.934	1.804	0.846	0.47	1.201	0.433	1.654
Gandhinagar	0.1584	0.478	0.0048	1.326	0.968	0.421	1.497	0.379	1.542
Kheda	0.2267	0.02	0.164	1.15	1.028	0.167	1.748	0.55	2.202
Kutch	0.7924	1.415	1.152	2.336	0.911	0.497	2.886	0.849	2.684
Mehsana	0.351	0.497	0.109	1.475	1.103	0.563	1.668	0.149	2.206
Narmada	0.5772	0.722	1.637	1.216	0.195	0.158	0.186	0.668	2.258
Panchmahals	0.019	0.833	1.024	1.966	0.854	0.493	1.164	0.304	1.99
Patan	0.190	0.918	0.085	1.745	1.286	0.035	2.216	0.112	2.298
Rajkot	1.060	1.599	0.44	2.1	0.778	0.558	2.059	1	1.211
SabarKantha	0.3146	0.133	0.74	1.427	1.364	0.089	1.571	0.275	0.821
Surat	1.198	1.3	0.223	0.043	0.629	0.998	0.818	0.323	3.887
Surendranagar	0.314	0.487	0.114	2.116	0.208	0.938	2.14	0.591	0.697
Dangs	0.692	0.216	0.651	0.179	0.524	0.548	0.072	0.18	3.416
Vadodara	0.707	0.009	0.64	1.315	0.825	0.059	1.23	0.26	0.318

From Table 1, lower the seasonality index value better the distribution of monthly Rainfall throughout the year. And the maximum seasonality index value show that rainfall occur mostly in 1-2 months [7].

From figure 3, Ahmedabad, Anand and Banas Kantha the decade 7th and 9th have higher value of seasonality index than 1.5 that shows maximum rainfall occur in 1 month and same in 1st and 2nd decade of Amreli. Kutch is having value higher than 1.5 in 4th, 7th and 9th decade, Kheda in 7th and 9th decades, Dahod in 3rd and 9th decade in this region rainfall occurs in one month. Same condition in 4th, 7th and 9th decades of Mehsana, Patan, Rajkot and 9th decade of Narmada and Panchmahals. From fourth graph Surat and Dangs is having high values in 9th decade.

The value below 0.15 was noted at 5th and 6th decade of Bharuch, 8th decade of Ahmedabad, 3rd decade of Gandhinagar, 2nd decade of Kheda, 1st decade of Dohad, 1st decade of Panchmahals, 3rd decade of Mehsana, 2nd and 6th decade of SabarKantha, 4th decade of Surat and 7th decade of Dangs which indicate rainfall occur very equable during this period.

Seasonal rainfall occur were value lies between 0.6 to 0.79 and that was noted at 2nd and 3rd decade of Bharuch, 7th decade of Bhavnagar, 2nd and 8th decade of Narmada, 5th decade of Surat, 9th decade of Surendranagar, 1st and 3rd decade of Dangs and Vadodara. This implies that rainfall was evenly distributed in 4 months.

When seasonality index is low that indicates that the rainfall occur in shorter day season. When the value is high that indicates most of the rainfall occurs within few months. Thus, an increasing trend in seasonality index is thus an indication of alarming situation for the agriculture [7, 14].

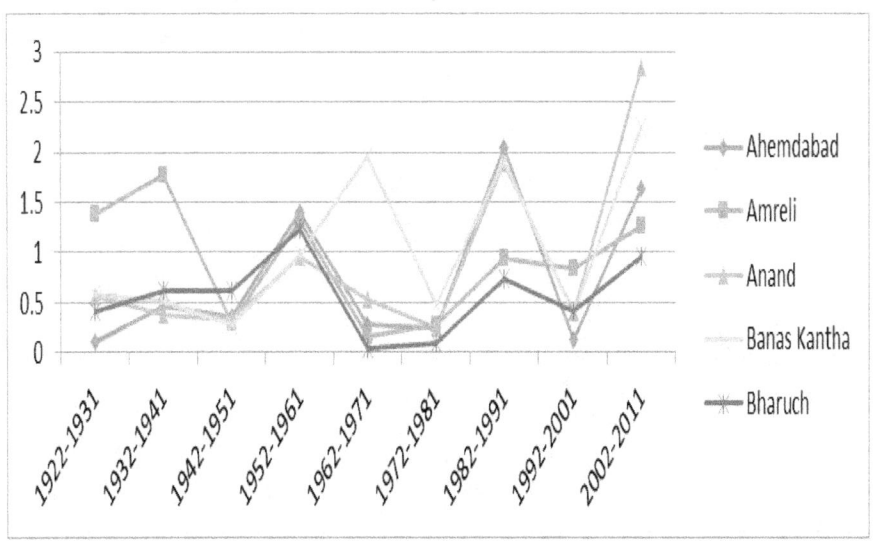

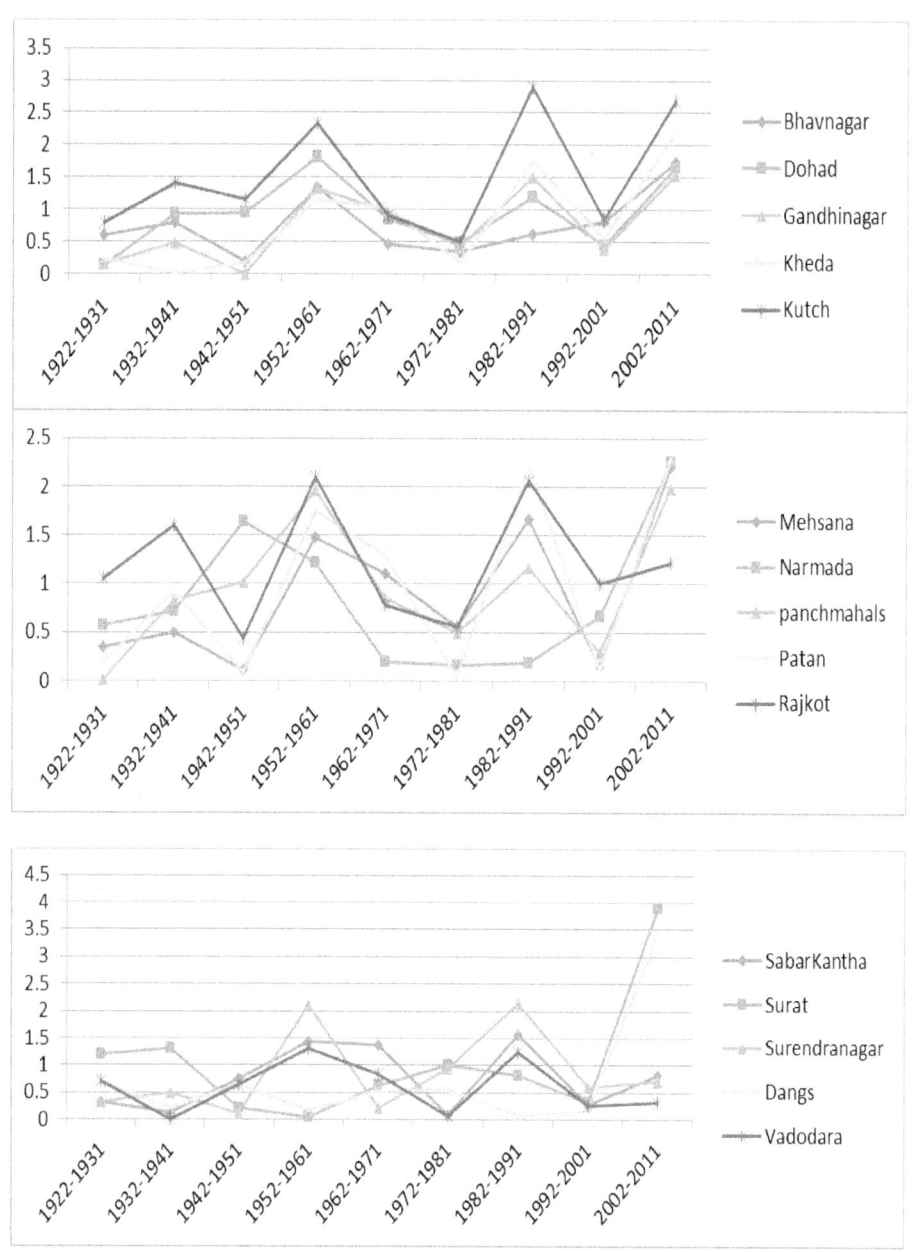

Figure 3: Showing Seasonality Index (SI) of different district

Table 2: Seasonality Index (SI) of different district for thirty- Thirty
year's data and Fourth five- fourth five years data

District	Thirty years data			Fourth five years data	
	1922-1951	1952-1981	1982-2011	1922-1966	1967-2011
Ahmedabad	0.930	1.360	0.536	0.2788	0.3855
Amreli	3.4425	0.8876	1.172	2.166	0.784
Anand	1.283	0.181	0.540	0.817	0.2559
Banas Kantha	0.169	0.508	0.736	0.124	0.1828
Bharuch	0.404	1.273	1.285	0.651	1.067
Bhavnagar	1.185	2.144	1.548	0.488	1.078
Dohad	1.736	1.4288	3.288	3.050	3.176
Gandhinagar	0.315	0.809	0.3347	0.527	0.368
Kheda	0.123	0.046	0.0967	0.4559	0.722
Kutch	3.361	1.922	0.647	1.679	0.889
Mehsana	0.036	0.935	0.3889	0.910	0.3771
Narmada	0.338	0.862	0.817	1.274	0.817
Panchmahals	1.877	1.605	3.462	3.339	3.3196
Patan	0.813	0.809	0.193	0.504	0.316
Rajkot	3.100	1.887	0.152	1.554	0.494
SabarKantha	1.188	0.151	1.025	1.996	1.6806
Surat	2.275	1.667	2.745	2.388	1.639
Surendranagar	0.951	2.847	2.247	1.14	1.497
Dangs	0.257	0.204	3.524	0.485	3.547
Vadodara	0.0866	0.550	1.181	0.638	1.35

When comparison is done for Thirty years data Banas Kantha,
Bharuch, Dohad, panchmahals, Dangs and Vadodara Seasonality
Index value is increasing with time that means maximum rainfall
occur in 1-2 month i.e. shorter period of intense rainfall which is
alarming situation for the agriculture. However, When comparison is
done for Fourth five years data Ahmedabad, Banas Kantha, Bharuch,
Bhavnagar, Dohad, Kheda, Surendranagar, Dangs and Vadodara all
are having increasing trend line. Out of with Dohad, Dangs and
panchmahals show the maximum value of SI.

Conclusion

Except Vadodara, Surendranagar, SabarKantha and Bharuch all the other district trend line is increasing at the final 9th decade which shows that shorter period of intense rainfall which is alarming situation for the agriculture. The maximum value of SI was seen in Dohad, Dangs and panchmahals. From this analysis variability of rainfall and change in spatial and temporal pattern of seasonality index is observed. These changes play an important role from water management and hydrological point of view. Due to increasing in seasonality trends most rain fall occurs in one or two month and no rainfall in first five month of the year have resulted in increase in heating. This may result in lowering of ground water and insufficient soil moisture. This result can be applied for mitigation plans and different water storage scheme in the area where the SI value is more than 1.5.

References

[1] Guhathakurta, P., and M. Rajeevan., Trends in the rainfall pattern over India, International Journal of Climatology, 28(11), 2008, 1453-1469.

[2] Pal, Indrani, and Abir Al-Tabbaa, Assessing seasonal precipitation trends in India using parametric and non-parametric statistical techniques, Theoretical and Applied Climatology 103(1-2), 2011, (1-11).

[3] Oguntunde, Philip G., Babatunde J. Abiodun, and Gunnar Lischeid. Rainfall trends in Nigeria, 1901–2000. Journal of Hydrology 2011, 411(3), 207-218.

[4] Adejuwon, Joseph O, Rainfall seasonality in the Niger Delta Belt, Nigeria, Journal of Geography and Regional Planning 5(2) (2012), 51-60.

[5] Wilson, Brent, and Richard A. Dawe, Detecting seasonality using time series analysis, Comparing foraminiferal population dynamics with rainfall data, The Journal of Foraminiferal Research 36(2) 2006, 108-115.

[6] Oguntunde, Philip G., Babatunde J. Abiodun, and Gunnar Lischeid, Rainfall trends in Nigeria, 1901–2000, Journal of Hydrology 411(3) 2011, 207-218.

[7] Guhathakurta, Pulak, and Elizabeth Saji, Detecting changes in rainfall pattern and seasonality index vis-à-vis increasing water scarcity in Maharashtra, Journal of Earth System Science 2013, 122(3), 639-649.

[8] Livada, I, and D. N. Asimakopoulos, Individual seasonality index of rainfall regimes in Greece, Climate Res 2005, 28, 155-161.

[9] Kumar, N., Yadav, B. P., Tyagi, A., & Jaswal, A. K. Trend and spatial distribution of rainfall & rainy days over Andaman & Nicobar Islands. Natural hazards, 2012, 63(2), 575-587.

[10] Kulkarni, Makarand A., Ankita Singh, and U. C. Mohanty. Effect of spatial correlation on regional trends in rain events over India. Theoretical and Applied Climatology 2012, 109(3-4), 497-505.

[11] Sen Roy, S., & Balling, R. C. Trends in extreme daily precipitation indices in India. International Journal of climatology, 2004, 24(4), 457-466.

[12] Pal I, Tabbaa AA (2009) Regional changes in extreme monsoon rainfall deficit and excess in India. Dynam Atmos Oceans 49(2–3), 204–214.

[13] Kanellopoulou, E. A. Spatial distribution of rainfall seasonality in Greece. Weather 2002, 57(6), 215-219.

[14] Website: http://blockprintwithflowers.blogspot.in

Chapter-XII

Population Growth, Environment and Food Security in India

Savita Ahlawat & Dhian Kaur

Abstract

The status of food security has been a matter of great concern in the era of increasing population, resource depletion and degrading environmental conditions. In India, after Green Revolution the growth rate of food grains production has however been higher than the population growth rate (in 1980's food grains growth rate was 3.5 % and population growth rate was 2.1%) and it tried to keep pace with the increasing population over the long time in order to sustain the increasing population. The per capita availability of foodgrains which improved after Green Revolution from 395 grams in 1951 to 468 grams in 1971 and 510 grams in 1991 has declined to 462 grams in 2012. The declining trend has serious implications for the country's food security situation. The degradation of environmental resources is being considered as a major cause of stagnation in foodgrains production. The present study intends to analyse the effects of above highlighted issues viz. increasing population, degrading environmental conditions and their effects on the status of food security in India. The results showed that due to agricultural intensification (irrigation intensity and excessive use of chemical fertilizers) problems such as land degradation, overexploitation of underground water resources, water logging, salinization and alkalinization have arisen in good agricultural areas of the country. These problems are more peculiar in Green Revolution areas mainly in north-western states where average decline of 12-16m in groundwater table has been recorded from 1980 to 2010. The study suggests that to have sustainable food security, degradation of environmental resources be paid due attention in various programmes and policies and region specific measures should be taken in this regard.

Keywords - Environment, Food Availability, Groundwater, Resource Depletion, Sustainable Food security

---

* Research Scholar and Professor, Department of Geography, Panjab University, Chandigarh, India

Introduction

Population is an important source of development, but when it exceeds the threshold limits of the support systems it also becomes a major cause for environmental degradation [1]. The United Nations Conference on Human Environment was also stated that increasing population is a great hurdle in the way of developmental programmes and safe environment [2]. As Population growth leads to increase in food demand, which typically results into heavy pressure on land and water resources.

According to Food and Agriculture Organisation population growth will result in increased in a doubling demand for food globally by 2050 [3]. In order to fulfil the demand the production should be increased and the foodgrains production can only be increased by two factors: (i) either increase in area under cultivation i.e. horizontal expansion (ii) or by increasing yield per hectare i.e. vertical expansion. In present scenario, horizontal expansion of land is not possible due population pressure therefore the only way to increase agricultural production is the vertical improvement in agricultural field i.e. use of HYV seeds, Fertilizers, Pesticides. Although agricultural production has increased by following vertical expansion techniques but on the other side these practices have also become a major cause for environmental degradation. Such conditions further effects the agricultural sustainability and food availability of an area. The Asian Development Bank has also expressed its concern about environmental degradation and future food production [4].

Thus, the growing trend of population is the main cause of environment degradation and depletion of natural resources. The rate of degradation of land and water resources is accelerating due to increasing population pressure which have become a great threat for food security situation in the country. The relationship between increasing population, environmental degradation and level of food security has been shown in Fig. 1.

This paper is divided into four sections; Section I. includes the introductory part of the research problem and shows linkages between population growth, environmental degradation and food security.

Fig. 1: Relationship Between Population Growth, Environmental Degradation and Food Insecurity

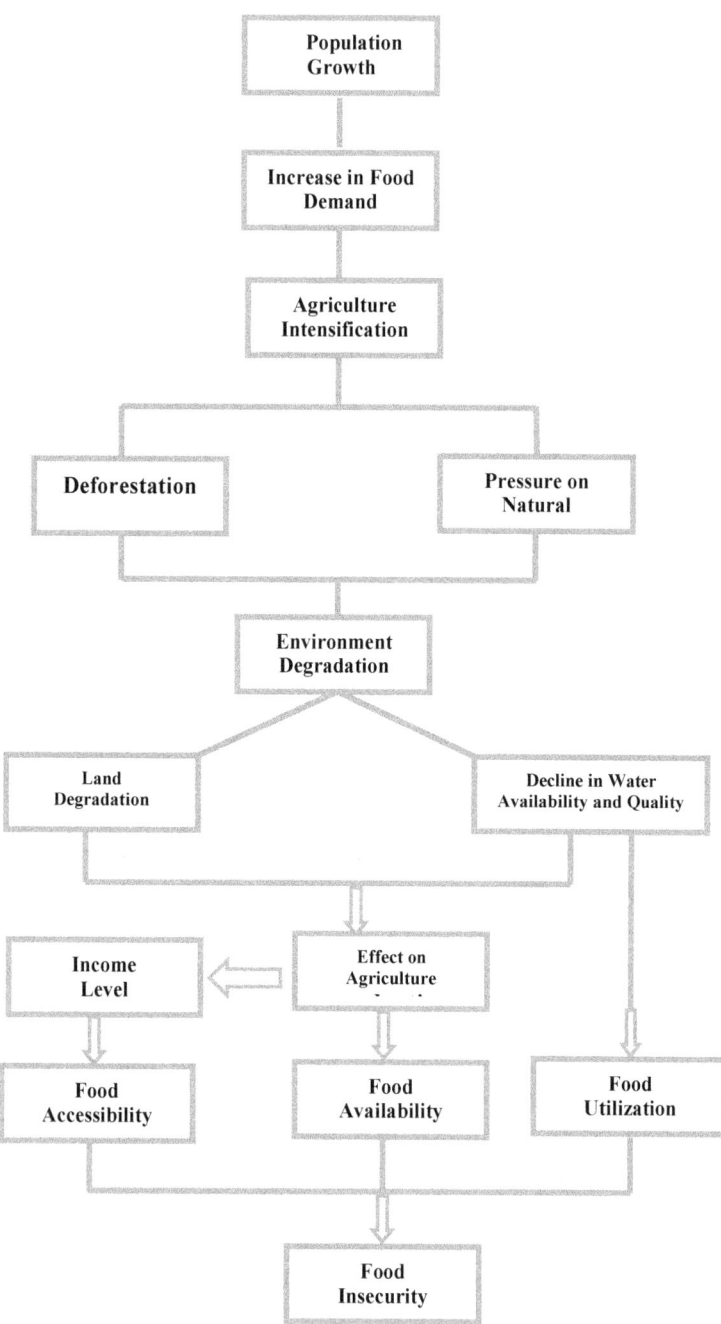

Section-II presents the details of the study area followed by objective, data Sources and methodology. Section III is devoted to the results and discussion and the last Section IV includes the concluding observations.

Study Area

The present research paper is written in context of India. As India is the second most populous country in the world (after China) having 1.22 billion population [5]. With the population growth rate at 1.58%, it is predicted that by the end of 2030 India will have more than 1.53 billion people and will surpass China in terms of total population [6]. Therefore, the population pressure on natural resources is very high due to which the country is facing the problem of environmental degradation and resource depletion.

Due to increase in population pressure and environmental degradation the status of food security has undergone a significant change in India. The per capita availability of agricultural land in rural areas has declined from 0.638 hectare in 1950-51 to 0.277 hectare in 2005-06 and per capita availability of forest land has also declined from 0.113 hectare in 1950-51 to 0.064 hectare in 2011. After Green Revolution the growth rate of foodgrains production has however been higher than the population growth rate (in 1980's foodgrains growth rate was 3.5 % and population growth rate was 2.1%) and it tried to keep pace with the increasing population over the long time in order to sustain the increasing population. The growth rate of foodgrains production stagnated during 1990s and it has become almost equal to population growth rate. The per capita availability of foodgrains which improved after Green Revolution from 395 grams in 1951 to 468 grams in 1971 and 510 grams in 1991 has declined to 462 grams in 2012. Even after achieving adequate food supply at the macro level, there is widespread poverty and malnutrition in the country. Out of India's 1.2 billion population an estimated 320 million people go to bed hungry. India has 25 percent of the world's hungry population and an estimated 43 per cent of children under the age of five years are malnourished and this situation is also getting worse due to increase in population pressure. India's rank on the 2012 Global Hunger Index of 63 among 120 countries reflects alarming levels of food insecurity [7].

Therefore, the present study is conducted in context of India as increasing population pressure and environmental degradation has serious implications for the country's food security situation.

Objective

The main objectives of the present paper are:
1. To show the general trend of population growth in India and its effects on different environmental aspects.
2. To analyze the collective impacts of population growth and environmental issues on the status of food security in India.

Sources of Data

Various governmental departments and their reports has been considered for the present study. Data on demographic characteristics (i.e. total population, population growth, population density) has been collected from Census Department. For environmental statistics related to land degradation, soil erosion, per capita availability of forest and agricultural land various issues of Economic Survey reports has been consulted. Agricultural data of various indicators such as total foodgrains production, agricultural growth rate, irrigated area, total cropped area has been taken from reports of agricultural census and agriculture department of India.

The collected data has been analyzed by using various statistical techniques and further the results are explained with the help of statistical diagrams and cartographic techniques.

Results and Discussion

The linkages between population growth, environment and food security have shown in Fig. 1 and the scenario of these indicators in context of India have explained in this section. This section has two sub-parts: first part explains how increasing population has been responsible for environmental degradation and second part deals with impacts of population growth and environment degradation on the level of food security in the country.

Population Growth and Environmental Degradation in India

India occupies only 2.4% of total geographical area of globe but it is a home to 17.31% of world's population. In contrast, the countries like USA accounts for 7.2 percent of the surface area with only 4.5 percent of the world population. This shows that the pressure on natural and environmental resources is very high in the country. The population growth rate in India is very high as compared to top ten most populous countries of the world and the decadal population growth rate in India has been shown in Fig. 2. The population has grown up from 360 million in 1951 to 1210 million in 2011. The State-wise population distribution shows that twenty states and union territories have a population of over ten million. Uttar Pradesh, Maharashtra, Bihar and Madhya Pradesh share the largest proportion of India's population.

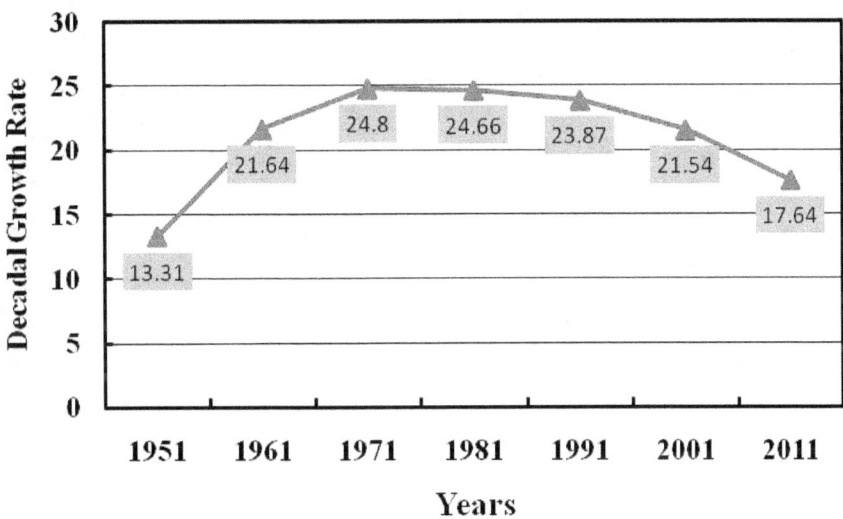

Fig. 2 Decadal Population Growth Rate of India Since 1951

The exponentially growing human population have negative implications for economic, social and environmental sectors. As the increasing population results into expansion of human activities which further leads towards degradation and depletion of natural resources. The consequent increasing demand for food, water, and housing have considerably altered land-use practices and severely degraded the environment [8]. Many scholars such as R. Shaw (1989); R. Scott et al. (1997), A. Dewaram (2007); J. Harte (2007);

C.M. Lakshmana (2013) have also analyzed the effects of increasing population on environmental degradation and resource depletion [9-13].

Effects of increasing population on environmental resources especially on land and water has discussed as follows:

Land

Land is the basic natural resource and is backbone of all economic activities. More than 99% of the world's food supply comes from the land, while less than 1% is from oceans and other aquatic habitats [14]. Due to increase in population pressure land is facing the following problems:

Man-Land Ratio (Pressure on Land)

Environmental situation is adversely effected by high man-land ratio i.e. higher population density. In India, the population density has increased from 77 person in 1901 to 382 in 2011 (Fig. 3). Population density is very high in northern part of India as compared to southern and eastern parts. Therefore, environmental degradation is also high in north India as compared to other parts.

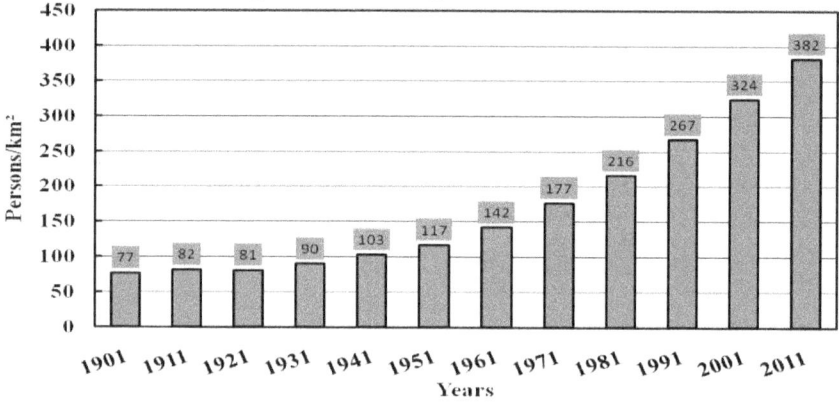

Fig. 3: India's Population Density Since 1901

Population pressure has also resulted into decline in per capita availability of arable land. The arable land in world has declined from 0.37 per hectare per person in 1961 to 0.2 per hectare in 2011.

The per capita availability of arable land in India at present is 0.128 per hectare per person which is slightly higher in comparison to some South Asian countries such as Indonesia (0.10), Malaysia (0.06), Sri Lanka (0.06) [15]. The projected estimates show that with increasing population pressure the availability of arable land will decline to 0.12 per hectare per person in 2025 and 0.09 per hectare per person in 2050 [16].

The per capita availability of agricultural land in rural areas has declined from 0.638 hectare in 1950-51 to 0.277 hectare in 2005-06 which is low as compared to 11 hectares in the developed world. In India, agriculturally developed states such as Punjab, Haryana, Uttar Pradesh are showing the declining trend in per capita availability of arable land. This decline in arable land will have serious impacts on people's livelihoods mainly in rural areas. As in the country, almost 69 percent population are living in rural areas which dependent on agriculture and allied sectors for their livelihoods.

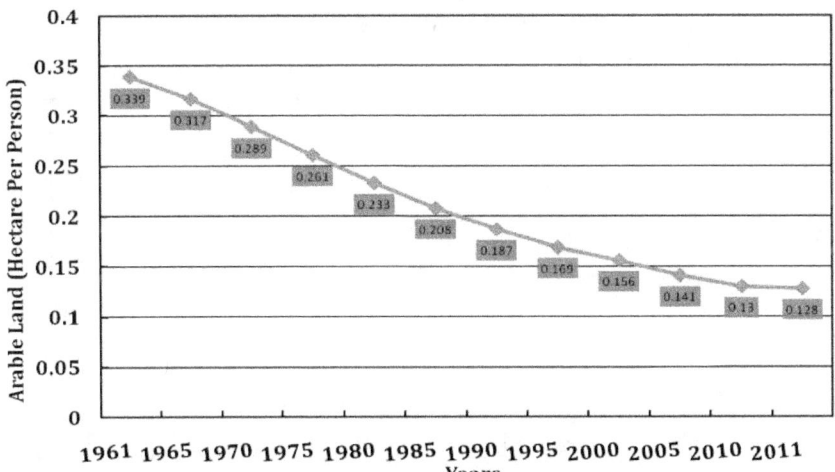

Fig. 4: Per Person Availability of Arable Land in India since 1961
        Land Degradation

It is a major threat to food security. It refers to the significant reduction in the productive capacity of the Land. Many natural and human induced factors are responsible for it. Among human factors fast growing population is the root cause of land degradation. Increase in size of population result into heavy pressure on agricultural land and give rise to agricultural intensification.

Agricultural intensification includes increase in cropping and irrigation intensification, heavy use of HYV seeds, pesticides, and fertilizers and these activities further contribute to land degradation, decline in soil quality and overexploitation of underground water resources.

Out of India's total geographical area 146.82 million hectare land is degraded. Extent of Land degradation in India has been shown in Fig 5. The ratio of degraded land is higher in north western parts where agricultural intensification took place after the introduction of Green Revolution during 1960s. In agriculturally developed Punjab state, about 39% soil is completely degraded while 50% of the soil is acutely low in nitrogen and 25% low in phosphorous content [17].

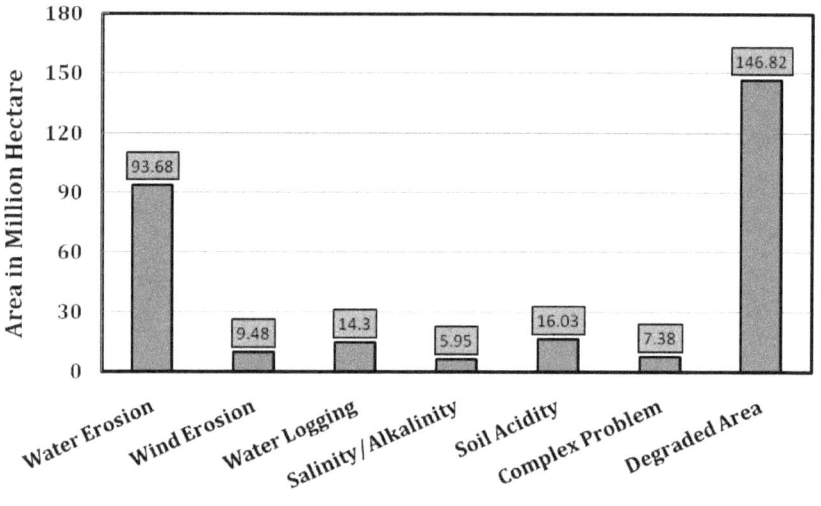

Fig. 5: Extent of Land Degradation in India

Land degradation results into decline in soil fertility which effects the country's foodgrains production. Scherr (1999) stated that land degradation is not only a great threat for developing country's food availability, but also have negative impacts on the agricultural income and food consumption of the rural poor [18]. About 15% of the world population is affected by land degradation which is likely to worsen unless adequate and immediate measures are taken to arrest the degradation processes.

Factors Responsible of Land Degradation-The factors which are responsible for land degradation are:

Agricultural Practices

Change in land use and agricultural practices is main cause of land degradation. Land use pattern shows the spatio-temporal changes in proportion of area under different uses while cropping pattern is the proportion of area under different crops at a point of time.

In the world, the cultivated area has grown by 12 percent over the last 50 years and irrigated area has doubled over the same period, accounting for most of the net increase in cultivated land.

Meanwhile, agricultural production has also grown between 2.5 and 3 times, due to increase in the yield of major crops. In India, over the past fifty years, the total population increased by three times, while the total area of land under cultivation increased by only 20.2 per cent i.e. from 118.75 Mha. in 1951 to 140.80 Mha. in 2010-11 (Fig. 6). Most of this expansion of agricultural land has taken place over fallow and grazing land.

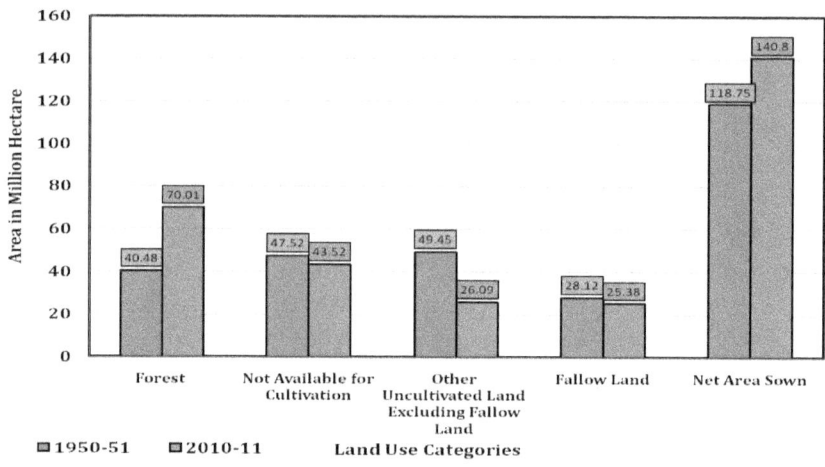

Fig. 6: Change in Land Use Categories Since 1950-51

After Green Revolution area under coarse cereals, millets and pulses has subsequently declined while area under wheat and rice has continuously increased (Fig.7). The changes in cropping pattern has shown in Fig. 7.

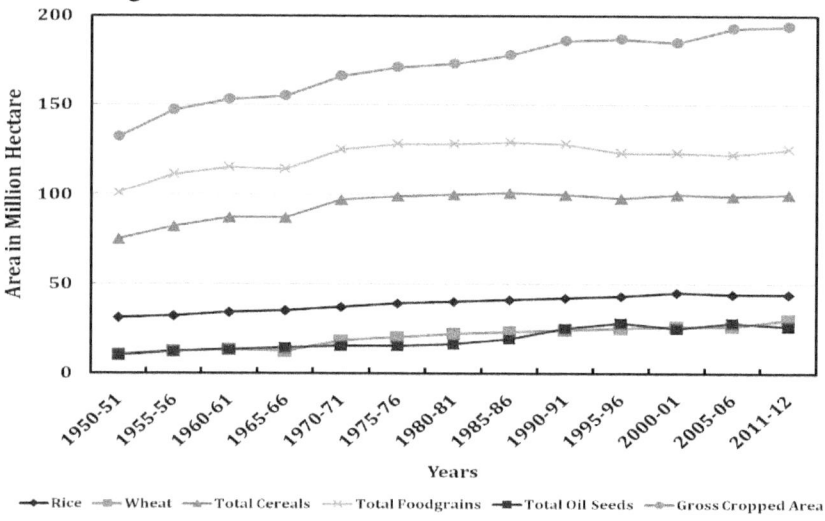

Fig. 7: Changes in Cropping Pattern in India

In the country, the gross irrigated area has increased from 23 Mha. in 1950-51 to 92 Mha. in 2011-12. This increase in irrigation intensity has further caused the problem of salinity and alkalinity. These changes in cropping pattern have mainly occurred due to population growth, increase demand for foodgrains, development in agricultural infrastructure and government policy for particular crops. At later stage these changes had become major cause for land degradation.

Excessive Fertilizer Consumption

In order to keep pace with foodgrains demand, fertilizers are added to soil to increase agricultural productivity and yield. But excessive use of fertilizers have become a major reason for land degradation.

In India, the annual consumption of chemical fertilizers in nutrient terms (N, P & K), have increased from 0.7 lakh MT in 1951-52 to 277.39 lakh MT 2011-12, while per hectare consumption of chemical fertilizers, which was less than 1 Kg in 1951-52 has also risen to 141.30 Kg in 2011-12 [19]. The fertilizer consumption on arable land has increased from 115.4 kg in 2004 to 178.5 kg per hectare in 2011 and during the same time period the world average fertilizer consumption has grown up from 110.6 kg to 133.5 kg per hectare.

Therefore, per hectare fertilizer consumption is very high in India in comparison to developed countries (U.S.A 120.5 Kg, Canada 66.9 Kg) and it is less in comparison to some Asian countries (China-548.3 Kg, Bangladesh -184.4 Kg, Malaysia -1096.5 Kg) [20]. In India, the Steering Committee of the Planning Commission has observed that as against the desirable NPK proportion of 4:2:1, now the average use of urea is 6:2 and 4:1 and this excessive use of urea has affected the soil profile adversely [21].

At regional level the overall fertilizer consumption in the country is more in West and North region as compared to East and South regions (Fig. 7). States such as Andhra Pradesh, Punjab, Haryana, Tamil Nadu, Uttar Pradesh, West Bengal, Maharashtra have fertilizer consumption higher than the national average and due to heavy usage of fertilizers the problem of land degradation/decline in soil fertility has also become very serious in these states.

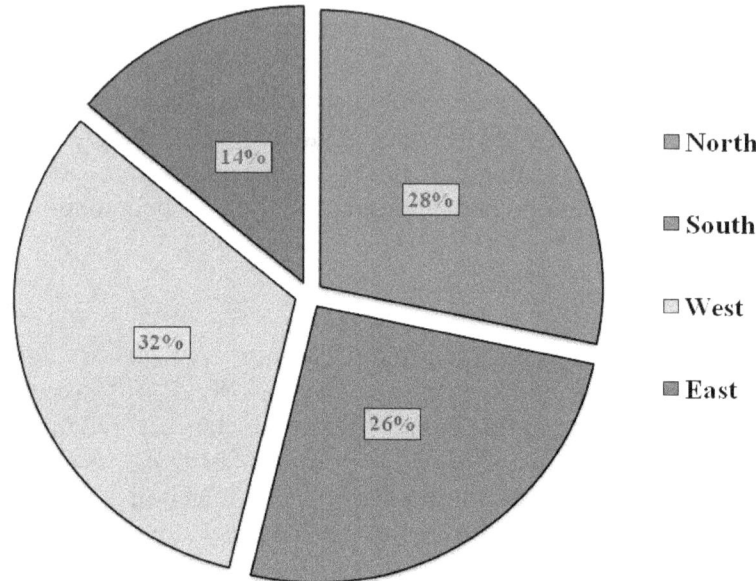

North

South

West

East

Source: Fertilizer Assosciation of India - 2011

Fig.7 Region-wise Fertilizer Consumption in India in 2011

Change in Forest Cover

Forests are a major part of the ecosystem and cover one-third of the world's land area. The forest products are the third most valuable commodity after gas and oil. 350 million of the world's poorest people depend almost entirely for their livelihoods on forests. The collection of firewood for sale in the market is the main source of livelihood for 11 per cent of the world's population [22].

World has 31 percent (4 million) of total land area under forests. Whereas in India forests despite having the second largest land use category, have less area under forest (23 percent) as compared to world's average and its surrounding countries (Bhutan, Sri Lanka and Nepal). The total forest area has increased from 40.48 million hectare in 1950-51 to 70.01 million hectare 2010-11 in the country. But on the other side the per capita availability of forest land has declined i.e. 0.113 hectare in 1950-51 to 0.064 hectare in 2011 against the world average of 0.64 ha i.e. only one-tenth of the world average [23].

More than 40 per cent of the forest in country are degraded and under-stocked. The loss of 4.5 million hectares forest land since 1950 through agricultural conversion and other uses [24].

This decline in per capita availability of forest land has a negative effect on food security dimensions. Firstly, deforestation causes soil erosion which effects soil fertility and further results into decline in agricultural production and food availability. Secondly, forest is a major source of income for rural people so decline in forest area effects their income level i.e. the economic accessibility of people. The decline in forest land has affected the livelihoods of 27 percent of rural population who entirely dependent on forest [25].

In India, the states having higher proportion of tribal population have higher proportion of forest area. Due to increasing population pressure the country is facing a problem of huge gap between supply and demand of forest products. At regional level, the forest land is showing a declining trend in Nagaland (296 sq. km), Manipur (173 sq. km), Madhya Pradesh (132 sq. km) and Chhattisgarh (129 sq. km) states [26].

Water

Water is very important aspect of life and it is needed to ensure food security, feed livestock, maintain organic life, and to conserve the biodiversity and environment. That's why the availability of water on earth makes it a habitable planet.

In present scenario, this essential resource is under threat and both the quantity and quality of water is declining at global as well as national level.

Availability

According to UNESCO estimates, 70% of the earth surface is covered with water, which accounts 1400 million cubic kilometres (m km3). The fresh water constitutes a very small proportion of it i.e. only 35 m km3 or 2.5% of total volume. Out of the total fresh water 30% is stored as underground and 0.3% water is available on the surface of the earth. Only 40% of fresh water is used by human beings. [27]. According to the international norms, a country having water availability less than 1700 m3 per capita per year is categorized as 'water stressed' and categorized as 'water scarce' if it is less than 1000 m3 per capita per year. Population growth has increased the demand for water resources to the extent that more than 40 percent of the world's rural population is living in water-scarce regions and water scarcity will affect 1.8 billion people by 2025. Situation of fresh water availability is very bad in Asian continent in comparison to Africa. As the former has 60% of world's population and has only access to 36% of the fresh water reserves; on the other side 13% of African population has access to 11% of the fresh water reserves [28].

In India where 17.3 per cent of the world's population resides has only 4 per cent of its water resources. It shows the huge stress on water resources in the country. The demand for domestic and agricultural usage of water has been increasing due to population growth and agricultural intensification. In the country, along with forest and agricultural land, the per capita availability of water has shown a declining trend in recent years. The per capita water availability has declined from 5177 m3 in 1951 to 2309 m3 in 1991, 1816 m3 in 2001 and 1545 m3 in 2011 and the projected estimates of Government shows that this water availability is likely to be reduced to 1401 m3 and 1191 m3 by the years 2025 and 2050, respectively [29].

Therefore, India will face severe scarcity of water in the near future. At present, Cauvery, Pennar, Sabarmati and East Flowing rivers and West Flowing Rivers of Kutch and Saurashtra including Luni are facing more acute water scarcity having per capita availability of water less than or around 500 cubic metre [30]. According to World Bank, only seven Indian states have full drinking water access in rural areas and 30% of rural population are lacking in drinking water accessibility in the country.

Along with surface water ground water also plays a very important role for drinking and irrigation purposes. 92 per cent of utilizable groundwater is devoted to agricultural sector in the country. This highly dependency on groundwater by the farmers for irrigation purposes have led to a serious depletion of the resource. Groundwater is depleted when pumping rates surpass the rate of natural recharge.

In India, total annual replenish able ground water potential has been estimated as 431 BCM and among the States, Uttar Pradesh ranks first (17.5%) in terms of share of replenish able ground water resources followed by Maharashtra (8.3%), Madhya Pradesh (7.9%), Andhra Pradesh (7.8%), West Bengal (7.1%) and Assam (7.0%). In India, groundwater table is dipping every year by 0.4 m and the country has also been categorized into safe, semi-critical and over exploited groundwater resources [31]. The areas of over exploited groundwater resources correspondence with the areas of green revolution and concentrated in arid, semi-arid areas of western and peninsular India, particularly in Punjab, Haryana, Rajasthan, Maharashtra, Karnataka, Gujarat, Andhra Pradesh, and Tamil Nadu [32]. In north-western states average decline of 12-16m in groundwater table has been recorded from 1980 to 2010. In the coastal areas of Gujarat, central Rajasthan, Madhya Pradesh, Uttar Pradesh, West Bengal, Karnataka and Tamil Nadu states also a decline of 4-8m in groundwater table has occurred during this time period. Due to depletion of groundwater 25 percent of India's harvest may be at risk in the coming years (Gleick 2000).

PD Chenoy stated that with increase in population and development level India's water needs are getting from bad to worse and the next big fight is clearly about water. Therefore, water availability is very important not only for consumption but also for agricultural activities and for ensuring food security in the country.

Quality

Along with quantity, the quality of water is also important. In India, the declining water quality has become a serious issue as impure water has serious implications for health status of people. The water quality is mainly affected by changing land use pattern, climatic conditions and anthropogenic activities i.e. excessive use of fertilizers, disposal of domestic sewage and extent of exploitation of ground water resources.

In India, out of 639 districts in pockets of 158 the groundwater has gone saline and it contains excessive fluoride, nitrates and iron content in 237, 385 and 270 districts respectively (TNN, 2012). In Andhra Pradesh, Tamil Nadu, Uttar Pradesh, Gujarat, and Rajasthan states 50-100% of the districts have excess level of fluoride content in drinking water sources and this consumption of high concentrations of fluoride lead to serious health issues. Western and North Western states particularly Rajasthan, Gujarat, Haryana, Punjab are facing the problem of salinity and the high concentrations of sodium ions contribute to certain heart disease and high blood pressure. Therefore, the protection and enhancement of groundwater quality has become a high-priority environmental concern because of its direct impacts on health status of people [36].

Implications for Food Security

"Food security [is] a situation that exists when all people, at all times, have physical, social and economic access to sufficient, safe and nutritious food that meets their dietary needs and food preferences for an active and healthy life" [37]. This definition includes the three dimension of food security i.e. food availability, food accessibility and food utilization. The interactions and combinations of these dimensions represent the status of food security and change in any one dimension will lead towards change in status of food security. In any area, the status of food security is directly related to the population growth, environment conditions and natural resources. The growing population and environmental degradation problems have both direct and indirect negative impacts on food security dimensions. In context of India, these are discussed as below:

Food Availability

Food availability is the major dimension and it remains the key concept of food security till 1980's when Amartya Sen (1981) raised the concept of food accessibility as an another dimension of food security [38]. It refers to the availability of sufficient quantities of food of appropriate qualities, supplied for all people at all times through domestic production. Therefore, sustained growth in agricultural activities is very important for the food security in the country. On one side, growth in agricultural sector increases food availability/ food supplies and on the other side, it also improve the purchasing power of many people, who earn their livelihoods through agricultural production [39].

Map Showing Availability of Food grain Pattern

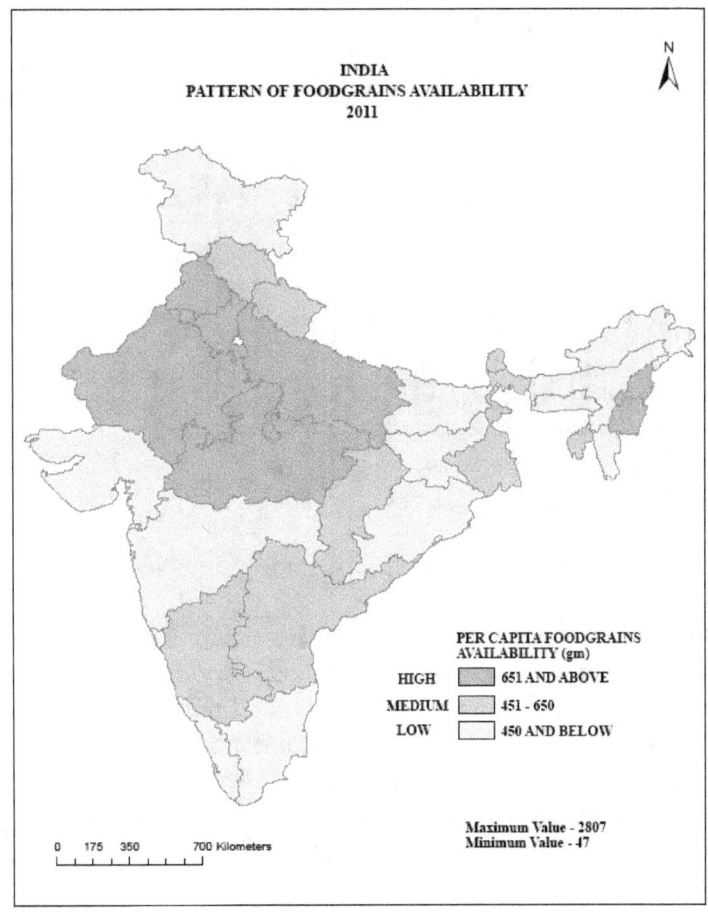

In India the total food grains production is 257.44 million tonnes in 2011-12 which was only 50.82 million tonnes in 1950-51. Only after green revolution the country has become self-sufficient in food grains production with annual growth rate of 3.5 percent which is higher than population growth rate. But during 1990s the growth rate of food grains production could not maintain its pace and annual growth rate has fallen to 1.7 percent just equal to annual population growth rate. Due to problems as discussed in above section (the land degradation, soil salinity/alkalinity, decline in ground water level) total food grains production and per hectare yield of food grains has been declining and this leads towards decline in per capita availability (which is highly dependent on average size of land-holdings, percentage area under food grains and irrigation facilities) of food grains in India (Fig. 8).

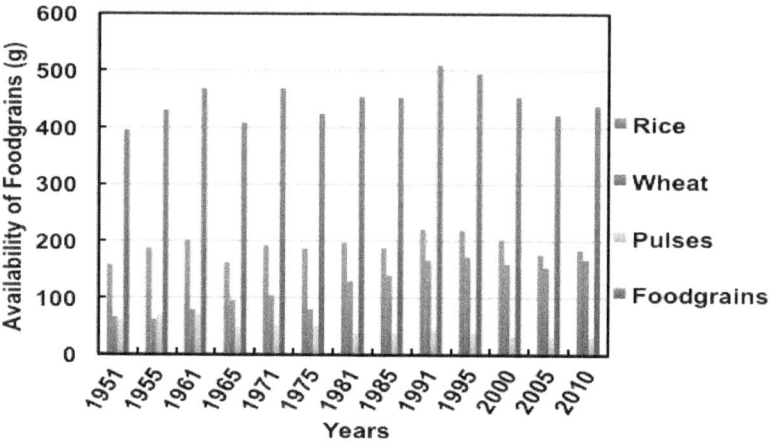

Figure Showing Per Capita Availability of Food grains in India

The spatial pattern of food grains availability (Map. 1) depicts that the per capita availability of food grains is very high in Green Revolution states i.e. in Punjab, Haryana, Uttar Pradesh, Rajasthan, Madhya Pradesh and it is low in eastern and north-eastern states (except Nagaland and Manipur). Results also reveal that the areas of high food grains availability are corresponding with areas facing more environmental degradation problems and due to which at present the growth rate of food grains production is almost stagnant in these areas.

Therefore, if this scenario of population growth and environmental degradation will be continue than the status of food security in the country will be under question.

Food Accessibility

It refers to economic access by individuals to adequate resources (entitlements) to acquire appropriate foods for a nutritious diet at all times. It depends on the purchasing power of people. FAO stated that the prevalence of widespread hunger is not due to the non-availability of food in the market but due to lack of adequate purchasing power among the rural and urban poor. Inadequate purchasing power, in turn, is due to insufficient opportunities for gainful employment. The famines of jobs and of purchasing power are becoming the primary causes for the famines of food in the households of the poor.

In India, approximate 69 percent population lives in rural areas and two - third of working population depends on agriculture for their livelihoods. As discussed in last section, increase in population size creates huge pressure on natural resources; this results into decline in per hectare arable land, forest land, size of land holdings and increase in problems of environmental degradation and resource depletion. Unemployment ratio has also increased which further results into lack of purchasing power of people. Due to increase in population size urban population has also grown-up and urban areas start expanding towards the periphery rural agricultural land. This results into transformation of agricultural land into non-agricultural uses and further leads towards increase in ratio of unemployed rural people. Most of agriculturally developed states in north India are facing this problem. This affects the livelihoods of people living in rural areas and makes them more vulnerable to food insecurity. Thus, agriculture is not only important for food availability but income level of rural people is also associated with it.

Therefore, in India, despite having marketable surpluses of food grains some areas are facing problem of food insecurity due to lack of economic access. As increasing population results into increase in food consumption, decline in natural resources, environmental degradation which further effects the status of food security in the country.

Food Utilization

It is related to utilization of food through adequate diet, clean water, sanitation, and health care, to reach a state of nutritional well-being for which all physiological needs are met. But due to huge population pressure access to basic services safe drinking water and sanitation is also limited. For poor countries with rapid population growth and depletion of groundwater, water-deficit induced food insecurity is a rising problem [40] [41].

As discussed in earlier section, the per capita water availability is declining in the country and this situation is very critical in rural areas of Rajasthan, Uttar Pradesh, Bihar, Maharashtra, Madhya Pradesh and Chhattisgarh [42]. This lack of water availability has also led towards poor sanitation facilities.

Along with water availability, the quality of water matters a lot for food utilization. Declining water quality have serious implications on health status of people. Worldwide, about 4 billion cases of disease are contracted from impure water and approximately 6 million deaths are caused by water-borne disease each year [43]. Approximately 4 billion cases of diarrhoea each year cause 2.2 million deaths. These problems are very severe in developing countries where about 90 per cent of the diseases can be traced due to a lack of pure water [44]. Water having high content of fluoride causes fluorosis disease which hits teeth and bones. Presence of nitrates in drinking water cause blue baby disease which hits infants and can lead to respiratory and digestive system problems. These situation are very worse in rural India where facilities to even detect chronic health problems arising out of water contamination do not exist.

Conclusion

As discussed above the magnitude of the threat to environment and natural resources is directly linked to human population size. If India's population will continue with the same growth rate the availability of natural resources will decline to low levels and in this scenario it will be very difficult to maintain sustainable food security in the country.

More people means less forest, water, soil, and other natural resources, but more waste, pollution, and greenhouse gases and this also leads toward climate change. It would not be exaggerated if stated that the major international wars in the future will mainly focus on natural resources [45].

A study conducted by MS Swaminathan Foundation shows that the most agriculturally developed states are facing problems of environmental degradation and resource depletion in India and these states will have less food sustainability in future [46]. Therefore, the growth of population should be checked and resource conservation techniques should be adopted for sustainable food security in the country. Region specific measures should be taken in this regard.

References

[1] P.D. Sharma, Population growth and environmental degradation, retrieved on 10th July, 2014 from http://safeenvirionment. wordpress.com.

[2] R. Buss, United Nations Conference on the Human Environment (UNCHE), Stockholm, Sweden. Retrieved on 21st June, 2014 from http://www.eoearth.org/view/article.

[3] FAO, WFP and IFAD, The State of Food Insecurity in the World 2013. Rome, FAO.

[4] Asian Development Bank, Emerging Asia, changes and challenges, ADB, 1978, Manila, Philippines.

[5] Census of India, General Population Tables-2011, retrieved on 15th March, 2014 from http://censusindia.gov.in.

[6] Sangappa.V.Mamanshetty, Growth of population impact on environmental degradation: an over view of India, Elixir Agriculture, 51, 2012, 10877-10880.

[7] Von Grebmer, D. Headey, L. Haddad, D. Wiesmann, H. Fritschel, S. Yin, C. Foley and B. Iseli, 2013 Global Hunger Index: The Challenge of Hunger, Bonn, Washington, DC, International Food Policy Research Institute, and Concern Worldwide.

[8] D. Pimentel, X. Huang, A. Cardova, and M. Pimentel, Impact of Population Growth on Food Supplies and Environment, Population and Environment, 19 (1), 1997, 9-14.

[9] R. Shaw, Rapid Population Growth and Environmental Degradation: Ultimate Versus Proximate Factors, Environment Conservation, 16, 1989, 199–208.

[10] R. Scott , J. K. Huang, L.X. Zhang, Poverty, Population and Environmental Degradation in China, Elsevier Science, 22, 1997, 229–251.

[11] A. Dewaram, Population growth and environmental degradation in India, Asia Pacific Journal on Environment and Development, 14, 2007, 41–63.

[12] J. Harte, Human population as a dynamic factor in environmental degradation, Population Environment, 28, 2007, 223–236.

[13] C.M. Lakshmana, Population, Development and Environment in India, Chinese Journal of Population Resources and Environment, 11 (4), 2013, 367-374.

[14] FAO, Food Balance Sheets, 1991, Rome: Food and Agriculture Organization of the United Nations.

[15] World Bank, Agricultural and Rural Development Database, Retrieved on 24th March, 2014 from http://data.worldbank.org/indicator.

[16] Nikos Alexandratos and Jelle Bruinsma, World Agriculture Towards 2030/2050, ESA Working Paper No. 12-03, Agricultural Development Economics Division of FAO.

[17] Times of India, Over 39% soil in Punjab completely degraded, 2013, Retrieved on 15th July, 2014 from http://timesofindia.indiatimes.com/india.

[18] S.J. Scherr, Soil Degradation: A Threat to Developing-Country Food Security by 2020, Food, Agriculture and the Environment Discussion Paper 27, 1999, FPRI, Washington.

[19] Fertilizer Association of India, Indian Fertilizer Industry Annual Report, 2011.

[20] World Bank, Fertilizer Consumption Database, Retrieved on 24th March, 2014 from **http://data.worldbank**. org/indicator.

[21] Food and Agriculture Organization, Fertilizer used by Crops in India, 2011, FAO, Rome.

[22] G.J. Nabuurs, O. Masera, K. Andrasko, P. Benitez-Ponce, R. Boer, M. Dutschke, E. Elsiddig, J. Ford-Robertson, P. Frumhoff, Forestry, in B. Metz, O.R. Davidson, P.R. Bosch, R. Dave, L.A. Meyer (eds.) Climate Change 2007: Mitigation. Contribution of Working Group III to the Fourth Assessment Report of the Intergovernmental Panel on Climate Change, Cambridge University Press, Cambridge.

[23] Food and Agriculture Organization, Global Forest Resource Assessment, FAO Forestry Paper 163, 2010, Rome.

[24] Bahuguna, K. Mitra, S. Saigal, Root to Canopy: Regenerating Forests through Community State Partnerships, 2004, Winrock International India / Commonwealth Forestry Association India 309–316.

[25] Aggarwal, V. Paul, and S. Das, Forest Resources: Degradation, Livelihoods, and Climate Change, in Datt D and S. Nischal, Looking Back to Change Track, 2009, 91-108, New Delhi: TERI.

[26] Forest Survey of India, India State of Forest Report 2011, Ministry of Environment and Forests, Government of India.

[27] Anon, Development of Environmental Information Tools for the Prediction of Water Quality Risks, ICREW Project Pilot Action 4 Final Report, 2006, A. Wither. Bristol, Environment Agency.

[28] Food and Agriculture Organization, The State of Food Insecurity in the World, 2013 Retrieved on 20th March, 2014 from http://www.fao.org.

[29] Govt. of India, Background note for consultation meeting with Policy makers on review of National Water Policy, 2009, Ministry of Water Resources, New Delhi.

[30] Central Water Commission, Water and Related Statistics, Water Resource Information System Directorate, Retrieved on 10th July, 2014 from http://www.cwc.nic.in.

[31] Central Ground Water Board, Annual Report 2011-12, Ministry of Water Resources, Government of India.

[32] R.P. Shaw, Rapid Population Growth and Environmental Degradation: Ultimate Versus Proximate Factors, Environment Conservation, 16, 199–208.

[33] P.H. Gleick, The Changing Water Paradigm: A look at Twenty-First Century Water Resources Development, Water International, 25 (1), 2000, 127–138.

[34] Hindustan Times, India Facing Water Crisis, 2011, Retrieved on 16th April, 2014 from http://www. hindustantimes.com/india-news/newdelhi.

[35] Times of India, Poison in India's groundwater posing national health crisis, 2012, Retrieved on 8th July, 2014 from http://timesofindia.indiatimes.com.

[36] W.M. Alley, Regional Ground-Water Quality, 1993, Van Nostrand Reinhold, New York.

[37] Food and Agriculture Organization, The State of Food Insecurity in the World, 2001, Retrieved on 15th July, 2013 from http://www.fao.org.

[38] Amartya Sen, Poverty and Famines: An Essay on Entitlement and Deprivation, Oxford University Press, 1982.

[39] United State Agency for International Development, Food Security Indicators for the Use in the Monitoring and Evaluation of Food security Program, USAID, 1999, Retrieved on 23rd September, 2013 from www.fantaproject.org.

[40] M. Rosegrant, X. Cai and S. Cline, World Water and Food to 2025. Dealing with Scarcity, 1992, Washington DC: International Food Policy Research Institute (IFPRI)

[41] H. Yang, P. Reichert, K.C. Abbaspour and A.J. Zehnder, A Water Resources Threshold and Its Implications for Food Security, Environmental, Science & Technology, 37, 2003, 3048–54.

[42] M.S. Swaminathan Research Foundation, Food Insecurity Atlas of Rural India, 2003, MSSRF and World Food Programme (WFP), United Nations.

[43] D. Pimentel, J. Houser, E. Preiss, O. White, H. Fang, L. Mesnick, T. Barsky, S. Tariche, J. Schreck, and S. Alpert, Water Resources: Agriculture, the Environment, and Society, Bio. Science, 47 (2), 1996, 97-106.

[44] WHO (World Health Organization) and UNICEF (United Nations Children's Fund). Global Water supply and sanitation assessment, Report, 2000, Geneva: UN.

[45] M.D. Kumar, Food security and sustainable agriculture in India: The water management challenge, Working Paper 60, 2003, Colombo, Sri Lanka: International Water Management Institute.

[46] M.S. Swaminathan Research Foundation, Atlas of Sustainability of Food Security in India, 2004, MSSRF and World Food Programme (WFP), United Nations.

Chapter-XIII

Renewable Energy and Green Buildings: Assessment of Hindrances and Catalysis Associated with Implementation of Renewable Energy in Green Buildings

Sohina Singh, Meenakshi Mital, Puja Gupta and Matt Syal*

Abstract

Encouraging renewable energy systems in buildings has tremendous potential to contribute to the energy needs of the building by providing a clean source of energy without affecting the environment. The study aims at assessing renewable energy in green buildings and was undertaken in three randomly selected green buildings. Case studies were developed for the same, focusing on the strategies and technologies used to attain the renewable energy points in green buildings and hindrances and catalysts associated with the same (on-site/off-site). Architects, Project managers, chief engineers and green building consultants associated with the buildings were interviewed to gather data.

The study showed catalysts and hindrances behind renewable energy (on-site/off-site). Also, the study helped analyzing the commonly and not so often used renewable energy strategies and technologies. The hindrances which have emerged from the study can be worked upon so that more and more buildings can take up renewable energy (on-site/off-site) as compared to the present scenario.

Keywords - Catalysts, Hindrances, Green building, Green building consultant, Renewable energy

* *Dept. of Resource Management and Design Application, Lady Irwin College, University Of Delhi, Delhi, India and School of Planning, Design and Construction, Michigan State University, USA*

Introduction

Energy is a basic requirement for the existence and development of human life. There has been an excessive reliance on the use of fossil fuel resources like coal, oil and natural gas to meet the power requirement of the country which is not suitable in the long run due to limited availability of fossil fuel as well as the adverse impact that they have on the environment and ecology [1]. Building construction and operation have extensive direct and indirect impacts on the environment. Buildings use resources such as energy, water and raw materials, generate waste (occupant, construction and demolition) and emit potentially harmful atmospheric emissions.

Encouraging renewable energy systems in buildings has tremendous potential to contribute to the energy needs of the building by providing a clean source of energy without affecting the environment [2]. Green building is the practice of creating structures and using processes that are environmentally responsible and resource efficient throughout a building's life cycle from siting to design, construction, operation, maintenance, renovation and deconstruction. This practice expands and complements the classical building design concerns of economy, utility, durability and comfort. Green building is also known as sustainable or high performance building [3].

The main objectives of green buildings are to avoid resource depletion of energy, water, and raw materials; prevent environmental degradation caused by facilities and infrastructure throughout their life cycle; and create built environments that are livable, comfortable, safe, and productive [4].

By adopting green building strategies, we can maximize both economic and environmental performance. Green construction methods can be integrated into buildings at any stage, from design and construction to renovation and deconstruction. Green building practices aim to reduce the environmental impact of buildings. Buildings account for a large amount of land use, energy and water consumption, and air and atmosphere alteration. Green building brings together a vast array of practices and techniques to reduce and ultimately eliminate the impacts of buildings on the environment and human health.

It often emphasizes taking advantage of renewable resources, e.g., using sunlight through passive solar, active solar, and photovoltaic techniques and using plants and trees through green roofs, rain gardens and for reduction of rain water run-off. Onsite generation of renewable energy through solar power, wind power, hydro power, or biomass can significantly reduce the environmental impact of the buildings [5].

Building rating systems are a popular tool to bring momentum in achieving energy efficiency and sustainability in buildings. Buildings are given ratings of platinum, gold, silver, or certified, based on green building attributes [6]. The Leadership in Energy and Environmental Design (LEED) Green Building Rating System provides a suite of standards for environmentally sustainable construction. There are seven categories under LEED NC and from all of those categories; the most important is the Energy and Atmosphere. The Energy and Atmosphere credits under LEED NC comprise a large component of the total credits needed for the certification and it give good opportunity to organizations to achieve large number of points under this category [7].

Hence it was considered important to investigate the technologies and strategies being used to implement the Energy and Atmosphere credits, especially renewable energy credits (on-site and off-site) and assess the catalysts and hindrances in implementing these credits. Not many buildings have gone for renewable energy credits in India. In addition even certified green buildings have not gone in for renewable energy criteria in a big way. The present study therefore investigates the hindrances and catalysts, towards implementing the energy and atmosphere credits with specific reference to renewable energy credits (on-site/off-site) under LEED NC.

Eligible renewable electrical energy generation systems

Solar: Solar electric or photovoltaic systems (PV) are the most likely to be used in urban settings. It is the most commonly used system, and it has several distinct advantages for use in a LEED project built on an urban or suburban site. The technology is clean and quiet, and the system can be of any size. Solar electric systems operate wherever there is sunshine. A building can also be designed and built so that future additions to the system can be incorporated at minimal cost.

Attractive roofing, awnings, siding materials and glazing are now available that incorporate photovoltaic technologies as part of their structure, so they serve double duty in the design. Referred to as Building Integrated Photovoltaic or BIPV, they have begun to capture the imagination of architects looking for ways to incorporate green energy while maintaining a high level of aesthetic quality. Installation costs tend to be lower for standard panel systems located on sunny roof areas as follows:

> Wind: Current wind turbine technology is occasionally appropriate on larger, typically rural project sites with a satisfactory wind resource and located at a distance from airports.
> Hydro, wave or tidal: Hydro, wave or tidal generation systems require the project to be located near a river or large body of water.
> Biomass: There are several types of bio-based generation systems that might be incorporated economically into a LEED-NC project, depending on the local availability of biomass resources. A biodiesel or biomass-fired cogeneration unit is potentially possible, as is methane-fired generation from landfill gas or anaerobic digestion of sewage or process waste [8].

Objectives

- To make a profile of the selected green buildings in terms of renewable energy credits
- To take a detailed account of the technologies and strategies used to implement the renewable energy in selected green buildings
- To study the catalysts and hindrances related with renewable energy systems in the selected buildings

Methodology

Locale

The study was carried out in three green buildings in Capital and National Capital Region selected randomly. These three buildings were developed as case studies for understanding the catalysts and hindrances associated with implementation of Renewable energy credits (on-site/off-site) along with strategies and technologies used.

Sampling

The sample consisted of three buildings which were developed as case studies. The units of enquiry were architects, project managers, chief engineers and building specific consultants who were involved in the process of LEED certification of the selected case studies. In addition, green building consultants were included as the units of enquiry who had worked on other LEED NC projects which had taken the renewable energy credit (on-site/off-site). It was done to gather a wider perspective of the hindrances and catalysts faced in the process of getting the renewable energy credits (on-site/off-site). Project managers and chief engineers provided information regarding details on technologies and strategies and catalysts and hindrances faced by them while implementing the Renewable energy credits (on-site/off-site). The consultants provided more details on the hindrances that they faced and the catalysts, which they felt, could accelerate the process of implementation of RE credits (on-site and off-site).

Tools for Data Collection

To collect the data, questionnaires were used. Questionnaires were prepared to sketch a profile of the buildings and to gather information regarding the catalysts and hindrances encountered while going for RE credits (on-site/off-site) under LEED NC. A checklist was made use of for understanding the LEED NC credits.

Analysis and Interpretation

The data collected from the three buildings was developed in the form of case studies. The data was analyzed quantitatively and qualitatively keeping in mind the objectives of the study. The responses obtained from the consultants were coded and tabulated.

A code sheet was devised for all the responses by first converting the open-ended questions into closed ended questions. After this, a master sheet was made in which the data was entered and inferences were made. Conclusions and inferences were drawn as per the objectives of the research.

Result and Discussion

Case Studies

The first building taken for the study got USGBC LEED platinum rating in 2009. More than 20% of the building's total energy use is generated from solar photovoltaic cells. It is the third building in Gurgaon to receive this esteemed distinction. The building has been operational since 2008. Refer to the table 1 for renewable energy details of the building.

Table 1: Technical data of the Solar Power

Type	Solar photovoltaic AC (alternate current) Hybrid Power Generating system by Tata BP Solar India
Application	To power AC operated office loads like computer, lights and fans
Total Maximum Load	35 KW
Energy Generation by solar photovoltaic systems	65514 KWh per annum
Total number of solar panels/systems	360, Standard modules:300 BIPV Laminates: 60
Total number of solar thermal systems	2

The second building is the first emission neutral office building in Asia which draws 100 percent of its electricity from photovoltaic plant. It needs some 50 percent less power than comparable buildings in the region.

This project has shown that approaches such as combining efficient insulation with renewable energies can help to dramatically reduce a building's energy consumption and, therefore, its CO^2 emissions. Refer to the table 2 for renewable energy details of the building.

Table 2: Technical data of the Solar Power

Type	Crystalline Silicon Grid Connected Solar System by Moser Baer Photo Voltaic Ltd
Application	To power AC operated office loads like computer, lights and fans
Total Connected Load watts	123 KW
Energy Generation by solar photovoltaic systems	88.9 MWh per annum
Total number of solar panels/system	270
Total number of solar thermal system	2

The US Green Building Council (USGBC) has awarded platinum rating to the third building, under LEED certification for the New Construction. It got the certification in the year 2006. It is one of the first buildings in India to get platinum rating under LEED NC category. They did not apply for the renewable energy credit because of space constraint. The building however, is using solar energy for all their hot water needs and water heated by solar thermal technology saves approximately 30,000 kilowatts per hour. Around 40 solar systems (solar panels + solar thermal systems) were installed for the purpose of lighting the Logo and heating the water. More panels could not be installed due to non-availability of space, and thus they could not apply for on-site renewable energy credit.

Comparative analysis of Strategies and Technologies used/not used by buildings

Under credit Renewable energy, all the three buildings have made use of solar passive design, out of which only two buildings have gone for renewable energy generation via solar photovoltaic cells and solar hot water system.

Also, the technologies other than solar have not been used like wind, geothermal, hydro, biomass and technology like solar process heating and cooling system. No building has gone for off grid source renewable energy technologies. Refer to table 3 for the technologies and strategies used/ not used by buildings.

Table 3: Comparative analysis of Strategies and Technologies used/not used by buildings

Renewable Energy	Using renewable energy from solar photovoltaic cells
	Using solar hot water system
	Wind, geothermal, biomass, hydro, and bio-gas strategies
	solar process heating and cooling system
	off grid source renewable energy technologies

☐ Technology/Strategy used by all three buildings
☐ Technology/Strategy used by two buildings

☐ Technology/Strategy not used by any of the buildings

Responses regarding implementation of Renewable energy in buildings

On-site renewable energy implementation was rated difficult as the cost pertaining to RE systems are high, buildings are not aware of the incentives and payback period is long. In addition to this, lack of space in buildings to install RE systems is a major problem.

Similarly off-site renewable energy implementation was reported as the most difficult credit as the requirements needed to fulfill the implementation process like approval of state laws etc. are difficult to implement. Also, it was felt that it is a cost intensive process.

Table 4: Responses regarding implementation of Renewable energy in buildings

Credits	Rating the credits in terms of difficulty in implementation Total Responses	Reasons
On-site Renewable Energy	5	High installation cost and space constraints
Off-site Renewable Energy	6	Unsupportive state laws, high cost

6 – Very difficult, 5 - difficult, 4 – somewhat difficult, 3 – average, 2 – somewhat easy, 1 – easy

Catalysts and Hindrances in the process of implementation of renewable energy

Mostly all the respondents felt implementation of renewable energy credits (on-site/offsite), results in improving the prestige and image of the organization. All the respondents felt that this acts as a major catalyst for the building owners to go for renewable energy credits.

Half of the respondents also reported that the social responsibility of the organisation is another big catalyst in taking the renewable energy credits. This is because the buildings account for major greenhouse gas emissions, thus encouraging the use of renewable energy systems will help encounter the problem of carbon emissions. All the respondents felt that better rental value is a minor building owners to go for renewable energy credits. The rent value of the building increases by taking RE credits and also renewable energy is one of the most sustainable options present over fossil fuels, which in a way improves organisation value.

Apart from the catalysts, there are also some hindrances in this process as per the respondents. Majority of the respondents felt that the high installation cost and lack of space are the major hindrances for renewable energy credits (on-site/off-site). Cost of the renewable energy system is very high, Building owners, architects and the consultants are not well aware regarding the incentives provided by the government thus, renewable energy credits are very cost intensive. Also, unavailability of space is an issue, as the buildings lack space to install renewable energy systems to get the required energy. All the respondents felt that improper orientation to sun is a minor hindrance. Majority of the respondents felt that the documentation of the renewable energy credits (on-site/off-site) is a complex process, and pose as a hindrance. Some consultants felt that lack of technological advancement in the field of renewable energy technology is also one of the minor hindrances faced by the buildings that limit the implementation of renewable energy credits (on-site/off-site). Also, most of the consultants felt especially for the green power credit, that hiring of third party to acquire this credit is expensive and is one of the constraints for the building to take up this credit. Refer to the table 3.3 and table3.4 for major and minor catalysts and hindrances.

Table 5: Catalysts for Renewable energy credits

Major	Minor	Reasons
Prestige and image	Cost savings	Prestige and image increases in the market, building's social corporate image is enhanced
	Better rental value	Greater control over the pricing strategy
	Social responsibility	RE systems reduce dependence on fossil fuels, save 30%-40% energy and shows pay back. Buildings want to show their responsibility towards environment

Table 6: Hindrances for Renewable Energy Credits

Major	Minor	Reasons
Lack of Capacity and Standard Quality Control	Improper orientation to Sun	Lack of capacity and inadequate expertise Inappropriate orientation leads to battery backup which is a conventional source
State Laws	Improper orientation to Sun	Laws that allow green power transmission are not supportive
Lack of Financial and Fiscal Incentives		Real Estate Industry not aware of the incentives

Conclusions

The study focuses on the renewable energy technologies and strategies being used by the green buildings. It gives an insight into the renewable energy technical specifics. It also showed that some of the strategies and technologies were used by all three buildings, giving an impression of them being easier to implement while some were not being used by either of them showing that they were more difficult to implement like offsite renewable energy (green power).

The study has also shown light on some of the major catalyst and hindrances faced while going for renewable energy. The study also indicates some of the areas which need to be worked on, to overcome the hindrances highlighted. Some of these are high installation cost, lack of space, state laws, lack of technology and high maintenance cost.

Thus, the hindrances which have been shown through the study can be worked upon so that more and more buildings can take up renewable energy credits (on-site/off-site) as compare to the present scenario where not many buildings have gone for renewable energy systems.

References

[1] Ministry of New and Renewable Energy (2010). MNRE Annual Report

[2] Rana, R. (2009). Energy efficiency in green building. Akshya Urja: MNRE

[3] USGBC. (2010). Renewable Energy in LEED projects: fact sheet.

[4] TERI: Sustainable Building- Design Manual, Vol. 1 and 2. The Energy and Resource Institute (TERI), New Delhi, India, 2004

[5] Reza, M., Mohammad, R. (2009). Handbook of green energy (pp. 87-95): Reza and Reza

[6] United Nations Environment Programme. (2007). Buildings and Climate Change – Status, Challenges and Oppurtunities (978-92-807- 3085-2)

[7] World Green Building Council. (2009). Green Building Rating Systems.

[8] Nayak, J., Prajapati, J. (2006). Handbook on Energy Conscious Buildings: Solar Energy Centre

Chapter-XIV

Traditional use of Medicinal Plants: An Ethno-medico botanical Study of Chamba Development Block in Himachal Pradesh

Sumit & P. Vishal Ahuja*

Abstract

Chamba is a rich repository of medicinal plants and precious herbs. People of Chamba have been using medicinal plants to cure common ailments for thousands of years. The indigenous traditional knowledge of medicinal plants of inhabitants of Chamba, where it has been transmitted orally for centuries, is fast disappearing from the face of the earth due to advent of modern technology and transformation of modern culture. It has been estimated that an average of 1 in 10 spp of vascular plants on this earth are endangered due to unplanned human activities. Therefore, sincere efforts should be made by all to conserve the rich Himalayan biological and cultural diversity. The objective of this study is to access the richness of medicinal plants used by the people in the anterior areas of Chamba district, and their traditional medical practices. This paper is a humble attempt to document their socio-ethnical knowledge of plants and uses thereof in their daily life. An ethnobotanical survey of medicinal plants was carried out in various rural pockets of Chamba block Distt. Chamba (H.P.) during 2006-2007. The information regarding the plants used to cure common ailments and various diseases was collected through interviews from knowledgeable people (traditional practitioners, old experienced farmers, family heads, housewives, eminent elderly persons of the community, etc. A total of 15 plants belonging to 15 genera and 13 families are listed in this paper. Details of medicinal plants are described alphabetically with their botanical names, vernacular name, family, plant part used and mode of administration.

Keywords: Chamba, traditional, ethnobotanical, ailments, vernacular.

_____

*Assistant Professor, Department of Botany, Govt. Post-Graduate College, Chamba H.P. and Researcher, Wildlife Information Liaison Development

Introduction

Ethnobotany, an interdisciplinary science, encompasses the entire realm of useful relationship between plants and tribals (Ford, 1978; Jain, 1986). Alcorn (1984) regarded ethnobotany as the study of contextualized plant use. This study of the plants in relation to people includes both wild and domesticated plants (Heiser, 1995). Of late, the subject of ethnobotany has been recognised as a rapidly expanding multidisciplinary natural science throughout the world, with many workers becoming involved in the practical application of its data in areas such as biodiversity prospecting and conservation biology.

India is blessed with a rich biological heritage. It has more than 45,000 spp (including 15,000 endemic spp), where the people worship the various elements of Mother Nature to express their indebtedness for sustaining them. At present, about 1500 plant spp are being used in the ancient Indian system of medicine, i.e. Ayurveda (Bhatnagar, 1997). Chamba is a rich repository of medicinal plants and precious herbs, diverse cultures and traditions. People of Chamba have been using medicinal plants to cure common ailments for thousands of years. Unfortunately, with the development of society and economy, traditional culture is declining largely due to influences of the mainstream culture. It has been estimated that an average of 1 in 10 spp of vascular plants on this earth are endangered due to unplanned human activities (Lucas & Synge, 1978). Therefore, sincere efforts should be made by all to conserve the rich Himalayan biological and cultural diversity. This attempt has been made to explore the empirical knowledge of the local inhabitants of Chamba subdivision. Moreover, due to increasing urbanization and development, lure of modern civilization and growing pressure of population, their rich traditions developed over years of observation by trial and error are on the verge of extinction. Therefore, an attempt is made to document their socio-ethnical knowledge of plants.

Methodology of Study

Ethnobotanical field surveys were undertaken to various rural pockets of Chamba block Distt. Chamba (H.P.). Firsthand information on ethno botanical aspects was collected through interviews from knowledgeable people (traditional practitioners, old experienced farmers, family heads, housewives, eminent elderly persons of the community, etc.), as suggested by Jain (1987a).

Botanical identification of the selected species was first done with the help of regional floras

Systematic enumeration of the plants is in alphabetical order of their botanical names, synonym of the species followed by their respective families in the parentheses. Besides this, there is information on English and Regional Names, parts used and folk uses. The data gathered were screened with help of available literature (Kirtikar & Basu, 1935; Anon., 1948-1976; Ambasta, 1986; Jain, 1991), besides many other books and articles published in different journals.

Results

Achyranthes aspera Linn.

Syn.: *Digera muricata* Mart.
Family: Amarantaceae
Vernacular: Puthkanda
Part used: Leaves
English: Prickly Chaff Flower
Folk Uses: 100 ml of leaves infusion is give twice a day to expel gases, flatulence and to relieve griping pains from the stomach and bowels.

Acorus calamus Linn.

Family: Araceae
Vernacular: Baryan
English: Sweet Flag
Part used: Rhizome
Folk Uses: Crushed rhizome is
applied on the area
affected by
rheumatism. 3 to 4
cups of the
decoction (1
teaspoon of dried
rhizome in 1 cup of
water) of rhizome is
given three times a
day for asthma.

Adhatoda vasica Nees.

Family: Acanthaceae
Vernacular: Basuti, Basaka
English: Malabar Nut
Part used: Leaves and Root
Folk Uses: 100 ml decoction
of leaves and the roots of this plant
along with ginger is given for all
sorts of coughs. 5 drops of juice
extracted from leaves in a
tablespoon of water is given every
three hours for diarrheoa and
dysentery.

Artemisia vulgaris Linn.
Syn.: *A. indica*

Family: Asteraceae
Vernacular: Charmar
English: Absinth
Part used: Leaves
Folk Uses: 1-2ml infusion of leaves given for dispersing yellow bile of jaundice from the skin. Plant considered as anthelmintic and is used against round worms.

Cannabis sativa Linn.

Family: Canabaceae
Vernacular: Bhang
English: Indian Hemp
Part used: Leaves
Folk Uses: 8 to 10 drops of leaf juice is poured in ear to and relieve earache and headache. 60 mg. dried leaf powder is given in spasmodic cough asthma.

Carum carvi Linn.

Family: Umbelliferae
Vernacular: Kala Zira
English: Caraway
Part used: Seeds
Folk Uses: 3 to 5 ml seeds decoction given thrice a day for painful swelling of the womb, dysentery and piles.

Emblica officinalis Gaertn.
Syn: *Phyllanthus emblica* L., *Cicca emblica* Kurz

Family: Euphorbiaceae
Vernacular: Amla
English: Indian Gooseberry
Part used: Fruit
Folk Uses: 1 teaspoon of dried fruit powder used to expel gases, in vomiting and considered as laxative in piles. Raw fruit in jaggery considered refrigerant and used in congestion of liver.

Ficus glomerata Roxb.

Family: Moraceae
Vernacular: Phagoora, Gular
English: Cluster Fig
Part used: Leaves
Folk Uses: The decoction of
leaves is given 1to 2 cups a day for
curing bronchitis. The latex is
externally applied over glandular
enlargement.

Foeniculum vulgare Linn.
S y n : *Foeinculum panmorium* DC. , Wight, Ic., *F. officinale*
                    Allion.

Family: Umbelliferae
Vernacular: Kaudi Saunph
English: Fennel
Part used: Seeds

Folk Uses: 2 g of seeds given
to promote flow of urine, expels
flatulence, relieves griping pains from
the stomach & bowels. Seeds given to
increase the milk in nursing mothers.
Seed oil used to expel hookworms.

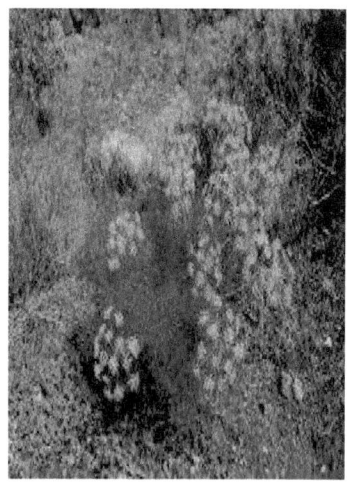

Mentha spicuta Linn.
Syn: *Mentha viridis*

Family: Lamiaceae
Vernacular: Padina
English: Spearmint
Part used: Leaves
Folk Uses: Leaves eaten raw
relieves flatulence and stomache.
Mint essence used for toothaches.
Plant decoction recommended as a
good bath additive for itching skin.

Ricinus communis Linn.
Syn.: *R. inermis* Jacq., *R. lividus* Jacq., *R. speciosus* Burm.

Family: Euphorbiaceae
Vernacular: Aerand
English: Castor
Part used: Leaves and
Seeds
Folk Uses: Poultice of
leaves applied locally in
rheumatism and headaches. Seeds
oil considered as a laxative.

Solanum nigrum Linn.
Syn.: *S. rubrum Mill., S. triangular Lamk.,*
A. villsoum Lamk., S. incertum Dunal.

Family: Solanaceae
Vernacular:Budhi Ke Tamatar, Makoi
English: Deadly Nightshade
Part used: Leaves
Folk Uses: Poultice of hot leaves
applied locally over wounds, sores,
ulcers and swollen and painful
testicles. Leaves infusion used in
enema for abdominal upset in the
infants.

Viola Canescens Wall.
Syn.: *V. serpens,* Wall.

Family: Violaceae
Vernacular: Banafsha
English: Violet
Part used: Leaves
Folk Uses: Decoction of leaves
                     and flowers given in
                     coughs,   malarial
                     fever, blood purifier
                     and   pulmonary
                     troubles.

Vitex negundo Linn.
Syn.: *V. bicolor* Willd., *V. arborea* Desf.

Family: Verbenaceae
Vernacular: Banah, Nirgunda
English: Indian Privet
Part used: Whole Plant
Folk Uses: 2 cups of
decoction of the leaves bark and the
roots given twice a day considered
good for rheumatism. Fomentation
of leaf extract, after boiling applied
on the swollen joints.

Withania somnifera Dunal.

Family: Solanaceae
Vernacular: Asgandh,
Ashwagandha   (Hindi)
English: Cherry
Part used: Roots and Leaves
Folk Uses: A spoonful of
powdered root given with milk
twice a day for all types of
weakness. Leaves used as a
febrifuge and applied externally to
lesions, painful swellings and sore
eyes.

Woodfordia fruticosa Kurz.
Syn.: *W. floribunda, Salisb.*

Family: Lytheraceae
Vernacular: Dhawa
English: Fire-flame Bush
Part used: Flowers
Folk Uses: A tablespoon of
dry powdered flowers are mixed
with honey is given in dysentery
and diarrhea.

Discussion and Conclusion

It is evident from the study that the rural inhabitants of Chamba Block are using wild as well as cultivated plants for their sustenance and healthcare needs. These plants are employed for the treatment to cure the stomach diseases, pulmonary troubles, kidney problems, eye infection, fever, arthritis, skin diseases, general weakness, wounds, sores, ulcers, dysentery and diarrhea.

The drugs are prepared in the form of paste, powder, decoction, extract, and even as tea or used directly in fresh. People use these Plants as cure because their elders told them and because these are readily available and cheap too.

Even the 'World Health Organization' is advocating for its use in primary health-care needs to achieve the goal of 'health for all (Akerele, 1987; WHO, 1993). Therefore, all possible efforts should be made to popularize and preserve this age-old knowledge of folk-medicine before it is lost forever. In fact, this data has to be screened on scientific lines for the welfare of humanity.

References

1. Ambasta, S.P. (ed.) (1986) *The Useful Plants of India*. CSIR, New Delhi.
2. Alcorn, J.B. (1996) Is biodiversity conserved by indigenous people? : 233-238. *In*: Jain, S.K. (ed.) *Ethnobiology in Human Welfare*. Deep Publ., New Delhi.
3. Anonymous, (1948-1976). *The Wealth of India, Raw Materials* Vol.–I-XI Publications & Information Directorate, C.S.I.R., New Delhi
4. Arora, R.K. 1981. Native food plants of the north-eastern tribals, 91-106. *In:* Jain S.K. (ed.) *Glimpses of Indian Ethnobotany*. Oxford & IBH, New Delhi.
5. Chauhan, N.S. 1988. Ethnobotanical study of medicinal plants of Himachal Pradesh. 187-198. In: Kaushik, P. (ed.) *Indigenous Medicinal Plants*. Today and Tomorrow Printers & Publ., New Delhi.
6. Ford, R.I. (ed.) 1978. *The Nature and Scope of Ethnobotany*. Anthropological Paper no. 67. Museum of Anthro. Univ. of Michigan, Ann. Arbor.
7. Jain, S.K. & Rao, R.R. (eds.) 1977. *A Handbook of Field and Herbarium Methods*. Today & Tomorrow's Printers & Publications
8. Jain, S.K. 1991. *Dictionary of Indian Folk Medicine and Ethnobotany*. Deep Publ., New Delhi.
9. Kirtikar, K.R. & Basu, B.D. 1935. *Indian Medicinal Plants*. Vol. I-IV. Lalit Mohan Basu, Allahabad, India.
10. Lucas, G. & Synge, H. 1978. *The IUCN Plant Red Data Book*. Surrey, England.
11. Martin, Marina, Mathias, Evelyn & McCorkle, Constance (ed.) 2001. *Ethno-veterinary Medicine-An Annotated Bibliography of Community Animal Healthcare*. Pub. ITDG Publishing, London.